Financing Politics

THIRD EDITION

Financing Politics

Money, Elections, and Political Reform

THIRD EDITION

Herbert E. Alexander
University of Southern California

a division of Congressional Quarterly Inc.
1414 22nd Street N.W., Washington, D.C. 20037

Politics and Public Policy Series

Advisory Editor

Robert L. Peabody

Johns Hopkins University

Tables on pages 121, 123, and 195 from *Financing the 1980 Election* by Herbert E. Alexander (Lexington, Mass.: Lexington Books, D.C. Heath & Co., copyright 1983, D.C. Heath & Co.). Reprinted with permission of the publisher. Table on page 148 from "The Cost of Becoming Governor" by Thad Beyle, *State Government,* Summer 1983. Reprinted with permission of the author.

Library of Congress Cataloging in Publication Data

Alexander, Herbert E.
    Financing politics.

    Bibliography: p.
    Includes index.
    1. Campaign funds—United States.   2. Campaign funds
—Law and legislation—United States.   I. Title.
JK1991.A6797   1984   324.7´8´0973   83-21079
ISBN 0-87187-280-3

To
Nancy, Michael,
Andrew, and Kenneth

Contents

Tables and Figures   ix

Foreword   xi

Preface   xiii

1. Money and Elections   1
    Money and Power   3
    Costs of Early American Elections   5
    Costs of Modern Elections   8
    Why Costs Rise   10
    Regulation of Campaign Finance   18
    Does Money Win Elections?   20

2. The Drive for Reform   31
    Early Efforts at Regulation   32
    Landmark Legislation of 1971   35
    1974 Amendments   37
    1976 Amendments   42
    1979 Amendments   43
    An Evolving Federal Election Commission 45
    Past and Prologue   52

3. Sources of Funds: Individuals   55
    Campaign Financing—Pre-1968   55
    1968 Campaign   59
    1972 Campaign   59
    Public Funding   62
    Ambassadorships for Big Donors   65
    Direct Mail Appeals   67
    Patterns in Political Giving   72

4. Sources of Funds: Groups   79
    Corporations   79
    Labor Unions   83
    Illegal Contributions   85
    Corporate and Labor PACs   88
    Other Special Interests   108

5. The 1980 Election: Public Funding Revisited   113
    The Prenomination Campaigns   113
    The General Election Campaigns   124
    Congressional Spending   132

6. The 1982 Election: Money, Strategy, and Organization   137
    Congressional Spending   138
    Independent Expenditures   147
    State Races   147
    Ballot Issues   154

7. Regulation of Political Finance: The States' Experience   163
    Disclosure   163
    Contribution Limits   165
    Bipartisan Election Commissions   171
    State Public Funding   173
    Implications of Public Funding   179
    State Tax Incentives   181
    Testing New Concepts   182

8. Past Reform and Future Directions   185
    Reform Proposals   185
    1984 and Beyond   192
    The Financial Future   196

Appendix   201
Bibliography   215
Index   223

Tables and Figures

Table

1-1   Costs of Presidential General Elections, 1860-1980   7

1-2   Expenditures for Radio and Television Time, Presidential General Election Campaigns, 1952-1980   13

3-1   Percentage of National Adult Population Solicited and Making Political Contributions, 1952-1980   74

4-1   Number of Registered PACs, 1974-1982   94

4-2   Financial Activity of PACs, 1972-1982   95

4-3   Adjusted Expenditures of PACs by Category, 1972-1982   96

4-4   Contributions to Congressional Candidates of PACs by Category, 1972-1982   98

4-5   PAC Contributions by Category to Incumbents, Challengers, and Open Seat Races (All Congressional Candidates), 1978-1982   103

4-6   PAC Contributions by Category to Democrats and Republicans (All Congressional Candidates), 1978-1982   105

5-1   Total Spending on Behalf of Republican Presidential Candidates in 1980 Campaigns   121

5-2   Total Spending on Behalf of Democratic Presidential Candidates in 1980 Campaigns   123

5-3   Candidate Sources of Funds, 1980 General Election   125

6-1   Congressional Campaign Expenditures, 1972-1982   138

6-2   Total Cost of Gubernatorial Elections, 1977-1982   148

6-3   Political Spending on State and Federal Races in California, Primary and General Election, 1981-1982   151

7-1   Regulation of Political Finance by the States   166
7-2   Public Financing of State Elections   175
7-3   Distribution of State Checkoff and Add-on Funds
       to Political Parties, 1980   177
8-1   Federal Income Tax Checkoff   195

Figure

1-1   The Campaign Spending Dollar in 1980   9
1-2   Total Political Spending in Presidential Election
       Years and Indexes of Total Spending, Total Votes
       Cast for President, and Consumer Prices, 1952-1980   11

Foreword

Since the advent of stabilized political communities around 5,000 B.C., money and politics have been inextricably linked, a means of progress as well as a source of contention. This uneasy pair has remained inseparable into the 1980s. Few politicians or close observers of the political scene would disagree with the old adage that "money talks." But how much influence does it actually have? Does money win elections? Has its voice been strengthened or weakened by recent forms of political participation—political action committees (PACs) and the public financing of presidential campaigns?

These are among the many important questions addressed in the third edition of Herbert E. Alexander's *Financing Politics: Money, Elections, and Political Reform.* Dr. Alexander, director of the Citizens' Research Foundation and a professor of political science at the University of Southern California, is the nation's leading authority on the subject of money and politics. In this comprehensive and data-rich book, the author reviews the development of campaign finance laws since the early 1970s and then takes a hard look at the 1980 and 1982 presidential and congressional campaigns.

Chapter 1 analyzes how the unequal distribution of money affects the assumption of political equality—"one person, one vote"—at the very heart of the American system of government. The chapter contrasts the campaigns of past and present elected officials and explains why the costs of running for office have soared. Chapter 2 discusses the landmark Federal Election Campaign Act of 1971; subsequent amendments in 1974, 1976, and 1979; and the controversial, eight-year history of the Federal Election Commission. Chapters 3 and 4 outline the sources of campaign funds and discuss how the regulations governing them have brought about change. The contributions of individuals as well as groups, such as corporations, labor unions, and corporate and labor PACS, are considered in detail. Chapters 5 and 6 examine campaign spending in the 1980 and 1982 elections with particular attention to the increased importance of computerized direct mail fund raising and the effects of the initiative movement on the political power of the New Right. Chapter 7 reviews important changes in state election laws and their implications for public funding. The author concludes with an arresting portrayal of the financial future of presidential and congressional campaigns and a critical appraisal of the success of spending reforms enacted during the past decade.

Alexander's timely treatise provides a sober, detached, and systematic look at the age-old questions of money and politics, questions of critical importance to the 1984 election and future contests. *Financing Politics* remains the most insightful analysis of this complex subject.

Robert L. Peabody

Preface

Political campaign money is once again front-page news. Not since the movement to reform campaign finance in the early 1970s has the role of money in politics commanded so much public attention. Journalists, political scientists, elected officials, and numerous interested citizens are participating, perhaps as never before, in a lively exchange over the place and influence of money in election campaigns and legislative politics. That is a salutary development, for money, I have long held, serves as a tracer element in the study of political power. Whatever light can be shed upon transactions involving money illuminates the political processes; that illumination reveals important aspects of political behavior and improves our understanding of influence and power.

This third edition of *Financing Politics* provides the background and analyses needed for rational exchange and informed decision making. A substantial portion of the book is new. There are chapters on the 1980 presidential elections and on the 1982 congressional and state elections. There is considerable discussion of new trends that generate publicity and controversy: the growth and influence of political action committees, the increasing use of independent expenditures, and the use by wealthy candidates of personal funds to finance their election campaigns. The evolution of the Federal Election Commission is traced and its impact analyzed, and recent developments in election campaign law and practice in individual states are described in some detail. The text has been updated throughout with the latest information available, and the most useful of the many recent studies of political finance have been discussed.

Special thanks are due to Mike McCarroll, vice president and general manager of Lexington Books, D. C. Heath and Co., for permission to use materials, including tables and appendices, from my book, *Financing the 1980 Election*.

Some historical data are derived from my article, "Financing Presidential Campaigns," in *History of American Presidential Elections, 1789-1968,* Volume IV, edited by Arthur M. Schlesinger, Jr. I appreciate the permission given by Chelsea House for use of materials from that article.

I am happy to thank members of the staff of the Citizens' Research Foundation for their devotion and help in the third edition: Brian A. Haggerty, CRF editorial consultant and research associate, for editorial assistance, rewriting, and redrafting throughout; Mike Eberts, my research assistant, who helped draft Chapter 6; and Gloria Cornette, CRF's assistant director, who always lightens my burdens and generously provides help and time in ways too numerous to list.

Joanne D. Daniels, director of CQ Press, conveyed her enthusiasm for this project to those of us at CRF who worked on it. Carolyn Goldinger, editor in the Book Department of Congressional Quarterly, was especially helpful in her editorial suggestions and added immeasurably to the final product. I also thank John L. Moore, who, with his wide knowledge of the subject matter, supervised the editing. Finally I thank Professor Robert L. Peabody, advisory editor of this series for CQ Press.

Herbert E. Alexander

Financing Politics

THIRD EDITION

Money and Elections 1

The American system of government is rooted in the assumption of political equality, "one person, one vote." But money—which candidates need to harvest those votes—is not distributed equally. The quest for political equality is hindered by the substantial inequities of campaign financing—a problem that has worried many Americans since the beginning of the Republic.

That worry has intensified as money has become indispensable to modern candidates—to enable them to buy advertising time, to pay pollsters and consultants, to hire direct mail experts, and to do the myriad other expensive things that running for office entails in the late twentieth century. With mounting public concern have come piecemeal efforts by the Congress and others to smooth out the impact of political money through contribution limits, public funding of campaigns, and various other regulatory devices designed to put candidates on a more equal financial footing.

Some of these devices have been declared unconstitutional by the U.S. Supreme Court or have otherwise failed; others have worked quite well. Yet great disparities remain in the amounts of money that candidates and the opposing political parties can raise and spend. Political financing continues to pose many other types of difficulties. Few candidates or political committees have found satisfactory ways to meet the expenses necessary to compete in a system of free elections. The implications of the ways in which we finance our politics are many, affecting candidates at all levels, from the White House to the courthouse, in both the nominating and electing phases of the electoral process; the two-party system and the structure of each party; and the decision-making process and public policy.

We will be looking in this book at how political campaigns are financed, the efforts to control associated abuses, the impact that laws have had, and the outlook for regulation in the future. We also will be looking at the scope of the problem—one in which the immensity is only hinted at by the vast amounts of money involved.

Scores of millions of dollars are needed—and spent—to elect our public officials. Consider the following:

● In 1952 about $140 million was spent on elective and party politics. By 1980 the costs rose to $1.2 billion, nearly nine times as much.

● Almost 500,000 public offices, from president to the proverbial dogcatcher, are filled by election in the United States, yet federal and state constitutions contain few provisions for the necessary—and costly—campaigns.

● In some states a campaign for the U.S. Senate may cost more than 10 times the salary paid to the winner during his term of office.

● The annual budgets of the major national party committees, the Republican National Committee and the Democratic National Committee, run many millions of dollars even in nonelection years—the size of the budget of a small corporation.

● The electorate is expanding and is well dispersed in urban, suburban, and rural areas. The development of communications media makes it easier—but also more costly—to carry on political campaigns.

These items add up to an important fact: Money—lots of it—is essential to the smooth conduct of our system of free elections. If one considers how much is spent in this country each year on chewing gum or cosmetics, the $1.2 billion does not seem overwhelming. It can be considered the cost of educating the American people on the issues confronting them. But there are several crucial questions for citizens in our democracy:

What effect has money on the ideal of equality of opportunity to serve in public office?

Who contributes to political campaigns—and why?

Do actual or potential contributions influence the behavior of officeholders or are contributions given in response to that behavior?

What is the impact of campaign money on public policy development? On agenda setting?

Can candidates buy their ways into office?

What effects have the reforms of the 1970s had on the ways we nominate candidates and elect our officials?

We shall return to these questions many times in this book and try to suggest answers.

Money and Power

In virtually all societies, money is a significant medium by which command over both energies and resources can be achieved.[1] The distinguishing characteristics of money are that it is transferable and convertible without necessarily revealing its original source. These are obvious advantages in politics.

Money is convertible into other resources. It buys goods, and it also buys human energy, skills, and services. Other resources, in turn, can be converted into political money through an incumbent's advantages of public office (for example, in awarding contracts and jobs), in controlling the flow of information, and in making decisions. Skillful use of ideology, issues, and the perquisites or promises of office attract financial support to political actors—in legitimate forms as contributions or dues, or in unethical or illegitimate forms such as those involved in recent years in the cases of Sen. Thomas Dodd, Bobby Baker, Spiro Agnew, and, of course, Watergate.

The convertibility of money, then, makes the financing of politics a significant component of the governing processes of all but the most primitive societies. But money is symbolic. The deeper competition is for power or prestige or for other values. In this sense, money is instrumental, and its importance lies in how it is used by people to try to gain influence, converted into other resources, or used in combination with other resources to achieve political power. Because of its universality, money is a tracer element in the study of political power. Light thrown upon transactions involving money illuminates political processes and behavior and improves our understanding of the flows of influence and power.

Power is distributed unequally in society; it does not vary directly with wealth, status, skill, or any other single characteristic. Rather, degree of power is determined by many such factors, no one of which stands alone and no one of which has meaning unless related to the purposes of the individual and the environment in which he or she acts. So money is but one element in the equation of political power. But it is the common denominator in the shaping of many of the factors comprising political power because it buys what is not or cannot be volunteered. Giving money permits numbers of citizens to share in the energy that must go into politics. In relatively affluent America, many individuals find it easier to show their support for a candidate or their loyalty to a party by writing a check than by devoting time to campaign or other political work. Of course, most citizens have no special talent for politics, or they will not give their time, so money is a happy substitute and at the same time a means of participation in a

3

democracy. If money is considered as a substitute for service, however, it does not require so firm a commitment; for example, one might give money to both parties, but one is less likely to give time to both. Money has an advantage over service, however, in that it is not loaded down with the personality or idiosyncrasies of the giver.

The problem of reconciling the "one person, one vote" theory with the unequal distribution of economic resources is compounded if one considers the operation of the American constitutional and political systems. The framers of the Constitution foresaw many of the problems that were to confront the new Republic and met them straight on. But for the most part they warned against the divisiveness and factionalism of political parties, as experienced in Europe, while at the same time requiring the election of officers of two of the three branches of government.

Most state constitutions also failed to provide institutional means for bridging the gap between the citizen and the government, while they too were requiring the popular election of numerous public officials. The gap was closed by the advent of political parties. The party system, however, never has been accorded full constitutional or legal status, nor has it been helped much financially by governments at the state and federal levels until recent years.

Of course, the Founding Fathers could not have foreseen all the developments that were to occur once the Republic began functioning. They could not have foreseen the rise of a highly competitive two-party system, nor the huge growth in the number of popularly elected officials, nor the direct election of U.S. senators, nor nomination campaigns, nor the democratization of the presidency, nor the advent of universal suffrage, nor the development of costly communications media—nor indeed the necessity for contenders to spend heavily on direct mail appeals designed to raise still more.

American history has witnessed an ever-expanding electorate, from the abolition of property qualifications through women's suffrage to civil rights legislation of the 1960s and the lowering of the voting age to 18 in the 1970s—all in addition to normal population growth. In 1919, for example, we doubled our voting potential by adopting the Nineteenth Amendment, granting nationwide suffrage to women. In the 1960s significant strides were taken to register blacks, with consequent increases in campaign costs, while the Twenty-sixth Amendment added millions of voters 18 to 20 years old to the electorate. Currently new efforts are being made to increase registration and voting by minorities, especially among blacks and Latinos.

Costs of Early American Elections

Before 1972 it was more difficult to measure all the costs of presidential campaigns, because money traditionally was spent at the national, state, and local levels by a multitude of committees and individuals (with no central accounting system necessary). Yet, because of the prominence of presidential elections, more historical information is available about them than about most other categories of election campaigns.

John Quincy Adams, sixth man to hold the office, argued that the presidency should neither be sought nor declined. "To pay money for securing it directly or indirectly," he asserted, was "incorrect in principle." [2] These were noble sentiments, but, in fact, all presidential candidates since George Washington have had to worry about campaign costs. From torchlight parade to "telethon," someone has had to pay expenses.

The data in Table 1-1 show the amounts spent by national level party and candidate committees on major party presidential candidates in the general elections since 1860, though the figures for years before 1912 are less reliable. A general upward movement in spending is revealed, with some startling differences in particularly intense contests. Much of the increase in expenditures over time is related to the growth in the size of the electorate and to general price increases. If expenditures are calculated on a per-vote basis, the sharp increase in costs is a recent phenomenon, beginning with the 1952 elections, the year, significantly, when the freeze on licensing of new television stations was ended; within the next four years, the number of commercial stations had quadrupled.[3]

Printing

Since the Republic's founding, printing has been the most basic campaign expense. In 1791 Thomas Jefferson asked Philip Freneau to come to Philadelphia, gave him a part-time clerkship for foreign languages in the State Department, and made him editor of the *National Gazette*, the subsidized organ of the Anti-Federalists. The Federalists had been financing their own paper, the *Gazette of the United States*, with money from Alexander Hamilton, Rufus King, and from public printing subsidies.[4]

The system of a newspaper supporting, and being supported by, one political faction or another quickly developed. Editors' fortunes rose and fell with the political success of their patrons. Newspapers vilified candidates mercilessly, and various factions spun off their own papers.

Much early campaigning for the presidency took place in newspaper columns. As late as 1850, when a wealthy backer wanted to further the political ambitions of James Buchanan, he contributed $10,000 to help start a newspaper for Buchanan's support.[5] In 1860 Abraham Lincoln secretly bought a small German weekly in Illinois for $400 and turned it over to an editor who agreed to follow the policies of the Republican party and to publish in both English and German.[6]

During the early 1800s books, pamphlets, and even newspapers often were handed from person to person until they were no longer readable. All that campaign publicity caused a reaction that seems quite modern. A letter writer to the *Charleston Gazette* complained that "We are so beset and run down by Federal republicans and their pamphlets that I begin to think for the first time that there is rottenness in the system they attempt to support, or why all this violent electioneering?" [7]

By 1840 more than just the printed word was used to spread the story. Pictures, buttons, banners, and novelty items appeared. According to one observer, William Henry Harrison's campaign that year had "conventions and mass meetings, parades and processions with banners and floats, long speeches on the log-cabin theme, log-cabin songbooks and log-cabin newspapers, Harrison pictures, and Tippecanoe handkerchiefs and badges." [8]

Active Campaigning

Active campaigning by the presidential candidates themselves is a fairly recent phenomenon. Andrew Jackson retired to the Hermitage after he was nominated, although his supporters did hold torchlight parades and hickory pole raisings. Political rallies came into their own in the mid-1800s. Campaigns provided an opportunity for a widely scattered population to meet and socialize. In those days, audiences judged orators by the length—not the content—of their speeches, and a two- or three-hour speech was not uncommon.

Stephen A. Douglas decided to barnstorm the country in his 1860 campaign against Lincoln, a practice not really tried again until 1896 when William Jennings Bryan, the "Boy Orator," traveled 18,000 miles giving some 600 speeches to at least five million people.[9] His opponent, William McKinley, by contrast, sat on his front porch and let the people come to him; special trains were run to his hometown of Canton, Ohio, with the railroads cooperating by cutting fares. The costs of these early forays into personal campaigning by Douglas and Bryan are not known, but because both candidates lost, they probably were not considered worthwhile expenses.

Table 1-1 Costs of Presidential General Elections, 1860-1980

Year	Republican		Democratic	
1860	$ 100,000	Lincoln*	$ 50,000	Douglas
1864	125,000	Lincoln*	50,000	McClellan
1868	150,000	Grant*	75,000	Seymour
1872	250,000	Grant*	50,000	Greeley
1876	950,000	Hayes*	900,000	Tilden
1880	1,100,000	Garfield*	335,000	Hancock
1884	1,300,000	Blaine	1,400,00	Cleveland*
1888	1,350,000	Harrison*	855,000	Cleveland
1892	1,700,000	Harrison	2,350,000	Cleveland*
1896	3,350,000	McKinley*	675,000	Bryan
1900	3,000,000	McKinley*	425,000	Bryan
1904	2,096,000	T. Roosevelt*	700,000	Parker
1908	1,655,518	Taft*	629,341	Bryan
1912	1,071,549	Taft	1,134,848	Wilson*
1916	2,441,565	Hughes	2,284,590	Wilson*
1920	5,417,501	Harding*	1,470,371	Cox
1924	4,020,478	Coolidge*	1,108,836	Davis
1928	6,256,111	Hoover*	5,342,350	Smith
1932	2,900,052	Hoover	2,245,975	F. Roosevelt*
1936	8,892,972	Landon	5,194,741	F. Roosevelt*
1940	3,451,310	Willkie	2,783,654	F. Roosevelt*
1944	2,828,652	Dewey	2,169,077	F. Roosevelt*
1948	2,127,296	Dewey	2,736,334	Truman*
1952	6,608,623	Eisenhower*	5,032,926	Stevenson
1956	7,778,702	Eisenhower*	5,106,651	Stevenson
1960	10,128,000	Nixon	9,797,000	Kennedy*
1964	16,026,000	Goldwater	8,757,000	Johnson*
1968	25,402,000	Nixon*	11,594,000	Humphrey
1972	61,400,000	Nixon*	30,000,000	McGovern
1976[1]	21,786,641	Ford	21,800,000	Carter*
1980[2]	29,188,188	Reagan*	29,352,767	Carter

* indicates winner

[1] 1976 represents the first time public funding was used for presidential elections. The Republican National Committee spent an additional $1.4 million on Ford's campaign. The Democratic National Committee spent an additional $2.8 million on Carter's campaign.

[2] In 1980 the Republican National Committee spent an additional $4.5 million on Reagan's campaign. The Democratic National Committee spent an additional $4 million on Carter's campaign.

SOURCES: 1860-1888 Republican and 1860-1900 Democratic: The best available figures, although disputed, are from the *Congressional Record*, vol. 45 (61st Cong., 2d sess., April 18, 1910), 4931, as cited in *Money in Elections* by Louise Overacker (New York: Macmillan, 1932), 71n; 1892-1924 Republican and 1904-1924 Democratic: Overacker, *Money in Elections*, 73; 1928-1944: Louise Overacker, *Presidential Campaign Funds* (Boston: Boston University Press, 1946), 32; 1948: Alexander Heard, *The Costs of Democracy* (Chapel Hill: University of North Carolina Press, 1960), 18, 20; 1952-1960: *Financing Presidential Campaigns*, Report of the President's Commission on Campaign Costs (Washington, D.C., Government Printing Office, April 1962), 10; 1964-1980: figures for 1964-1980 were compiled by the Citizens' Research Foundation and reported in the quadrennial series of financing the presidential elections by Herbert E. Alexander, cited in Bibliography.

Costs of Modern Elections

With the growth of the electorate has come a sharp increase in the cost of reaching it either directly through jet travel or indirectly through the mails and mass media. Politics today has become a major industry.

In 1952, the first presidential election year for which total political costs were calculated, it was estimated that $140 million was spent on elective and party politics at all levels of government. Twenty years later it was three times that much—$425 million. The 1972 total represented a huge jump of 42 percent over the 1968 amount and a significant actual increase in spending beyond the factor of inflation.

In 1976 several factors combined to halt the trend, at least temporarily. Disclosure laws, passed by Congress in 1971 and strengthened in 1974, and contribution limits passed in 1974 diminished the role of wealthy, "fat cat" contributors in all federal election campaigns. Moreover, in 1976 public funds were used for the first time to pay some of the costs of presidential primary and general election campaigns, with the money coming from taxpayers' optional use of an income tax form checkoff designating $1 of their tax payment for the Presidential Election Campaign Fund. The federal funding and the related expenditure limits and prohibition of private contributions to presidential general election campaigns held presidential campaign spending in check. Total campaign-related spending at all levels in 1976 reached $540 million. That figure represented a 27 percent increase over 1972, but the increase did not keep pace with inflation, which rose 33 percent during the same four-year period.

In 1980, however, total campaign spending amounted to about $1.2 billion, a 120 percent increase over 1976, far beyond the 35 percent rise in the cost of living during the four-year period. Several factors contributed to the dramatic increase, including the stepped-up use of high technology and the experts needed to apply it to campaigns: pollsters, media specialists, and computer experts. Further, individuals and groups interested in participating financially in presidential campaigns discovered ways to circumvent laws regulating contributions and expenditures. These are described in Chapter 5. Finally, federal campaign laws enacted throughout the 1970s required more persons and committees than ever before to disclose their financial activity. Thus political spending has been more meticulously reported than in the past.

Even with public funding, presidential campaigns still account for the largest single portion of the country's total political campaign bill. The Citizens' Research Foundation has estimated that $275 million of the $1.2

Figure 1-1 The Campaign Spending Dollar in 1980

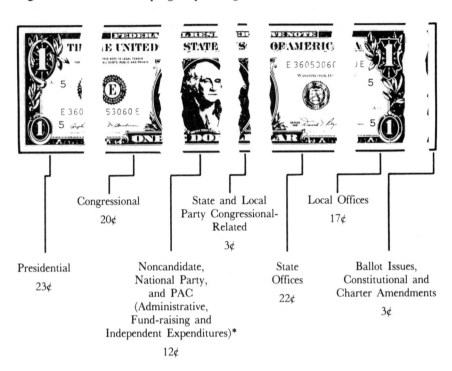

Congressional
20¢

State and Local
Party Congressional-
Related
3¢

Local Offices
17¢

Presidential
23¢

Noncandidate,
National Party,
and PAC
(Administrative,
Fund-raising and
Independent Expenditures)*
12¢

State
Offices
22¢

Ballot Issues,
Constitutional and
Charter Amendments
3¢

* Not including party and PAC contributions to presidential and congressional candidates; party and PAC contributions to these candidates are included in the presidential and congressional categories.

billion spent on 1980 campaigns, 23 percent of the total, went for presidential campaign costs (Figure 1-1).[10] Included in the $275 million are the costs of prenomination campaigns—some dating from 1977—third party and independent candidate campaign spending; national, state, and local party committee spending on behalf of the presidential campaigns; and the costs of the presidential nominating conventions.

Congressional campaigns continued to account for a large share of political spending. Approximately $239 million was spent to nominate candidates and elect a Congress, including party and interest group contributions to the candidates.[11] That figure represents an increase of 21 percent over 1978 and 90 percent over 1976. Inflation and the large number of candidates running for Congress contributed significantly to the increase.

In 1980 a record 2,288 candidates—1,944 House candidates and 344 Senate candidates—were entered at some stage of the congressional primary and general election campaigns, 379 more candidates than in 1978. In 1982 the number of candidates was down a little to 2,239, of whom 1,956 ran for the House and 283 ran for the Senate.

Other major areas of total political spending in 1980 included the following:

● $150 million in noncandidate spending by the national parties ($55 million) and by political action committees ($95 million). These funds were spent mainly to cover administrative and direct mail costs, and, in the case of the political action committees, communications costs and independent expenditures in congressional campaigns. Party and nonparty committee contributions to candidates and coordinated expenditures on their behalf are included in the presidential and congressional spending totals cited above.

● $34 million in congressional election-related state and local party committee spending. This money was used to pay for activities such as voter registration and turnout drives to benefit candidates for Congress.

● $265 million to nominate candidates and elect governors, other statewide officials, and state legislators.

● $200 million to nominate candidates and elect to office scores of thousands of county and local public officials.

● $40 million to wage campaigns related to state and local ballot issues and amendments to state constitutions and county and municipal charters.[12]

Why Costs Rise

Prior to 1952 the gradual rise in political spending, indicated in Table 1-1, could be accounted for by inflation and by the growth in the size of the electorate. In the last 30 years, however, several additional factors have contributed to the sometime dramatic increases in the cost of election campaigns.

Impact of Radio and TV Spending

The quantum jump in campaign spending that began in the 1950s can be attributed in considerable measure to the use of television. Between the 1948 and the 1952 elections enough Americans had bought television sets for the medium to figure seriously for the first time in the 1952 campaigns; by then, it was estimated that there were 19 million television sets and 58 million viewers.[13]

Candidates who choose to use broadcasting facilities pay dearly for the opportunity. Spending by the two major party candidates in the 1980 presidential general election for television and radio time combined amounted to approximately $30.7 million, about 52 percent of the $58.8 million in federal funds allotted to the two candidates.

Radio. Radio was first used in the 1924 election. In that campaign, the Republicans opened their own stations in their eastern campaign headquarters and broadcast every day from October 21 until election day, spending $120,000 for air time (one-third the amount they spent on either

Figure 1-2 Total Political Spending in Presidential Election Years and Indexes of Total Spending, Total Votes Cast for President, and Consumer Prices, 1952-1980

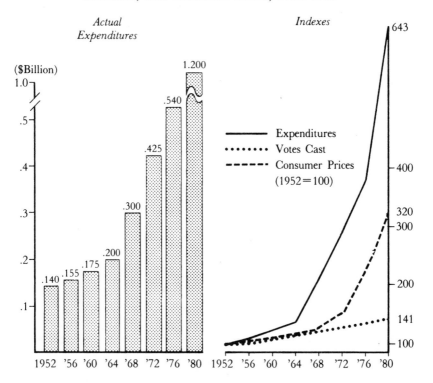

SOURCES: Expenditures 1952-80, Herbert E. Alexander, data derived in part from Alexander Heard, *The Costs of Democracy* (Chapel Hill, N.C.: The University of North Carolina Press, 1960), 7-8; consumer price index and votes cast for president, U.S. Bureau of the Census.

pamphlets or speakers). The Democrats spent only $40,000 on air time in 1924. Four years later, the new medium was more fully utilized by both parties. The Democrats spent $650,000 and the Republicans, $435,000. Such levels of spending for radio were fairly constant for 20 years.

After television came into wide use, candidates continued to buy radio air time. In the 1968 presidential general election, radio costs were double what they had been in 1964, while TV costs were only 55 percent higher. Between 1968 and 1972, TV costs in the general election declined $2.5 million while radio costs increased slightly by $200,000. In the 1976 presidential campaign, candidates spent approximately one million dollars more on radio than they did in 1972. The Carter and Ford campaigns combined spent $2.8 million for radio time. In 1980 Ronald Reagan's and Jimmy Carter's campaigns combined spent $4.1 million.

Some candidates prefer radio to TV because it is much cheaper per message. They also like radio for its potential to reach "trapped" audiences, such as commuters traveling to and from work, and its ability to pinpoint special groups. Both Richard Nixon's campaign in 1972 and the Reagan campaign in 1980 used radio spots designed to appeal to ethnic, age, and occupational groups.

Television. With television came sharp increases in the cost of broadcast time. When Adlai Stevenson was told that one television speech would cost $60,000 he said: "Now every time I start to put a word on paper, I'll wonder whether it's an expensive $10 word, or a little, unimportant word like 'is' or 'and' that costs only $1.75." [14] Abraham Lincoln's successful 1860 campaign cost $100,000. A century later, that much or more was spent for a single half-hour of television air time.

The highest level of broadcast spending came in 1968. That year Richard Nixon had a carefully programmed campaign calling for non-controversial television spots and live regional broadcasts that featured the candidate answering prescribed questions from a panel of well-rehearsed supporters. The total of $58.9 million that Federal Communications Commission (FCC) reports show was spent in 1968 by candidates at all levels was 70 percent above the total spent only four years earlier ($34.6 million). On the presidential level, about $12.6 million was spent on broadcasting for the Nixon campaign, and about $6.1 million worth of broadcasting was devoted to Hubert Humphrey's campaign; these were large amounts in relation to the value of the dollar at that time.

The 1972 broadcast spending totals were only slightly above the 1968 totals, but broadcast spending declined as a proportion of the total political

Table 1-2 Expenditures for Radio and Television Time, Presidential General Election Campaigns, 1952-1980

Year	Republican	Democratic
1952	$ 2,046,000	$1,530,000
1956	2,886,000	1,763,000
1960	1,865,000	1,142,000
1964	6,370,000	4,674,000
1968	12,598,000	6,143,000
1972	4,300,000	6,200,000
1976	7,875,000	9,081,321
1980	12,324,000[1]	18,400,000

[1] Does not include about $245,000 in coordinated expenditures by the Republican National Committee for media buys on behalf of Reagan-Bush or approximately $4.2 million spent by the RNC during the general election period on a media campaign supporting all Republican candidates.

spending from about 20 percent in 1968 to 14 percent in 1972. Among the reasons for this decline were the emergence in importance of nonbroadcast communications and the provisions of the 1971 election law.

Much of the decline was accounted for by a drop in Republican presidential broadcast spending—down from $12.6 million in 1968 to $4.3 million four years later. Recognizing that what became known as the "selling of the presidency" [15] by TV in 1968 had in fact done little to bolster their candidate's showing in the polls, the Nixon campaign made a major shift in campaign strategy in 1972 to emphasize spending on direct mail aimed at particular groups in the electorate. Nixon's opponent, George McGovern, spent $6.1 million for air time.

In the 1976 presidential general election campaigns, more money was spent than in 1972 for TV broadcast time, but the total still was lower than the comparable 1968 total. Public financing and spending limits led Jimmy Carter and Gerald Ford to channel large portions of their funds into advertising that would enable them to reach the largest number of voters. Inflated network costs also accounted for the increase. In 1972 the cost of a network minute was approximately $40,000; in 1976 it jumped to about $90,000 and even higher, to about $120,000, for selective prime time.

Ford and Carter allocated about half their general election budgets to media and related expenses in 1976. Carter spent $10.3 million on media, including $7.8 million to buy TV air time. Ford spent $11.5 million for media, $6.4 million of it used to purchase television broadcast time.

In the 1980 presidential general election campaigns, spending for TV broadcasts continued to increase, although when inflation is taken into account, costs did not reach the high-water mark of 1968. Reagan and Carter spent $35 million on media advertising and production, including $10.8 million on television time for Reagan and $15.8 million for Carter. The cost of TV time also continued to rise. Network charges could range from $26,000 for a five-minute spot at 10:55 p.m. to $94,000 for a 30-second spot adjoining a top-rated, weekday prime-time show, and $144,000 for a 30-second spot during a popular Sunday evening prime-time show.[16]

Broadcast Industry Regulation. Congress has recognized the potential power of radio and television to influence electoral politics and has enacted laws to regulate the political uses of broadcasting. Some of the laws have an impact on campaign costs.

To prevent a broadcasting facility from improperly influencing an election by giving only one candidate access to its audience, Congress enacted what now is Section 315 of the Communications Act of 1934. Essentially Section 315 requires a broadcast station licensee who gives or sells time to a "legally qualified candidate for any public office" to give or sell "equal opportunities" to use the broadcast station to all other candidates for that office. The only exceptions to the law are appearances by candidates on newscasts, news interviews, news documentaries, and on-the-spot coverage of news events. The law, as amended, also requires broadcast stations to charge candidates equally and, during an election campaign, to charge them no more than the lowest unit rate offered to the station's most favored commercial customers.

Section 315 requires licensees to allow candidates reasonable access to the use of the station's broadcasting facilities. This provision became a matter of litigation in the 1980 presidential campaign. The three major commercial television networks refused to sell candidates Reagan, Carter, and John Connally broadcast time in late 1979 to announce and advance their candidacies, maintaining it was too early for such advertisements. When the FCC sided with the Carter campaign committee, which had filed a complaint based on the reasonable-access provision of the Communications Act, the networks brought suit against the FCC. The matter was carried to the U.S. Supreme Court, which ruled in July 1981 that the First Amendment rights of candidates to present their views and of voters to obtain information outweigh the constitutional rights of broadcasters.

The so-called "fairness doctrine," codified in Section 315 of the Communications Act, also became a matter of litigation in 1980. The fairness doctrine requires licensees to devote a reasonable amount of broadcast time to discussing controversial issues of public importance and to allow reasonable opportunity for the presentation of opposing viewpoints. The fairness doctrine also requires licensees to give individuals whose honesty, integrity, or similar personal qualities are attacked during the presentation of views on such issues access to the broadcast facilities to defend themselves. In September 1980 the Carter-Mondale campaign sought a declaratory ruling from the FCC that it was entitled to free time under the fairness doctrine to respond to broadcast advertisements paid for by independent groups supporting Ronald Reagan. In October 1980 the commission unanimously ruled that broadcasts sponsored by independent groups supporting Reagan did not entitle the Carter-Mondale Committee to free air time. But the commission did rule that such broadcasts obligated radio and television stations to sell the committee or any independent groups supporting the Democratic candidates equivalent time at equal rates.

Compliance

The reporting requirements of the 1971 Federal Election Campaign Act (FECA) and its subsequent amendments have imposed additional financial burdens on all federal candidates. Publicly funded presidential candidates in both the prenomination and general election campaigns incur additional costs because they must supply the Federal Election Commission (FEC) with substantial documentation to claim matching funds and to prove their campaigns have remained within the various expenditure limits stipulated by the FECA. Lawyers and accountants who can lead candidates through the complexities of campaign laws and devise systems to keep track of campaign receipts and expenditures have become as prominent in the campaigns as political operatives.

The 1976 FECA Amendments sought to mitigate the financial burdens imposed by compliance requirements on publicly funded presidential candidates by exempting from the definitions of contribution and expenditure money paid for legal and accounting services to comply with the FECA or with tax laws applying to political activity. The maximum amount an individual could donate for these purposes was $1,000. The 1979 FECA Amendments were intended in part to relieve all federal candidates of some of the burdens of compliance by reducing the number and frequency of compliance reports.

Nevertheless, the costs of compliance remain substantial. For example, Jimmy Carter's 1980 prenomination campaign reported spending about

$1.9 million on compliance, approximately 10 percent of the $18.6 million it collected. Ronald Reagan's 1980 prenomination campaign reported spending more than $1 million in compliance-related legal and accounting costs, about 4.6 percent of the campaign's total receipts of $21.4 million. In the 1980 general election, as in 1976, the candidates were permitted to raise private money to cover compliance costs. According to a 1980 year-end report, the Reagan campaign raised almost $1.6 million to pay for legal and accounting costs related to compliance. An additional $500,000 was raised subsequent to that report to cover campaign wind-down expenses and the costs of litigation with the FEC over the agency's audit of the committee. The Carter campaign reported total compliance costs, including wind-down expenses, of almost $1.5 million.

Fund Raising

Fund-raising expenses also have become a major cost component in campaigns for federal office. The FECA contribution limits make it necessary for candidates to undertake broadly based drives that often are more expensive than soliciting a smaller number of large contributors. The 1974 law sought to take these costs into account by allowing a 20 percent overage beyond expenditure limits for fund-raising operations in presidential campaigns.

In 1980 the Reagan prenomination campaign spent about $3.5 million to raise $21.4 million, including the $7.3 million the candidate was certified to receive in matching funds. Fund-raising costs represented about 16 percent of the amount the campaign raised. The campaign's fund-raising methods included extensive use of direct mail appeals, which accounted for a substantial portion of its receipts but which also were costly, especially early in the campaign when potential contributors still were being identified. The campaign spent about $1.6 million on direct mail fund raising but only about $633,000 on fund-raising events and their associated costs.

The Carter prenomination campaign reported nearly $3 million in fund-raising costs, 16 percent of the $18.6 million it received. The campaign relied heavily on $1,000 donations, solicited personally or through fund-raising dinners and events.

Whether raising money for fund-raising overage or other campaign expenditures, the difference between the fund-raising strategies of the two campaigns is evident in a comparison of the number of contributions each campaign submitted to the FEC for matching funds. Only contributions of

$250 or less are matchable, although individuals may contribute up to
$1,000. The Reagan campaign submitted 213,103 contributions for match-
ing, and Carter's campaign submitted 63,336.

Professionalization of Politics

Candidates incur additional costs by retaining political specialists.
Some consultants run the candidate's entire campaign, advising on basic
strategy decisions, such as what issues the candidate should stress or how
best to utilize limited time and funds. Others specialize in polling, fund
raising, organizing volunteers, or media advertising. Some consultants
handle only particular aspects of a campaign; for example, putting voters'
names on computer tapes for direct mail appeals, fund raising, or election
day get-out-the-vote reminders. Other firms provide automated telephone
equipment and operators who can make thousands of calls to voters, play a
message from the candidate, or record responses.

The proliferation of consulting firms points to the increasing professionalization of electoral politics. This trend may be irreversible but has
been criticized on the grounds that profit-making companies have no base or
interest in the candidate's constituency and often supplant established party
organizations and traditional volunteer campaign staffs. Few party organizations, however, are geared to provide services with the competence and
reliability that some professional consultants demonstrate. Moreover, campaign managers often have looked upon volunteers as of marginal help.
With the complexities of new regulations, some campaign directors feel that
the amateur efforts are more often a burden than a boon.

In presidential campaigns, the increase in the number of primary
election contests and the growing length of the prenomination campaign
period also have contributed to rising costs. In 1968 there were only 15 primaries in which about 40 percent of the party convention delegates were
chosen. Due in large part to a movement toward greater mass participation
in the Democratic party's selection of delegates to its presidential nominating convention, the number of primaries gradually was increased in an
effort to diminish the influence of the party hierarchy and to make the
choice of the party more responsive to the electorate. In 1972, 23 states conducted presidential primaries; in 1976 the number increased to 30. In 1980,
35 states, Puerto Rico, and the District of Columbia held presidential
primary elections. Seventy-six percent of the Republican delegates and 71
percent of the Democratic delegates were elected in primaries or were
chosen by a separate process that was bound to reflect the primary results.[17]

In primary contests candidates are required to reach mass audiences. Newspaper and broadcast advertising and other means of communicating with large numbers of people are far more expensive than the means employed formerly to influence state and interest group leaders who used to control the delegate selection process.

The campaign finance reforms enacted in 1974 helped lengthen the prenomination campaign period, thus increasing the candidates' costs. Because candidates no longer may rely on large contributors to cover campaign start-up costs, they have been forced to begin their fund raising early in order to gather from many small contributions the seed money they need. As noted, the costs of such fund-raising drives are significant. So are the costs of the campaign publicity required to generate the name recognition candidates hope will inspire potential contributors to donate to their campaigns.

Regulation of Campaign Finance

Until Watergate and other recent scandals brought intense scrutiny to the role that money plays in U.S. elections, reform of the political finance system since the turn of the century invariably yielded piecemeal legislation which, ironically, may have helped further the very corruption that was the original target. The controls imposed by the legislation were mostly negative, restricting spending even as needs and costs were rising.

To prevent candidates from becoming obligated to special interests, limits were set on the amount of contributions. Funds from suspect sources or heavily regulated industries were prohibited. To dilute the "spoils system," career civil servants were protected from political demands for cash. If there was danger that partisans would dominate the airwaves, all sides were guaranteed equal opportunity for free time—although opportunities to buy time were equal only for those who could pay for it. One after another, traditional sources of political funds were cut off without provision for new sources of supply.

The application of new technology to political campaigns exacerbated the financial problems. The use of television, jets, polling, and computers caused costs to mount and to outpace contributions. Consequently, fund-raisers developed innovative methods of gathering money. New contributors and new sources emerged as improved solicitation and collection systems developed with computerized mail drives and sophisticated fund-raising organizations. Labor and business pioneered in forming political action committees (PACs) to raise funds and support candidates. Other organizations—trade associations, peace groups, environmentalists, and other issue-oriented groups—emulated them. Millionaire candidates raised the ante for other candidates, escalating costs but also focusing attention on wealth as a factor in electoral candidacy.

During the first half of the 1970s, federal laws regulating election campaigns were changed fundamentally through enactment of the Federal Election Campaign Act of 1971, the Revenue Act of 1971, and the FECA Amendments of 1974, which significantly altered both the 1971 laws. From 1972 to 1976, 49 states also revised their laws regulating political money. The states undertook much experimentation, living up to their description by Justice Louis D. Brandeis as "laboratories of reform." [18]

Although there has been little uniformity in recent laws governing political finance, certain patterns can be discerned. The regulations have taken four basic forms, each of which will be discussed at greater length later. Stated briefly, they are:

1. Public Disclosure—to provide the public, both during and after campaigns, with knowledge of monetary influences upon its elected officials and to help curb excesses and abuses by increasing the political risk for those who would undertake such practices.

2. Expenditure Limits—to meet the problems created by rising costs and by some candidates having more funds than others.

3. Contribution Restrictions—to meet the problems of candidates obligating themselves to certain interests.

4. Public Funding—to provide an alternative source of funding for candidates to replace contributions that have been prohibited or limited.

This recent wave of reform, a tide unmatched since the Populists and Muckrakers triggered reform at the turn of the century, has been primarily an effort to improve a system perceived by many as fraught with favoritism and corruption. It had been widely felt in recent years that the American system of financing elections through sometimes secret, often unlimited private donations had given undue influence in politics and government to wealthy or well-organized donors at the expense of the unorganized public.

Reform is not neutral. When the rules of the game are changed, advantages shift and institutions change—sometimes in unforeseen ways. As Douglas Rae has pointed out, election laws can be used—in fact are being used—as instruments to achieve certain political goals.[19]

The problem of the election reformer in the final quarter of the twentieth century is how to apply democratic principles to elections in an age of media politics, seemingly dominated by an atmosphere of dollar politics. The $61.4 million reported for Richard Nixon's successful campaign to retain the presidency in 1972—the year of the last presidential campaigns conducted under the old election laws—represents six times the amount reported for John F. Kennedy's attaining that office in 1960 and more than 600 times the amount to elect Abraham Lincoln a century earlier. In the 1976 presidential campaigns—the year of the first such campaigns to be funded by public monies—Jimmy Carter spent $21.8 million of public funds in the general election in his successful effort to gain the presidency. Before declaring the election reforms an unqualified success, however, several questions must be asked. Do expenditure limits mean there will be more or less communication between candidates and voters? Is voting turnout affected when expenditure limits reduce candidate opportunities to communicate with potential voters? Do contribution limits and expenditure limits encourage more competition, or do they favor incumbents or discriminate among candidates in differing jurisdictions and circumstances? How will government funding of political campaigns alter the political process? Will government intrusion be an opening wedge for control over various political activities? Are floors (minimal levels of public funding) better without ceilings or limits on spending?

The consensus among reformers and their supporters (who, at least since Watergate, appear to make up a majority of the citizenry), seems to be that democratic principles cannot be upheld in an atmosphere of unfettered and often unpublicized campaign fund raising and spending. The secrecy or incomplete disclosure surrounding political giving prior to the enactment of reforms permitted widespread abuses that at times constituted a fundamental corruption of the election process. Several events in recent years, some of which are described in the following chapters, provide dramatic evidence of the corruption by political money that can occur at both the federal and state levels. Such events have given impetus to the reform movement.

Does Money Win Elections?

Popular lore has it that the candidate who spends the most wins, and, on the surface, the record in some recent elections would seem to bear this out. During the presidential general election in 1980, because both Reagan and Carter accepted public funding, each spent approximately the same amount. But, as described in Chapter 5, about $10 million more was spent on Reagan's behalf by individuals and groups outside his campaign's direct control than on behalf of Carter. During the prenomination campaign, both Reagan and Carter outspent their opponents. Reagan spent $19.8 million to gain the Republican nomination. George Bush, the Republican opponent who won the next highest number of convention delegates, spent $16.1 million. On the Democratic side, Carter outspent his opponent, Sen. Edward M. Kennedy, D-Mass., $18.5 million to $12.2 million.

Work and Organization

The outcome of an election, however, usually depends upon much more than money. Reagan's capture of the Republican nomination was in large part the result of the hard work and efficient organization of his campaign staff. Although he did not declare his candidacy until November 1979, his campaign organization had been working to build support for his presidential bid since the beginning of 1977. Reagan's name recognition and head start gave him a fund-raising advantage over his opponents, and his early primary victories undoubtedly brought in the kind of money only successful campaigns can attract. Carter's fund raising benefited from his incumbency as well as from Kennedy's late start.

Voters sometimes refuse to respond favorably to frills, blitz campaigns, or wealthy candidates, creating a backlash that may turn voters off. It is worth noting that, despite the record spending on the presidential campaigns of 1972, the turnout of voters was the lowest since 1948. Survey data indicated that many people did not vote simply because they were not interested or did not care for any of the candidates.[20]

A number of factors can compensate for a shortage of cash. Low-budget candidates may be campaigning in areas predominately favorable to their parties or they may be well-entrenched incumbents; they may be swept into office by a national trend or benefit from a presidential landslide. Any of these circumstances can bring victory if candidates have sufficient resources to enable them to present their qualifications and positions— sometimes merely their names and faces—to the voters.

Counterbalance

In broad terms, money may be considered as a countervailing force to a natural majority, or to large aggregates of voters, with the candidates of the minority party feeling compelled to spend more money than the candidates of the party that otherwise would command the most votes.

During the twentieth century, at the national level, Republicans in general election campaigns consistently have had more money at their disposal than the Democrats, even when independent labor funds are added to Democratic spending. Yet, from the 1930s through the 1970s, the Democrats have been able to command a majority of voters more often than the Republicans. In his eight years in office, Dwight Eisenhower had a Republican-controlled Congress for only two years; Nixon and Ford from 1969 through 1976 faced large Democratic majorities in Congress. And although the Republicans controlled the White House and the Senate from 1980 through 1984, the Democrats remained in control of the House.

In the 1936 presidential election, the Republican party together with the wealthy Liberty League spent $9,411,095 (a total not topped until 1960) against the Democrats' $5,964,917. Yet, despite this 3-to-2 financial advantage, the Republicans carried only two states for their nominee, Alfred Landon. Some historians have expressed doubt that any of the presidential elections in the twentieth century would have ended differently had the losing candidate been able to spend more money. The closer the election results, however, the greater the chance that any one factor could make a difference. For example, the Kennedy-Nixon contest in 1960, the Nixon-Humphrey race in 1968, and the Carter-Ford race in 1976 all were won by such small margins—1 to 2 percent of the vote—that additional expenditures could well have changed the result.

The predisposition of voters, the issues of the moment, the advantages of incumbency, and the support of various groups are always related to the final vote totals and are often more important than cash. Independent decisions by the news media—particularly TV—about what aspects of a campaign to cover can provide more exposure than advertising purchased by the candidates. Most campaigns now spend substantial amounts of travel money to put the candidate at events where free television coverage is certain. Campaign schedules are now drawn up with a view to obtaining media coverage, in time to make the morning or evening newspapers, or to get on the evening newscasts. National nominating convention sessions usually are scheduled for prime viewing hours.

If not decisive, money at least is capable of reducing severe handicaps for most candidates. No candidate can make much of an impression without it, especially a maverick who contests the regulars or a candidate who challenges an incumbent.

How Much Is Enough?

One reason candidates seem to spend so lavishly is that little scientific evidence is available about the incremental value in votes of various levels of campaign spending or about the effectiveness of different campaign techniques. Traditionally, candidates spend as much as their supporters expect them to or as their opponents spend—and then some. New techniques win acceptance and to some extent displace older ones, but few candidates are willing to pioneer with unconventional methods alone. For example, although the electronic media are now widely used, most campaigns still make major expenditures for print media advertising. Indeed, new uses of old techniques develop. As an example, the print media have been enhanced by applications of computer technology, bringing increased use of direct mail that can be specially targeted to groups of potential voters or contributors. Contribution limits have produced pressures in the same direction, requiring candidates to attempt to reach a broader base of financial support by soliciting more small contributions. Matching fund plans have produced similar pressures. A provision in the 1974 FECA Amendments, for example, requires that, to qualify for public funds, a candidate for the presidential nomination receive a minimum number of relatively small contributions in at least 20 states.

Other new pressures are at work; for example, statutory expenditure limits as well as contribution limits mean less money is available for spending, forcing campaigns to undertake vigorous "cost-benefit" budgeting of available resources. This may lead to the reduction or elimination of certain marginal campaign activities. Of course, there is no agreement on what activities are considered marginal, and, in fact, marginality differs for the various levels of campaigning. Neither social science nor market research has been able to tell candidates what kinds of spending achieve the most votes per dollar; indeed, the impact will not be the same in a national or statewide campaign as in a local one. Perhaps half of all campaign spending is wasted—but no one knows which half. In any case, political campaigns are not comparable to advertising campaigns selling products such as soap. The candidate's personality and unanticipated events both impinge on campaigns in ways that cannot be controlled as easily as can the environment for selling commercial products.

Significant spending also occurs from largely psychological motives: the candidate spends to quiet his anxieties (in most campaigns, plentiful), to stimulate workers, or to show that he attracts money and is serious about winning. For example, the high expenditures for President Nixon's 1972 reelection campaign grew in part from his need to build confidence in his ability as a vote-getter. Politicians often feel they must do something, anything, to keep the campaign going and morale high. The candidate's morale is bolstered when he sees his picture on posters or billboards along the route; some campaign managers spend a considerable amount of money just to keep the candidate happy and enthusiastic. Indeed, the costliest election is a lost election.

Relatively, the dollar price of U.S. elections is not high. The $1.2 billion spent for campaigns in 1980 was less than the total of the advertising budgets for that year of the two largest corporate advertisers, Procter and Gamble and Sears, Roebuck and Company. It was a fraction of 1 percent of the amounts spent by federal, state, county, and municipal governments— and that is what politics is all about, gaining control of governments to decide policies on, among other things, how tax money will be spent.

Nevertheless, U.S. political costs tend to be higher than in some countries because the season for concentrated political advertising is relatively short, growing in intensity just before an election. Moreover, unlike those countries where political parties receive free broadcast time on government-controlled radio and television stations, in the United States candidates and parties do not merely compete with each other; they also must compete for media time and space with commercial advertisers with large budgets who often dominate the best time slots on popular television and radio programs.

In this competitive situation, there are two conditions we can point to that, if all other things are fairly equal, enhance the power of money. First, we have found that money is most important in prenomination campaigns. Second, there is evidence that wealthy candidates do have a head start on those without wealth.

Importance of Prenomination Spending

Because of its ability to buy the kinds of services that produce name recognition and exposition of positions, money wields its greatest influence on campaigns—particularly in presidential races—during the prenomination period. This is the period before the national nominating convention when the candidate's name and image must get publicity, when a number of national and local organizations must be created to win delegates, when the serious national candidate probably will need to contest a string of primary elections in states across the country.

John F. Kennedy's prenomination campaign of 1960 reported spending $912,500; additional outlays by state and local groups added unknown amounts to that total. In addition, Kennedy was able to threaten to spend enough money to discourage competition, as in California and Ohio.

The 1964 Republican prenomination fight was essentially a battle between Nelson A. Rockefeller's personal wealth and Barry Goldwater's broad financial base consisting of many small contributions from his conservative supporters. The $10 million spent for the 1964 Republican nomination campaigns doubled the record $5 million spent in the Eisenhower-Taft contest of 1952.

These totals, however, paled in comparison with the sums spent on the 1968 nomination when, for the first time since 1952, there was serious rivalry in both parties. In all, about $45 million was spent before Nixon and Humphrey finally got their parties' nominations. Nixon's campaign accounted for more than half the $20 million spent by the Republicans, and Humphrey spent about $4 million of the $25 million expended by a large field of Democratic candidates that included Lyndon Johnson (before he decided not to seek reelection), Robert Kennedy (before his assassination), and Eugene McCarthy.

With Nixon's nomination assured in 1972, his Committee for the Reelection of the President directed most of its spending toward the general election. But the Democrats topped the record $25 million they had reported spending four years earlier. George McGovern, the eventual nominee, and 17 other candidates spent $33.1 million in the party's prenomination battles.

In 1976 candidates for the Democratic nomination spent more than $46 million, with Jimmy Carter accounting for $12.4 million of that sum. On the Republican side, Gerald Ford and Ronald Reagan spent some $26 million on their prenomination campaigns.

In 1980, nine Republican candidates spent $69.7 million in their efforts to gain the nomination; Ronald Reagan led the way with expenditures of $19.8 million. Four candidates seeking the Democratic nomination spent $35.6 million, $18.5 million of it spent by Jimmy Carter. Prenomination campaign spending in 1980 is treated in greater detail in Chapter 5.

Wealthy Candidates

Four of the last nine chief executives were considered wealthy men when they took office (Franklin D. Roosevelt, Dwight D. Eisenhower, John F. Kennedy, and Lyndon B. Johnson). Personal wealth, however, was a factor only in the nomination of Kennedy. Adlai E. Stevenson and Barry Goldwater were well-to-do, but their fortunes bore no relation to their nomination or subsequent defeats; at most, their wealth may have helped them to enter politics. George McGovern, Hubert Humphrey, Harry Truman, Thomas Dewey, Richard Nixon (in 1960), and Gerald Ford were not even moderately wealthy when they first ran for president.

Although Jimmy Carter may have been moderately rich when he entered presidential politics, his personal wealth does not appear to have been a factor in his attaining his party's nomination. The success of his family's peanut warehouse business, however, did permit Carter to guarantee loans to his campaign during a difficult period in 1976 when matching government funds were not available because of legal challenges to the then-new public financing system for presidential campaigns. Ronald Reagan also was a man of moderate wealth when he undertook the 1980 presidential campaign. His wealth, however, did not figure in his nomination, although it gave him the freedom to devote his full attention to campaigning.

But, even though it was not a factor in the nomination of most recent presidential candidates, personal wealth has been an important factor in several modern political campaigns. The most conspicuous examples of self-contributors on the record are the Rockefellers. When he appeared before the House Judiciary Committee in November 1974 as the vice president-designate, Nelson Rockefeller said that in his 18 years in public office he and members of his family had spent more than $17 million on his various political campaigns. He noted that this family spending had been necessary because "it's very difficult for a Rockefeller to raise money for a campaign. The reaction of most people is, 'Why should we give money to a Rockefeller?' " [21]

Rockefeller submitted to the Senate Rules Committee a summary of his own political contributions during the years 1957-1974. He said his political spending since 1957 totaled $3,265,374, which included $1,000,228 in his own presidential campaigns, $80,599 in his New York gubernatorial campaigns, and $1,031,627 to the New York State Republican party and local committees and clubs. In addition, Rockefeller's brothers and sister had supported his political activities with contributions totaling $2,850,000.

In 1971 passage of the Federal Election Campaign Act diminished the role personal wealth could play in federal campaigns. But the Supreme Court, in a 1976 decision, *Buckley v. Valeo*, removed FECA's limits on a candidate's contributions to his or her own campaign. The law subsequently was revised to reinstate the personal and family limits of $50,000 in presidential and vice presidential elections, but only if the candidate accepts government funding. (The *Buckley* decision is discussed in Chapter 2.)

Because federal funds are not provided for congressional elections, there is no limit on the amounts these candidates may contribute to their own campaigns. In the 1976 Republican senatorial primary in Pennsylvania, for example, Rep. John Heinz financed almost 90 percent of his successful campaign against former Philadelphia district attorney Arlen Specter with loans from his personal fortune—$585,765 out of a total of $673,869. Specter spent only $224,105 on the primary, according to his campaign reports; of this total, Specter lent his campaign $38,744. Counting the general election race, which he also won, Heinz made loans to his own campaign amounting to $2,465,500.

In more recent congressional elections, the incidence of substantial self-contributions increased considerably. In 1978, for example, a total of 58 congressional candidates gave or lent at least $100,000 to their own campaigns.[22] Often both candidates in the general election relied heavily on their own money. Sen. Charles Percy, R-Ill., spent $675,000 of personal funds in a successful effort to defeat Democratic challenger Alex Seith, who spent $1.1 million of his own money.

In 1982 several candidates contributed extremely large amounts to their own campaigns, including Democrat Mark Dayton of Minnesota, who spent $6.9 million of personal wealth in an unsuccessful bid to defeat Republican Sen. David Durenberger, and New Jersey Democrat Frank Lautenberg, who gave or lent $5.1 million to his own Senate campaign in defeating Republican Millicent Fenwick, who gave or lent $877,000 to her own cause.

Several candidates for state government offices also have spent considerable sums of their own money on their campaigns. In 1980 Democratic Gov. John D. "Jay" Rockefeller IV of West Virginia spent $11.6 million in personal funds on a successful reelection bid. In 1982 New York Republican Lewis Lehrman spent $3.7 million of his own and his brother's money to win his party's gubernatorial nomination and then disbursed additional millions in an unsuccessful general election campaign.

Two concerns usually are raised in discussions of wealthy candidates. One is that their personal resources give them too great an advantage over other candidates; the second is that their advantage gives the rich overrepresentation.

Advantages. Even with the limitations that now obtain on spending by a wealthy presidential or vice presidential candidate accepting government funds, wealth still would seem to bring a candidate incalculable advantages. His or her name makes news, and items about the candidate's family draw attention—all part of the process of building valuable name recognition. The budding politician from a wealthy family frequently is able to run for high office from the outset, whereas men and women of less wealth (with the possible exception of actors, athletes, and astronauts) usually must begin at lower elective levels and earn their way upward.

Other advantages for wealthy candidates derive from their access to wealthy friends. Well-connected persons obtain credit with ease and can guarantee that loans or bills will be paid. Their ability to pick up the tab at lunches and dinners, to phone long-distance without worrying about the cost, is helpful too.

Superficially, at least, rich candidates seem less likely to seek personal gain from public office. They may, in fact, incur fewer obligations to contributors and thereby preserve more freedom of action—and wealthy candidates have at times used just such an argument in their campaigns.

All this is not to say that wealthy candidates may not lose: they frequently do. But political realities continue to favor the wealthy candidate. Wealth propels, quickens, and catalyzes. And it is only folklore that the average American admires the impecunious candidate who wins elections on a shoestring. Voters often have cast their ballots willingly for the well-to-do individual with an expensive organization and a substantial war chest. American voters have been strongly drawn to the Roosevelts, Tafts, Kennedys, and Rockefellers.

Representation. As to the concern that the rich are overrepresented in politics, it is necessary to point out that wealthy candidates often are surrogates or in effect representatives of those who might not otherwise have strong voices in government. This tradition goes back to the Virginia squire who was the first president, and it carries up through wealthy candidates such as Robert Kennedy, with his appeal to blacks and the poor.

Contrary to the common assumption, wealthy candidates are not all conservatives who represent vested interests. Associated Press reports in 1983 noted that at least 23 senators and 19 representatives disclosed assets exceeding $1 million.[23] Those members of Congress represented all points on the political spectrum, from liberals, such as Sen. Edward Kennedy of Massachusetts and Rep. Fortney Stark of California, to moderates such as Sen. John Glenn of Ohio and Sen. John Heinz of Pennsylvania, to conservatives, such as Sen. William Armstrong of Colorado and Sen. Malcolm Wallop of Wyoming.

To the extent that wealthy candidates help shore up the two-party system or give voice to minority interests, they make an important contribution to the political dialogue. The main problem of wealth in elections may not be in the outcome of financially imbalanced contests but rather in depriving the voters of potential leaders who do not have the money to consider running for office.

Notes

1. Derived from Alexander Heard, "Political Financing," *International Encyclopedia of Social Sciences* (New York: Macmillan, 1968), vol. 12, 235-241.
2. *Memoirs of John Quincy Adams*, (1875, vol. 7, 468-470, as quoted in *Money and Politics*, Jasper B. Shannon (New York: Random House, 1959), 15.
3. For a brief history of the uses of radio and television broadcasting in political campaigns, see Herbert E. Alexander, "Financing Presidential Campaigns," in *History of American Presidential Elections 1789-1968*, ed. Arthur M. Schlesinger, Jr. (New York: Chelsea House Publishers in association with McGraw-Hill Book Co., 1971), 3873-3875. Other historical information in this chapter is drawn from the same source.
4. Eugene H. Roseboom, *A History of Presidential Elections* (New York: Macmillan, 1957), 25.
5. Shannon, *Money and Politics*, 21.
6. Shannon, *Money and Politics*, 23.
7. Jules Abels, *The Degeneration of Our Presidential Election: A History and Analysis of an American Institution in Trouble* (New York: Macmillan, 1968), 83.
8. Roseboom, *A History of Presidential Elections*, 121.
9. M. R. Werner, *Bryan* (New York: Harcourt, Brace & Co., 1929), 95.
10. Herbert E. Alexander, *Financing the 1980 Election* (Lexington, Mass.: D. C. Heath, 1983), 103-116.
11. Alexander, *Financing the 1980 Election*, 116-122.
12. Alexander, *Financing the 1980 Election*, 122-131.
13. Newton N. Minow, John Bartlow Martin, and Lee Mitchell, *Presidential Television* (New York: Basic Books, 1973), 34.
14. Robert Bendiner, *White House Fever* (New York: Harcourt, Brace & Co., 1960), 147n.
15. Joe McGinniss, *The Selling of the President 1968* (New York: Trident Press, 1969).
16. Dom Bonafede, "Campaigning by TV—It's Expensive, But Does It Make Any Difference?" *National Journal*, October 11, 1980, 1704.
17. Rhodes Cook, "Attention Shifts to First Presidential Primaries," *Congressional Quarterly Weekly Report*, February 2, 1980, 281.
18. Louis D. Brandeis, "What Publicity Can Do," *Harpers Weekly*, December 20, 1923, 10.
19. Douglas W. Rae, *The Political Consequences of Electoral Laws* (New Haven: Yale University Press, 1967).

20. The Gallup Opinion Index, *Campaign '76* (Report No. 125) shows that nearly four of ten nonvoters in 1972 did not vote because of lack of interest in politics or because they did not like the candidates.
21. Reported by UPI in *Trentonian*, November 22, 1974.
22. Steven Dornfeld, "Candidates: Importance of Pocketbook Power Grows," *St. Paul Pioneer Press*, September 23, 1980.
23. See "19 in House List Assets of $1 Million, *Los Angeles Times*, May 18, 1983; "Senators Report $2.4 Million Total '82 Honorariums," *Los Angeles Times*, May 20, 1983; "Wealth Walks the Halls of Power," *USA Today*, February 16, 1983.

The Drive for Reform 2

For decades official apathy toward serious reform of political finance was a Washington habit. The federal and state laws that were enacted tended to be predominantly negative—their chief purposes were to prohibit and restrict various ways of getting, giving, and spending political money.

From the early twentieth century—when President Theodore Roosevelt proposed disclosure laws, a prohibition on corporate political giving, and government subsidies—until 1961 several presidents went on record in favor of reform, but none took vigorous action.[1] President Kennedy was the first president in modern times to consider campaign financing a critical problem, and he showed this concern in 1961 by appointing a bipartisan Commission on Campaign Costs. This started the reform era, but it was not until 1971 when, in the short space of two months, efforts to revise the antiquated system of political finance came to a sudden climax. Congress passed two measures—the Federal Election Campaign Act of 1971 (FECA),[2] which replaced the 1925 Federal Corrupt Practices Act, and the Revenue Act of 1971.

Until the time the Kennedy Commission was appointed, most of the laws affecting political finance were devised to remedy or prevent flagrant abuses. It evidently was assumed that honest politicians could afford to pay their campaign expenses with their own money or with "untainted" gifts. Efforts to free candidates from dependence upon any one person or interest group usually took the form of restricting or prohibiting contributions from presumably dubious sources. Moreover, arbitrary ceilings were set to prevent excessive spending.

As restrictive laws were passed, however, new methods of raising and spending money soon were devised. When the assessment of government employees was prohibited by the Civil Service Reform Act of 1883,

31

attention shifted to corporate contributions. When they in turn were barred by the Tillman Act of 1907, gifts from wealthy individuals—including many stockholders or officers in corporations—were sought. When direct contributions from the wealthy were limited by law, ways to circumvent the limitations quickly were found.

In this chapter we sketch briefly the history of campaign finance regulation and describe the major laws that currently govern our system of electing candidates for federal office, including the public financing of presidential elections.

Early Efforts at Regulation

After the 1904 election—during which it was charged that corporations were pouring millions of dollars into the Republican campaign to elect Theodore Roosevelt—a move for federal legislation that would force disclosure of campaign spending led to formation of the National Publicity Law Association (NPLA). Under the banner of the NPLA were gathered prominent figures such as Charles Evans Hughes (later chief justice), William Jennings Bryan, Harvard President Charles William Eliot, and American Federation of Labor President Samuel Gompers.

The first federal prohibition of corporate contributions was enacted in 1907, and the first federal campaign fund disclosure law was passed in 1910. The following year an amendment required primary, convention, and preelection financial statements and limited the amounts that could be spent by candidates for the House and Senate. The law was contested in a famous case in 1921 in which the U.S. Supreme Court overturned the conviction of Truman Newberry—a candidate for the Senate in 1918 who defeated Henry Ford in the Republican primary in Michigan—for excessive campaign spending.[3] The Court held that congressional authority to regulate elections did not extend to primaries and nomination activities; most of the questionable expenses in Newberry's campaign had preceded the Republican primary. This narrow interpretation of congressional authority was rejected in 1941 in another Supreme Court case relating to federal-state powers, but Congress did not reassert its power to require disclosure of campaign funds for prenomination campaigns until 1971.[4]

Corrupt Practices Act

Relevant federal legislation was codified and revised, although without substantial change, in the Federal Corrupt Practices Act of 1925. That act remained the basic law until 1972, when the 1971 FECA became effective.

Essentially, the 1925 law required disclosure of receipts and expenditures by candidates for the Senate and House (not for president or vice president) and by political committees that sought to influence federal elections in two or more states. The law also imposed ceilings on expenditures by candidates for federal office, but by establishing multiple committees—thereby decentralizing campaign management—candidates were able to circumvent the limit. The Hatch Act of 1940 limited to $5,000 the amount an individual could contribute to a federal candidate, and the federal gift tax imposed progressive tax rates on contributions of more than $3,000 to a single committee in any year. But under both laws individuals could give up to that amount to numerous committees, each working for the same candidate. Thus, gifts totaling $25,000 or $100,000 or more from one individual to one candidate were legally acceptable. The bar on corporate giving that had been on the books since 1907 was extended temporarily to labor unions in the wartime Smith-Connally Act of 1943 and then made permanent in the Taft-Hartley Act of 1947.

The post-World War II years witnessed a series of congressional gestures, usually no more than committee reports, toward reform. Presidents Truman and Eisenhower expressed concern about the methods used to raise money for political campaigns and, as ex-presidents, both endorsed the Kennedy Commission recommendations.

Commission on Campaign Costs

Kennedy had expressed concern about campaign finance before he became president. He was sensitive to the advantages wealth gave a candidate. Having himself been accused of buying public office, Kennedy was aware of the public's cynicism. Before his inauguration, he set in motion the activities that led to creation of the Commission on Campaign Costs.

Taken as a whole, the commission's report presented a comprehensive program for reforming the financing of the political system, covering not only federal legislative remedies but also bipartisan activities, certain party practices, and state actions.[5] One alternative presented for the first time called for matching funds (or matching incentives) for presidential candidates. Some of the proposals were not to be adopted for more than 12 years, but the report's purpose was more immediate: to get things moving in this area of legislation by detailing a comprehensive program for reform.

The recommendations were received without enthusiasm on Capitol Hill, where certain members of Congress were distrustful of a presidential initiative in a field traditionally considered a legislative prerogative. Nor was there applause from such groups as the U.S. Chamber of Commerce, which was concerned that the tax incentive features would erode the tax base, or from the labor movement, which objected to proposals on public reporting and tax incentives. Press comments were favorable, but election reform remained dormant for several years after Kennedy was assassinated.

The program was one of the few Kennedy creations to suffer seriously in the transition that followed his death. Lyndon Johnson gave the subject no public attention until 1966 when reports of criticism about the President's Club (a group composed of contributors of $1,000 or more, including some government contractors) and other political fund-raising activities moved President Johnson to act. In his 1966 State of the Union address he stated his intention to submit an election reform program. His proposals, however, were not transmitted in time for passage by the 89th Congress.

Forerunners of the FECA

Although neither bill became effective, legislation considered by Congress during the Johnson administration—the Ashmore-Goodell Bill and the Long Act—helped pave the way for election reform measures that later became law.

Ashmore-Goodell Bill. In 1966 the controversy surrounding Connecticut Sen. Thomas Dodd's alleged use of political funds for personal purposes helped spark new interest in reform, and the House subcommittee on elections produced the bipartisan Ashmore-Goodell bill, the most comprehensive bill considered in Congress until that time. The bill was a mixture of the stronger portions of the Johnson and Kennedy proposals and of other bills and proposals. Most important, it called for creation of a bipartisan Federal Election Commission to receive, analyze, audit, and publicize spending reports by all candidates and committees in federal elections. A weakened version of the bill, eliminating the FEC as the single repository of the reports, passed the Senate the following year by a surprising 87-0 vote. But the House failed to act, and the legislation died.

Long Act. The never-implemented Long Act was enacted by Congress in 1966 largely as the result of the persuasion and parliamentary skill of its sponsor, Russell Long of Louisiana, then chairman of the Senate Finance Committee. The bill provided a federal subsidy for presidential elections, a scheme contrasting sharply with a Johnson administration proposal to provide tax incentives for political contributors. Caught off guard, the

White House at the last hour chose to shelve its own recommendation and to support Long's plan.

Long's bill, attached as an amendment to an unrelated bill, called for federal subsidies to be paid to political parties according to a formula based on their presidential candidates' performances in the previous election. Despite a clear lack of visible support from the public, the press, or opinion leaders, the bill passed on the last day of the second session of the 89th Congress and was signed into law by President Johnson.

The new law soon met with negative response. In the spring of 1967, Sen. Albert Gore of Tennessee and Sen. John Williams of Delaware cosponsored an amendment to repeal the Long Act. One of the leaders of the floor fight for repeal, Robert Kennedy, argued that the subsidy put a dangerous amount of power into the hands of the national party chairs. Through promises of distribution of money in the general election, Kennedy argued, the party leaders would be able to influence the delegations of the large states to support their choices for presidential candidates. Rather than repeal, Congress voted to make the act inoperative after May 1967.

Landmark Legislation of 1971

The Long Act and the Ashmore-Goodell bill might be termed the parents of the two laws that constituted a major turning point in the history of campaign finance reform: the Federal Election Campaign Act of 1971 (FECA), which replaced the Federal Corrupt Practices Act of 1925, and the Revenue Act of 1971.

Federal Election Campaign Act

The FECA of 1971, which passed in January 1972, a month after the Revenue Act, required fuller disclosure of political funding than ever before—a factor that was to play a key role in the Watergate affair.[6] Among its provisions, the FECA:

● Set limits on communications media expenditures for candidates for federal office during primary, runoff, special, or general election campaigns. This provision was replaced in the 1974 Amendments with limitations on total spending by candidates (which were then in part declared unconstitutional by the Supreme Court in 1976).[7]

● Placed a ceiling on contributions by candidates or their immediate families to their own campaigns of $50,000 for president or vice president; $35,000 for senator; and $25,000 for representative, delegate, or resident commissioner. This provision later was ruled unconstitutional by the Supreme Court, but the $50,000 limit was reinstated in the 1976 Amendments for presidential election campaigns in which the candidate accepts public funding.[8]

- Stipulated that the appropriate federal supervisory officer to oversee election campaign practices, reporting, and disclosure was the Clerk of the House for House candidates, the Secretary of the Senate for Senate candidates, and the Comptroller General for presidential candidates and miscellaneous other committees. This provision was changed partially by the 1974 Amendments, which established the Federal Election Commission.

- Required candidates for the Senate and House and their committees to file duplicate copies of reports with the secretary of state, or a comparable officer in each state, for local inspection. This provision was designed to help provide information to local voters about the funding of campaigns.

- Required each political committee and candidate to report total contributions as well as the full name, mailing address, occupation, and principal place of business of each person whose aggregate contributions or loans for a calendar year exceed $100; and to report total expenditures, as well as to identify in a similar way, each person to whom are made expenditures whose total value exceeds $100 for a calendar year, including expenditures for personal services, salaries, and reimbursed expenses. The $100 amount in both cases was raised to $200 by the 1979 Amendments.

- Required candidates and committees to file reports of contributions and expenditures on the 10th day of March, June, and September every year, on the 15th and 5th days preceding the date on which an election is held, and on the 31st day of January. Any contribution of $5,000 or more was to be reported within 48 hours if received after the final preelection report. These provisions were partially changed in the 1974 Amendments and again in the 1979 Amendments.

- Required a full and complete financial statement of the costs of a presidential nominating convention within 60 days of the convention.

Revenue Act

The Revenue Act of 1971 provided tax credits or, alternatively, tax deductions for political contributions at all levels and also a tax checkoff to subsidize presidential campaigns during general elections. The act provided that political contributors could claim a tax credit against federal income tax for 50 percent of their contributions (to candidates for federal, state, or local office and to some political committees), up to a maximum of $12.50 on a single return and $25 on a joint return (increased to $25 and $50 in the 1974 Amendments and to $50 and $100 in the Revenue Act of 1978, PL 95-600). Alternatively, the taxpayer could claim a deduction for the full amount of contributions up to a maximum of $50 on a single return and $100 on a joint return. (The deduction, which had been increased to $100 and $200 in the 1974 Amendments, was repealed in the 1978 law that increased the tax credit.)

The tax credits and deductions had an easy passage, but the accompanying tax checkoff provisions have had a long and stormy history. The checkoff represented a revival of a provision of the Long Act of 1966, but it was revised to provide money directly to presidential candidates, not to the political party committees on their behalf. The checkoff provided that every individual whose tax liability for any calendar year was $1 or more could designate on his or her federal income tax form that $1 of this tax money be paid to the Presidential Election Campaign Fund; married couples filing jointly could designate $2. This provision has remained in force ever since.

1974 Amendments

The Watergate scandals brought new pressures for campaign finance reform, but consideration of reform proposals proceeded slowly. Action on a Senate-passed reform bill was stalled throughout 1973 in the House, where the necessity of running for office every two years traditionally made it the more conservative body when dealing with campaign reform. There the bill faced Wayne L. Hays of Ohio, chairman of the Committee on House Administration and a vocal opponent of reform and public financing.

In 1974 campaign reform was a major item on Congress's agenda. President Nixon sent his own proposals to Capitol Hill, but they pleased almost no one in Congress. The Nixon proposals were viewed by many as combining "safe" reforms with others that could not be passed. Nixon called public financing "taxation without representation." [9]

Finally, on August 8, 1974, a few hours before Nixon announced his resignation as president, the House passed, 355-48, a campaign reform bill that differed sharply from a second reform bill the Senate had passed while Hays was delaying consideration of the 1973 bill. The second Senate bill combined the original bill with a call for public funding of presidential and congressional primary and general election campaigns. The more limited House version provided for public funding of presidential nominating conventions and elections.

As finally passed by large margins in both chambers, the bill provided public financing only for presidential elections, including matching funds for the prenomination period; flat grants to the political parties for their national nominating conventions; and larger grants to the major party nominees for their general election campaigns. The bill also created a Federal Election Commission and established a variety of expenditure limitations on political campaigns.

President Ford signed the bill October 15, 1974, and the 1974 FECA Amendments became law. A longtime opponent of public funding, the president expressed doubts about some sections of the law but said that "the times demand this legislation." [10]

Ford's reservations about portions of the bill were borne out when the Supreme Court in 1976 found parts of the legislation unconstitutional (discussed later in this chapter). Among the provisions of the 1974 Amendments invalidated by the *Buckley* decision were expenditure limitations on Senate and House campaigns, found unconstitutional because public funding was not provided for congressional elections. The 1974 Amendments also affected the development of political action committees, to be discussed in detail in Chapter 4.

Federal Election Commission

Established by the 1974 Amendments, the Federal Election Commission was organized formally in April 1975. It was designed to draw together the administrative and enforcement functions that previously were divided among three supervisory officers—the Comptroller General, the Secretary of the Senate, and the Clerk of the House of Representatives—as mandated by the FECA of 1971. [11]

The FEC had a stormy first year. It was in existence only nine months when the Supreme Court, in *Buckley v. Valeo*, declared unconstitutional the method by which the commission members were appointed (some by Congress, some by the president). [12] That meant that for a time the commission could not enforce the FECA or certify matching fund payments to presidential candidates. Congress subsequently changed the procedure for appointing the members, and the FEC was reconstituted.

From the outset, a potential conflict was apparent between the new commissioners' experience and friendships on Capitol Hill and their need for impartial handling of congressional elections. The first appointments to the commission included four former representatives. To achieve credibility as an independent agency, there was a clear need to establish the FEC's freedom from the Congress it was in part established to regulate. Some members of Congress, it turned out, did not want the FEC to be very independent where congressional elections were concerned.

Early FEC Regulations Rejected

Another problem for the FEC arose because the regulations it wrote had to be submitted to Congress along with an explanation and justification. If neither the Senate nor the House disapproved by a formal vote within 30 "legislative" days (days each house is in session), the regulation would have the force of law. Such review of regulations (later declared unconstitutional) threatened the independence of the affected agency, in this case the FEC.

Commissioners claim the FEC seeks a balanced relationship with Congress, but discord developed very early in its existence. In fact, Congress rejected the first two FEC regulations, one dealing with congressional expense accounts and the other with "point of entry"—the question of which office would first receive reports from candidates for federal office.

The proposed regulation regarding congressional expense accounts, submitted to Congress in July 1975, sought to treat donations received by members of Congress, ostensibly to supplement money appropriated for office expenses, as political rather than legislative funds. As such they would be subject to the same limits and disclosure requirements as campaign contributions. In October 1975 the Senate vetoed the proposal, and the FEC was forced to submit a compromise version that was weakened further under pressure from some members. Although the revised proposal was cleared finally by Congress, the release of the Supreme Court's *Buckley* decision intervened before the regulation could be issued.

The proposed point-of-entry regulation required that all candidate and political committee fund reports be filed originally with the FEC; then the FEC would provide microfilm copies of the reports to the Secretary of the Senate and the Clerk of the House within two working days. Such a system would have provided more effective disclosure under efficient procedures, but it was rejected by the House.

Opponents of the proposal argued that House custody of the original reports was essential if the House was to pass judgment in any cases of contested elections or alleged unethical behavior in campaign fund raising or spending. House members also were concerned that the FEC would not provide them with the same services offered by the Office of the Clerk of the House: that of checking their disclosure filings before they submitted verified reports, thus helping them avoid possible violations of the law.

Reluctantly, the FEC bowed before the opposition and revised its proposal, reversing the procedure so that candidates filed first with the clerk and the secretary, who then passed on copies to the FEC. Although the re-written proposal subsequently was cleared by Congress, as in the case of the congressional expense account regulation, the Supreme Court's *Buckley* decision was handed down before the regulation could be issued.

In mid-1983 the Supreme Court ruled unconstitutional use of the legislative veto by which Congress had rejected the two sets of regulations proposed by the FEC. The Court's decision had its origins in a deportation case involving the Immigration and Naturalization Service and the attorney general, but the ruling applied to all congressional use of the veto technique to limit the power of the president, executive branch officials, and federal regulatory agencies, such as the FEC.[13] A 7-to-2 majority of the Court held that the legislative veto provisions Congress had written into laws giving the executive branch qualified authority to act violated principles of separation of powers and the system of checks and balances embodied in the Constitution. Time will tell how the decision will affect the operation of the FEC and its relationship with its congressional overseers. Congress, of course, retains the power of the purse as well as the power to refuse to dele-gate authority to executive agencies or to require that proposed regulations be enacted by Congress in statute form.

Constitutional Challenge

In addition to its early liaison and communications problems with Congress, the new FEC's future was clouded almost immediately by a legal suit challenging not only the constitutionality of most of the major provisions of the 1974 Amendments but also the commission's very existence.

In *Buckley v. Valeo*, the courts confronted a difficult judicial task. The dilemmas to be resolved made the issue one of appropriate debate for the decade in which the United States marked its bicentennial. The problem, in its simplest form, was for the courts to balance the First Amendment rights of free speech and free association against the clear power of the legislature to enact laws designed to protect the integrity of the election system. Involved were questions of public discussion and political dialogue. Basi-cally, the plaintiffs sought to ensure that the reforms, however well meant, did not have a chilling effect on free speech or on citizen participation.

An unusual feature of the law had authorized any eligible voter to start federal court proceedings to contest the constitutionality of any provision of the law. The provision, sponsored in the Senate by James L. Buckley, New York Conservative-Republican, had been designed to speed along any case by permitting questions of constitutionality to be certified directly to the federal court of appeals, which was obliged to expedite the case. A case was brought a few days after the law became effective on January 1, 1975. Plaintiffs covered a broad spectrum of liberals and conservatives, both individuals and organizations, and included Senator Buckley, Eugene J. McCarthy, former Democratic senator from Minnesota, and Stewart R. Mott (a large contributor). Defendants included Secretary of the Senate Francis R. Valeo, the attorney general, the FEC, the Clerk of the House, and three reform groups: Common Cause, the Center for Public Financing of Elections, and the League of Women Voters.

On January 30, 1976, a little over a year after the case was initiated, the Supreme Court reversed many major points that had been considered and upheld by the court of appeals. The impact of the decision has been great not only on the regulation of federal elections but also on state and local law.

The central question was posed by Justice Potter Stewart during oral arguments: Is money speech and speech money? Or, stated differently, is an expenditure for speech substantially the same thing as speech itself, because the expenditure is necessary to reach large audiences by the purchase of air time or space in the print media? The decision resolved the conflict by asserting the broadest protection to First Amendment rights to assure the unrestrained interchange of ideas for bringing about popular political and social change. Accordingly, the court majority concluded that expenditure limitations imposed direct and substantial restraints on the quantity of political speech. This applied to limits on candidates' personal expenditures on their own behalf as well as on spending by or on behalf of a candidate. An exception was made, however, with reference to overall candidate expenditure limits, with the Court holding that candidates who accepted public funding when provided by the government also could be obliged to accept campaign expenditure limits as a condition of the granting of the public money. The Court made clear that independent spending by individuals and groups could be considered a protected form of free speech only if the spending were truly independent. Independent spending, then, could not be coordinated with candidates or their campaign organizations nor consented to by candidates or their agents.

On the other hand, the Court upheld the limits on individual and group contributions to campaigns, asserting that these constitute only a marginal restriction on the contributor's ability to engage in free communication. Saying that free expression rests on contributing as a symbolic act to help give a candidate the means to speak out, the Court also asserted that the quantity of speech does not increase perceptibly with the size of the contribution. Hence limits on contributions were constitutional. The Supreme Court found that there was a real or imagined coercive influence of large contributors on candidates' positions, and on their actions if elected, leading to corruption or the appearance of corruption, and it said that contribution limits were acceptable because they serve to mute the voices of affluent persons and groups while also restraining the skyrocketing costs of political campaigns.

The Court sustained all the disclosure requirements of the law, sanctioned the forms of public funding provided by the federal law, and upheld the concept of a bipartisan regulatory commission to administer and enforce the law so long as the agency was within the executive branch of the government and its members were appointed by the president. This last point required Congress to reconstitute the FEC, whose six members had been appointed by the president, the Senate, and the House.

1976 Amendments

Although the Supreme Court required appointment of all members of the commission by the president within 30 days, the actual reconstitution of the FEC took 111 days. The process was complicated by proposals for controversial changes in the law, including the public funding of congressional campaigns. When Congress failed to act within the 30-day period, an additional delay of 20 days was granted by the Court. On March 22, 1976, after Congress again failed to act promptly, the FEC lost its executive functions and consequently could not certify payments of matching funds to candidates then seeking their parties' presidential nominations. Until the law was revised, government funds could not be paid out, forcing the candidates to economize while relying solely on private funds.

Much of the delay occurred because Congress was unable or unwilling to act promptly. President Ford requested a simple reconstitution to permit the FEC to continue to operate through the 1976 election. He argued against becoming bogged down in other controversial changes. Instead, Congress undertook significant revisions dealing with compliance and enforcement procedures, the issuing of advisory opinions, and the role of corporate and labor political action committees. It was clear that the initiative in campaign finance regulation was passing from reformers and the media supporting them to those directly affected by the regulations: incumbents, political parties, and major interest groups.

Finally, in May 1976 the commission was reconstituted according to the Supreme Court ruling. Within a few hours of being sworn in, the commission certified $3.2 million due to various candidates and $1 million to the major party national conventions. The FEC had continued to process submissions for matching funds while certifications were suspended.

The Ford campaign was relatively healthy financially throughout the hiatus. Ronald Reagan, Ford's main rival for the Republican nomination, charged that the president benefited from "interest-free credit" from the government, which billed the President Ford Committee while other candidates needed advance money before their chartered planes would fly. The effect on Ford's campaign was not clear, because Reagan went into debt in this period yet won primaries in Texas, Indiana, Georgia, and Alabama. As the campaign became more heated, Ford's financial advantage was slowly dissipated. The delays did not hurt Carter seriously, although he lost nine of the last 14 primaries in a winning campaign for the nomination. Given his momentum, prompt matching funds could have helped him in the later primaries.

1979 Amendments

Throughout the 1976 campaigns and in the years following, there was considerable discussion among those regulated by the FECA about the effects of the law and its amendments on the conduct of campaigns and on election outcomes. Recommendations for further changes in the law were offered by the White House, the FEC, and members of Congress. In August 1978 the House Administration Committee commissioned Harvard University's Institute of Politics to study and report on the impact of the FECA and its amendments. The study, which took nearly a year to complete, singled out three problems caused by the implementation of the act and its amendments: the individual contribution limits were set too low; political parties were weakened further; and the laws imposed burdensome reporting requirements on election campaigns.[14] In order to alleviate these and other problems it cited, the report recommended numerous legislative changes.

Although not all the recommendations made in the report were acceptable to Senate and House members for immediate action, several of its recommendations were influential in mid-1979, when the matter of revising the FECA was taken up by the Senate Rules Committee. In December

1979, after differences between Senate and House versions of the proposed law had been worked out, Congress passed the 1979 Amendments to the FECA, and on January 8, 1980, President Carter signed them into law.[15]

The amendments were designed to be "noncontroversial" to ensure passage. They were intended to ease candidate and political committee reporting requirements, to give political parties an expanded role in federal elections, and to change other procedural matters. Thus they represented a relaxation of some of the constraints earlier reforms had imposed on the electoral process. Nevertheless, some of the changes—particularly those expanding the role of state and local party committees—had far-reaching effects in the 1980 election, as is described in Chapter 5.

Essentially the 1979 Amendments simplified record keeping and public reporting requirements, increased the permissible role of state and local political parties, and refined the procedural requirements of the enforcement process.

Among its major provisions, the new law:

● Exempted candidates receiving or spending $5,000 or less from filing disclosure reports; the same applied to local party committees under certain circumstances.

● Changed some political committee organizational requirements.

● Increased the amount that volunteers may spend on travel and home entertainment on behalf of a candidate without reporting it as a contribution from $500 to $1,000 and on behalf of a political party from $1,000 to $2,000.

● Permitted state and local party committees to spend unlimited amounts on certain voter registration and get-out-the-vote activities, and on certain campaign materials used for volunteer activities.

● Raised the level of itemized reporting of contributions and expenditures from amounts in excess of $100 to amounts in excess of $200, and raised the threshold for reporting of independent expenditures from amounts in excess of $100 to amounts in excess of $250.

● Reduced certain public reporting filings and changed filing dates.

● Permitted the FEC to initiate random audits but only when there is indication of significant violations.

● Clarified certain compliance and enforcement actions.

● Prohibited personal use of excess campaign funds except in limited circumstances.

● Raised from $2 million to $3 million the amount that major political parties may receive to operate their national nominating conventions.

One of the differences between the House and Senate versions of the 1979 FECA Amendments that had to be worked out before passage could be assured was the matter of conversion of excess campaign contributions to personal use. Senate rules prohibited personal use of campaign contributions by both sitting and retired members. House rules prohibited sitting members from converting campaign funds to personal use but permitted retired members to do so. No provision to exclude the personal use of such funds was included in the House version of the bill. Legislative redistricting following the 1980 census meant more incumbents than usual probably would be defeated. Some congressional incumbents apparently looked forward to excess campaign contributions to cushion their possible defeat—a sort of consolation prize for losers. In the compromise version of the amendments, House incumbents were excepted from the prohibition on personal use of excess campaign funds.

Studies published in 1982 and 1983 maintained that despite House and Senate rules, personal use of campaign surpluses by sitting members of both houses of Congress was neither isolated nor inconsequential.[16] Such funds, the studies reported, continue to be used for a wide variety of non-campaign-related purposes, including foreign travel expenses, loans to congressional staff members, automobile repair bills, and country club dues, as well as for campaign-related purposes, including presidential campaigns undertaken by congressional incumbents.

An Evolving Federal Election Commission

Since beginning its operations early in April 1975, the FEC has been a focus of considerable controversy. Some criticism of the commission is inevitable, for inherent in the idea of creating an agency to regulate elections rests a philosophical dilemma: how closely can elections be regulated in order to preserve the integrity of the electoral process and still allow for free and untrammeled political exchange?

The actual criticisms leveled at the commission do not address the philosophical dilemma directly. Instead they take the form of allegations of violations of due process by the agency and its enforcement procedures; of administrative inefficiency, particularly regarding its conduct of campaign audits; of favoritism in hiring and appointment practices and in enforcement procedures; and excessive zeal in enforcing the letter of the law. Consequently the commission has suffered from uncertainty about its mandate, both on Capitol Hill and at times among the commissioners and staff, and thus has been unable to achieve clarity of purpose. The agency has had to spend substantial time and resources defending itself, which has detracted from its primary responsibility of administering and enforcing the election laws.

Commission Structure

In accord with the 1976 FECA Amendments, the FEC is composed of eight members: the Secretary of the Senate and the Clerk of the House, or their designees, who serve ex officio and without the right to vote; and six members appointed by the president and confirmed by the Senate. The terms of the appointments are staggered and are for six years each. No more than three of the appointees may be affiliated with the same political party. The commission elects from its members a chair and a vice-chair—each of a different political party—and the chair serves a term of only one year, in order to prevent a particular party or interest from dominating agency decisions and actions.

In 1979 the Campaign Finance Study Group of Harvard University's Institute of Politics recommended that the FEC chair be appointed to a four-year term and that he or she be responsible for administering the agency. The chair's responsibilities also would include appointing the staff director and general counsel and preparing the agency's budget. Under existing law, the commission decides administrative and fiscal business by majority vote; the chair represents the agency and presides over the commission meetings, but has little authority. The Harvard Study stated:

> This intentionally "weak" commission structure creates ... problems that need to be addressed: an absence of adequate accountability on the part of appointed officials; indirect delegation of responsibility to staff without adequate policy direction; and the likelihood that the staff, faced with such absence of direction, will either focus on non-controversial, minor paperwork matters, or, worse, assume policymaking functions properly reserved to publicly accountable officials.[17]

In 1981 Common Cause, a self-styled citizens' lobbying organization that had supported campaign reform legislation in the early 1970s, made similar recommendations in a study of its own. The organization agreed with the Campaign Finance Study Group that much of the blame for the agency's administrative inefficiency and lack of clear direction must be directed at Congress. "It is quite clear that the Congress was uncomfortable with the concept of a strong and independent commission established to protect the public's interest in clean and competitive elections," said the Common Cause study. "Instead, when forced to establish an election commission in the face of public outrage over Watergate, Congress deliberately weakened the commission with structural defects and a continuing congressional presence that undermines the very concept of independent enforcement." [18]

Appointments

The process of appointing members to the Federal Election Commission has been a continuing source of conflict. The opposing influences of labor and business frequently are brought to bear on appointments. The conservative and liberal wings of both parties screen each nominee, giving special attention to his or her views. Expertise and political cronyism often vie as criteria for appointments. Ideally, the commission should be comprised of elections experts or persons experienced in election administration, political party or campaign management, and those who have run for office. In fact, according to some critics, appointments to the FEC have been unduly influenced by the appointees' political connections and leanings.

Despite the Supreme Court's 1976 *Buckley* decision mandating appointment of the commissioners by the president, President Ford continued to make his appointments with congressional wishes clearly in mind. Some of President Carter's appointments, however, encountered criticism. He was forced to withdraw his first choice as a Democratic nominee, Susan King, in the face of opposition from House Speaker Thomas P. O'Neill Jr. and House Majority Whip John Brademas. Carter then nominated John W. McGarry, at the suggestion of O'Neill, but that choice met with resistance from critics who questioned whether the independence of the commission could be maintained if McGarry, a close friend of O'Neill's, were approved. Because of opposition from Republicans and from the corporate community, McGarry twice failed to receive Senate approval. Finally, in October 1978, Carter made a recess appointment, replacing outgoing Commissioner Neil Staebler with McGarry. He succeeded in having the appointment approved in February 1979, when he submitted it in tandem with that of popular Republican Max Friedersdorf.

Carter's first choice of a Republican nominee, Samuel Zagoria, also met with strong opposition from the Republican leadership and corporate interests, who were concerned that Zagoria had been endorsed by some labor representatives and that he would support public financing of congressional elections. Carter was forced to withdraw Zagoria's name, and he nominated Freidersdorf instead.

Carter's second pair of appointments also encountered opposition. In May 1979 the president renominated Democrat Thomas Harris for a six-year term and Republican Frank P. Reiche, who had served as unpaid chairman of the New Jersey Election Law Enforcement Commission, to replace outgoing Commissioner Vernon Thomson. Although Harris was questioned about problems the FEC had experienced during his term at the agency, his nomination was approved the following month. Reiche's nomination, however, was held up by conservative Republican opponents who maintained that the New Jersey lawyer supported public financing of congressional campaigns and that he would not be sufficiently partisan as a Republican nominee to the FEC. Finally, Reiche's nomination was approved, and he became the first FEC commissioner to have had election-campaign regulation experience prior to his appointment.

During the first year of his presidency, Ronald Reagan had an opportunity to make three appointments to the commission, two to replace commissioners whose terms were scheduled to end in April 1981 and a third to replace Commissioner Friedersdorf, who had resigned in December 1980 to become President-elect Reagan's chief liaison with Congress. After some haggling among themselves, congressional Democrats submitted a list of Democrats competent to serve on the FEC. Reagan chose one of them, Danny McDonald, a former member of the Tulsa Board of Elections. Reagan's two Republican nominees were Joan Aikens, a member of the FEC since its inception, whom he appointed to complete the two years remaining of Friedersdorf's term, and Lee Ann Elliott, a Chicago Republican who had served for 16 years as associate executive director of the American Medical Political Action Committee (AMPAC). Although Elliott's nomination made some liberals within and outside Congress uncomfortable, both because of her work with AMPAC and her support for corporate PACs, it was confirmed by the Senate, along with the nominations of McDonald and Aikens. In 1983 Aikens and McGarry were reappointed and confirmed without controversy.

Advisory Opinions

When Congress rewrote the FECA in 1976 it set new standards for the FEC in writing advisory opinions (AOs) to guide candidates and other interested parties in complying with the law. The commission itself had stopped issuing AOs following the 1976 *Buckley* decision and began evaluating them in light of the decision. Many of the 76 AOs that it had issued through December 1975 had been criticized by practitioners and scholars for being narrow and legalistic, for inflexibly following the rigidities in the law, and for failing to consider traditional political practices.[19]

The new standards set in the 1976 Amendments stipulate that the FEC cannot issue rules of general applicability but must apply AOs only to specific facts presented in a request. Any rules of general applicability must be incorporated into the regulations. But the commission itself determines how broadly or narrowly to interpret the law.

Since the enactment of the 1976 Amendments, the FEC responds in two ways to new requests for advisory opinions. It issues formal advisory opinions if they are applicable to specific factual situations. In other cases, the FEC issues responses to advisory opinions (AORs) that clearly state that they are not formal advisory opinions but responses based on proposed regulations. While the AOs provide the full protections and immunities granted by the law, the responses to advisory opinions, which involve reliance on proposed regulations, do not afford the same protection to the requesters.

The 1979 Amendments extend the right to request an advisory opinion from the FEC to any person who has an inquiry about a specific campaign transaction. They also require the agency to respond to advisory opinion requests within 60 days, and within 20 days if the request is made within the 60-day period prior to an election.

Voluntary Compliance

A major goal for the commission has been to induce voluntary compliance. After enactment of the 1971 FECA, expertise in fulfilling compliance requirements began to develop in the private sector, as candidates and political committees turned to lawyers, accountants, and computer specialists for advice on how to comply. Numerous booklets, manuals, and guides eased the burden of compliance. Once it began functioning, the Federal Election Commission supplanted these as the major source of compliance information. It established a toll-free "hot-line" to answer questions and held seminars throughout the country in preparation for the 1976 campaigns.

During the 1976 prenomination period, candidates and convention committees found increasing compliance costs particularly burdensome. In the general election campaign, public financing helped ease these financial problems for the two major presidential contenders. Moreover, an FEC ruling in the midst of the 1976 campaign clarified a provision of the 1976

Amendments that allowed compliance-related expenditures to be counted separately and not be charged against statutory limitations. If necessary, money could be raised from private sources for this purpose.

Prior to the establishment of the FEC, the Department of Justice had sole authority in cases of campaign finance law violation. From 1975 to 1979, the FEC and the Justice Department divided jurisdiction by mutual agreement. All "serious and substantial" violations of the act were the responsibility of the Department of Justice, and the commission assumed responsibility for handling less serious violations. The 1979 Amendments, however, gave the commission "exclusive jurisdiction" over all civil matters relating to the act. The Justice Department can pursue unilaterally criminal enforcement matters or follow through on referrals from the commission. Such referrals, which usually require the commission's determinations of a "knowing and willful" violation that cannot be resolved through the agency's own resources, have not been common. Further, most provisions of the act do not easily lend themselves to criminal violation. Thus the Department of Justice regularly refers reporting and organizational offenses to the commission.

The act specifically mandates the commission to encourage voluntary compliance with the law, and the commission has committed itself to correct or prevent violations by seeking conciliation before resorting to civil enforcement actions. Candidates and committees, however, may agree to conciliation for a variety of reasons. The exceptional pressures of time and publicity may make a candidate under investigation by the FEC reluctant to choose any other course. Further, fines levied by the FEC regularly are less than the anticipated costs of litigation. Finally, although the FEC does not formally adjudicate, the commission does interpret matters of law, determine matters of fact, and publicly declare violations of law. These powers cannot be easily ignored.

Audits

The commission's exercise of its audit authority has been a matter of contention almost from the beginning. Both the slow pace of its audits and the conduct of random audits of congressional campaigns were the focus of controversy and criticism during and after the 1976 elections. Critics complained that it took nearly three years for the agency to release the Carter prenomination and general election campaign audits and that the audits either revealed only minor infractions or left some matters unresolved. Members of Congress expressed concern that the commission's random audits of their campaigns would confuse the public, giving them the appearance of wrongdoing where none existed; would subject the members to attack by their opponents; and would be unproductive and a waste of money and resources.

In 1978, under continuing congressional pressure, the FEC eliminated the random audit procedure and set up a schedule that gave top priority to candidates and committees needing assistance in reporting and record keeping. In 1979 the agency contracted with Arthur Andersen and Company, a major accounting firm, and Accountants in the Public Interest to study its political campaign auditing process. Both organizations made a number of recommendations for change,[20] but a management plan drawn up to implement the recommendations was withdrawn in favor of a plan that would give greater emphasis to presidential campaign audits.

In the 1979 Amendments, Congress eliminated the FEC's authority to conduct random audits and required a vote of four FEC members to conduct an audit after it determined that a committee had not complied substantially with the election campaign law.

Although the agency completed its 1980 presidential nomination and general election campaign audits of publicly funded committees far more quickly than it had completed similar audits of 1976 campaigns, critics of FEC audit policy and procedures still found cause for complaint. In April 1981 lawyers representing nine of the campaign committees of the 1980 Democratic and Republican presidential contenders and the two major national political parties sent joint letters to the commission and to Congress attacking the FEC's audit methods as "insensitive to the realities of the presidential campaign process and the First Amendment expression which is at the heart of every political campaign."[21] The Campaign Counsel Group, as it called itself, complained in particular that the commission staff substituted its judgment for that of the campaign committees, which had acted in good faith to comply with the law. The FEC subsequently rejected the group's complaint and defended the commission's audit procedures.

Open Meetings

The FEC, which decided at the outset to be a "sunshine" agency, holds regular open meetings except when dealing with personnel actions or enforcement, operates under code of ethics for its members and employees, and provides easy public access to its records and discussions, including the maintenance of a public room for inspection of political fund reports. It also seeks to provide ample information to induce voluntary compliance.

Under the FECA, the FEC assumed responsibility for the Clearing-house on Election Administration that carries on activities and publishes studies relating to registration of voters, voting, and election administration. Until 1979 the Clearinghouse served as a communication link among federal, state, and local election agencies. It contracted with the Congressional Research Service of the Library of Congress to publish periodically a federal-state election law survey analyzing federal and state legislation and judicial decisions and to issue an occasional survey of state election laws. But in the 1979 Amendments, the Clearinghouse role was pared back to deal with federal elections only. Some of its functions have since been restored.

Past and Prologue

By the beginning of the 1980s, the United States had in place an election regulation system that had taken most of the previous decade to enact and "debug." Federal elections were subject to strict rules for disclosure of spending and contributions, with the role of the wealthy donor greatly diminished and with public money available for the campaigns of presidential candidates. Unlike the negative reforms of the past, which attempted to prevent election abuses by telling candidates and vested interests what they could not do, public funding was a positive step forward in that it provided a substitute for the source of funds that the law partially dried up.

The new election system was under the administration of an independent commission, and units throughout the country performed a similar function for state and local elections. The states' experience with campaign finance laws will be discussed in Chapter 7.

In contrast to the early 1970s, when the House was more conservative than the Senate on campaign reform matters, in the early 1980s the Republican-controlled Senate is the more conservative body. Indeed, in recent years the House has taken the initiative on campaign finance reform. In 1979, for example, the House passed a bill—described in Chapter 4—limiting aggregate PAC contributions to candidates and lowering individual PAC contribution limits. It almost passed a congressional public financing bill. The Senate, however, stalled action on the PAC bill by threat of filibuster and took no action on the matter of congressional public funding. In the immediate future, campaign reform proposals probably will have greater chance of success in the House than in the Senate.

Notes

1. This chapter is derived in part from: Herbert E. Alexander, *Money in Politics* (Washington, D.C.: Public Affairs Press, 1972), 183-251. See also Louise Overacker, *Money in Elections* (New York: Macmillan, 1932), 107; Alexander Heard, *The Costs of Democracy* (Chapel Hill: University of North Carolina Press, 1960), 334-335; and David W. Adamany and George E. Agree, *Political Money: A Strategy for Campaign Financing in America* (Baltimore: Johns Hopkins University Press, 1975).
2. For a case study of the enactment of FECA, see Robert L. Peabody, Jeffrey M. Berry, William G. Frasure, and Jerry Goldman, *To Enact a Law: Congress and Campaign Financing* (New York: Praeger Publishers, 1972).
3. *Newberry v. United States*, 256 U.S. 232 (1921).
4. *United States v. Classic*, 313 U.S. 299 (1941).
5. *Financing Presidential Campaigns*, Report of the President's Commission on Campaign Costs (Washington, D.C.: Government Printing Office, 1962).
6. P.L. 92-225.
7. P.L. 93-443.
8. P.L. 94-283.
9. Christopher Lydon, "President Urges Campaign Reform with Gift Limits," *New York Times*, March 9, 1974.
10. John Herbers, "Bill to Reform Campaign Funds Signed by Ford Despite Doubts," *New York Times*, October 16, 1974.
11. Paul T. David, "The Federal Election Commission: Origins and Early Activities," *National Civic Review* 65 (June 1976): 278-283.
12. *Buckley v. Valeo*, 424 U.S. 1 (1976).
13. *INS v. Chadha*, 462 U.S. — (1983).
14. U.S. Congress, House, House Administration Committee, *An Analysis of the Impact of the Federal Election Campaign Act, 1972-78*, from the Institute of Politics, John F. Kennedy School of Government, Harvard University (Washington, D.C.: Government Printing Office, 1979).
15. P.L. 96-187.
16. Bill Hayes, Diane Kiesel, and Alan Green, "The New Slush Fund Scandal," *New Republic*, August 30, 1982; and "The Senate's Secret Slush Funds," *New Republic*, June 20, 1983. See also Correspondence, "Senator Cranston's View," *New Republic*, June 27, 1983, 2, for a response from Sen. Alan Cranston, D-Calif., who, according to the latter article, used his unofficial office account to pay for a variety of items and services related to his presidential campaign.
17. U.S. Congress, *An Analysis of the Impact*, 17.
18. Common Cause, *Stalled from the Start: A Common Cause Study of the Federal Election Commission* (Washington, D.C.: Common Cause, 1980), iii-iv.
19. *Annual Report*, Federal Election Commission, Washington, D.C., March 1976, 30-32.
20. Arthur Andersen & Co., "Review of the Political Campaign Auditing Process" (September 1979); and Accountants for the Public Interest, untitled study of the Federal Election Commission's audit process (September 1979).

21. Edward L. Weidenfeld et al., letter from the Campaign Counsel Group to John McGarry, chairman of the FEC, April 30, 1981.

Sources of Funds: Individuals 3

The 1976 Supreme Court ruling on the campaign finance laws left areas where "big money" might still influence campaigns—notably the unlimited spending permitted certain candidates in their own campaigns and the unlimited independent expenditures permitted so long as the effort is not co-ordinated with a candidate. On the other hand, the court upheld the $1,000 individual contribution limit, which reduced the possibilities of a candidate's becoming beholden to a few large donors. The effect of the reform laws becomes apparent when sources of campaign funds for the 1976 and 1980 presidential elections—the first to be conducted with public funding and under the contribution limits—are compared with sources of funds for earlier presidential election campaigns.

Campaign Financing—Pre-1968

Money collected from the candidates themselves and assessments on officeholders were sufficient to finance some of the earliest American presidential campaigns. Yet the system was expensive for those participating, and only a few could afford to run for office. Even after election, the salary was low, there was entertaining to do, and there were other demands on personal funds. Thomas Jefferson was almost insolvent at the end of his second term as president.[1]

By the 1830s regular assessments were being levied on the government employees in the New York Custom House, and it was observed that those who refused to pay lost favor.[2] Soon, however, the money raised this way was not enough. Andrew Jackson generally is credited with bringing in the "spoils system," rewarding with favors and government jobs those who had contributed to campaigns. The payoff, of course, might include favorable government policies as well as jobs and contracts.

When August Belmont, an American who represented the House of Rothschild, set up the Democratic National Committee (DNC) in 1852, he did so to raise funds for the party's presidential candidate, Franklin Pierce. His solicitations apparently were not successful, for it was reported that "at the opportune moment Belmont stepped in and contributed a large sum to the national committee. Thus the matter of funds was taken care of." [3] He would not be the last chairman to contribute money to the party.

With the end of the Civil War, the great corporations and individuals who had amassed fortunes from American industry began to pay a major share of presidential campaign costs. Ulysses S. Grant is said to have entered office in 1869 more heavily mortgaged to wealthy contributors than any candidate before him.[4] His $150,000 campaign was largely financed by men such as Commodore Cornelius Vanderbilt, the Astors, and Jay Cooke.[5] They represented the railroad and land grant interests that, along with major corporations, supplied most of the Republican money. Then, as later, only a small number of the wealthy were on the Democrats' side, but they included individuals such as Belmont, Cyrus H. McCormick, and Samuel J. Tilden. Accordingly, the Democrats were only relatively disadvantaged.

Throughout the 1860s and 1870s, Jay Cooke held intimate fundraising dinners in Washington, D.C., for the benefit of the Republican party.[6] That businessmen should support the political party that most clearly favored their financial interests was accepted practice. "Frying the fat" was a phrase used to describe the means of acquiring campaign contributions from Pennsylvania manufacturers.

The Democrats attempted to raise money in the same way. In 1868 eight Democrats including Belmont, still chairman of the DNC, signed a business contract with the treasurer of the party in which each agreed to give $10,000 "to defray the just and lawful expenses of circulating documents and newspapers, perfecting organizations, etc., to promote the election of Seymour and Blair." [7]

In 1876 the Democrats nominated Samuel J. Tilden, said by some to be worth as much as $10 million.[8] Cartoonist Thomas Nast showed him supporting the Democratic campaign chest out of his own "barrel." [9] Actually, Tilden was notoriously tightfisted. He may have lost the election to Rutherford B. Hayes (although he led the Republican contender in both popular and, initially, electoral votes) because he was unwilling to spend enough money to win over more electoral votes.

James A. Garfield, in his presidential campaign in 1880, appealed to his managers to assess government employees for the money he would need.

That was the last election, however, in which that source could be tapped legally.[10] Reformers had launched a concerted attack on that system, and the Civil Service Reform Act of 1883 began to protect federal workers from the demands of the parties for tribute money.

The financing of campaigns found its genius in Mark Hanna, who rose from wholesale grocer in Cleveland to maker of presidents because of his ability to raise funds for the Republican party. In 1888 he raised more money than the Republican National Committee (RNC) could spend; he returned the excess to the donors on a pro rata basis.[11]

In Hanna's view, there were few things that could not be bought; his battle to secure the Republican nomination for William McKinley in 1896 reportedly cost $100,000.[12] Hanna was named chairman of the RNC that year and on McKinley's behalf proceeded to organize a presidential campaign on a scale never seen before. In a style that pioneered the fund-raising techniques of later generations, quotas were set and contributions were determined by ability to pay. Banks were assessed at one-quarter of 1 percent (.0025) of their capital. Life insurance companies, together with many other business organizations, contributed.

Hanna tried to make it clear that there were to be no favors in return for contributions; McKinley wanted to remain clean. In 1900 Hanna returned a $10,000 gift to a Wall Street brokerage firm that he believed was making a specific demand.[13]

The Republicans might not have had such easy access to large funds if the business community had not thought the stakes so large. The free silver issue threatened the existing economic policies of the United States, and William Jennings Bryan and the people around him struck fear in many a Republican heart. These campaigns pitted the rich against the poor, the Eastern establishment against Western farmers.

Bryan never had access to funds in amounts the Republicans had. In 1896 he attempted to match the Republican campaign with resources of only $675,000, about 20 percent of the GOP total. Bryan lost some wealthy "Gold Democrats" to McKinley; most of the contributions Bryan received came from a group of wealthy silver mine owners.[14]

Of the $3.5 million estimated cost of the 1896 Republican campaign, about $3 million was said to have come from New York City and vicinity and the rest from Chicago.[15] Harold L. Ickes, who worked in that election for McKinley, later wrote: "I never doubted that if the Democrats had been able to raise enough money, even for legitimate purposes, Bryan would have been elected." [16]

Elected vice president in 1900, Theodore Roosevelt succeeded to the presidency on the death of McKinley in 1901. For his campaign in 1904, TR turned down the suggestion of Lincoln Steffens that he depend on small gifts of from $1 to $5.[17] He solicited funds from two of the country's richest men, railroad magnate E. H. Harriman and Henry C. Frick, a partner of Andrew Carnegie. According to one account, Frick later reported: "He got down on his knees to us. We bought the son of a bitch and then he did not stay bought." [18] Despite the immense corporate and individual contributions to his campaign, Roosevelt showed little appreciation for the "hand that had fed him" as he began to attack the trusts and the men who had given to his campaign.

It took a long time to recognize the need to avoid obligations to special interests, although as early as 1873 in a speech at the University of Wisconsin, Chief Justice Edward G. Ryan of the Wisconsin Supreme Court had said: "The question will arise . . . which shall rule—wealth or man; which shall lead—money or intellect; who shall fill public station— educated and patriotic free men, or the feudal serfs of corporate capital." [19] Charles P. Taft, the brother of William Howard Taft, contributed $250,000 to his brother's campaigns in 1908 and 1912 because he did not want him to have to go begging to the large corporations or be under obligation to anyone as president.[20] In 1907 Roosevelt made several proposals to Congress to improve the political finance system, including government funding of political campaigns. One proposal, prohibiting direct corporate contributions to federal campaigns, was adopted that year and remains the law today.

The 1936 presidential campaign was one of the most expensive on record—the total was not exceeded until the 1960 race—and it gave birth to a new fund-raising technique that quickly became a staple, the $100-a-plate dinner. The technique is credited to Matthew McCloskey, a Philadelphia contractor and later treasurer and finance chairman of the DNC, who arranged a dinner at the time of Franklin Delano Roosevelt's inauguration to raise money for the Democrats.[21] The idea spread quickly and widely; the $100-a-plate dinners, luncheons, breakfasts, and brunches became common at all levels of the political system. With affluence and increased needs, $500-a-plate and $1,000-a-plate affairs were held for more select groups. In 1968 Richard Nixon held just one fund-raising dinner, but 22 cities were linked by closed-circuit television for that one event. The dinner grossed $6 million; the net profit, $4.6 million, was close to one-fifth the to- tal cost of the campaign.

Big contributors continued to play a major part in the campaigns of the 1940s, 1950s, and 1960s. In 1948, for example, close to 7 of every 10 dollars (69 percent) contributed to the Democrats' national level committees came from donations of $500 or more. In 1956 the comparable proportion for the Republicans was 74 percent. In 1964, 69 percent of the Democrats' money came from large donors; four years later, the Democrats' national level committees received 61 percent of their funds from $500-plus donors.

1968 Campaign

A great deal more information about large contributors, both on and off the record, was available in 1968. That was especially the case in the prenomination period. Nixon, Eugene McCarthy, and Robert F. Kennedy are believed to have had at least one $500,000 donor to their prenomination campaigns; McCarthy may have had two. One political contributor, Stewart R. Mott, spent $100,000 trying to persuade Nelson Rockefeller to run as an anti-Vietnam War candidate. When he was unsuccessful, Mott gave his support to McCarthy, contributing $200,000 to his campaign.

One of the largest known contributions in 1968, just under $1.5 million, came to light unexpectedly. Before 1972 no federal law required disclosure of campaign funds in the prenomination period, and most campaign committees were legally set up in states (such as Delaware) that had no disclosure laws. But for an unknown reason, one major Rockefeller committee was set up in New York, which did have a reporting law. The committee received $1,482,625 from Mrs. John D. Rockefeller, Jr., Nelson Rockefeller's stepmother. Her contribution was an unusual one in American politics in that she subsequently was required to pay gift taxes of $854,483. Because gift taxes applied only to contributions in excess of $3,000, the larger donors normally would split up their gifts into numerous smaller contributions made to numerous paper committees, all supporting the same candidate and established for the purpose of tax avoidance.

The largest single contributor in the 1968 election was W. Clement Stone, chairman of the Combined Insurance Company of America. Stone gave more than $2.8 million to the Republicans—all but $39,000 of that amount to Nixon's nomination and general election campaigns.

1972 Campaign

Donors of large amounts reached what seems almost certain to stand as their highest level of participation in campaign financing in the 1972 election. The information available about those largest of donors—contributors of $10,000 or more—indicates that they donated money to the 1972 campaigns in extraordinary amounts. Just 1,254 individuals contributed a total of $51.3 million.[22]

Broader Data Base

Beginning with the 1972 election, much more than ever was known before came to light about sources of funds and categories of expenditures, providing data for a more systematic analysis. The Federal Corrupt Practices Act of 1925 did not apply to primary candidates, and it required reporting only by committees operating in two or more states. Adoption of the Federal Election Campaign Act (FECA) in 1971 brought primaries and runoffs under coverage of the law. It also brought under coverage any committee raising or spending in excess of $1,000 and seeking to influence federal elections.

In the 1972 election, the General Accounting Office (GAO), the Clerk of the House, and the Secretary of the Senate each began to receive thousands of detailed reports. For the period covering April 7 (when the law took effect) to December 31, 1972, the three offices together received well over a quarter-million pages of data, excluding instruction pages and audit notices.

Although the reporting arrangement meant considerable overlap and duplication, the massive amounts of data provided scholars and journalists with the opportunity to study and report campaign practices in greater detail and with greater certainty than ever before.

Voluntary Disclosure

Spurred on by the new law and seeking favorable campaign publicity, several of the presidential candidates disclosed voluntarily some of their contributions prior to April 7, 1972, adding considerably to the data base. Sen. George McGovern, a Democratic contender, and Rep. Paul N. McCloskey, Jr., a Republican challenger to incumbent president Nixon, made full disclosure of all contributions their central campaign committees received. Partial disclosures were made by four other Democrats—Sen. Hubert Humphrey, New York mayor John Lindsay, Sen. Edmund S. Muskie, and Alabama governor George C. Wallace. Almost 1,500 contributions in sums of $500 or more were disclosed voluntarily by the six candidates. They totaled almost $4 million.[23]

The other candidates flatly refused to make voluntary disclosures, although some data were collected subsequently and made public by the

Citizens' Research Foundation from filings in states requiring disclosure. Common Cause sued to force disclosure of the pre-April 7 receipts and expenditures of the Nixon reelection campaign. The legal action resulted in court-stipulated partial disclosure just before the November election; full disclosure was agreed upon and complied with in September 1973. Ironically, full disclosure meant that Nixon's campaign, otherwise noted for its secret funds and undercover operations, became the first presidential campaign in history whose financing was fully a matter of public record.

The postelection disclosures revealed that during the period from March 10, 1972—the date for the last filing required under the 1925 Federal Corrupt Practices Act—to April 7, 1972—the date the FECA became effective—Nixon committees raised $11.4 million, almost half of it on April 5 and April 6. It was uncertain whether contributions received during this period were subject to any disclosure, and the Committee for the Reelection of the President (CRP) sought to exploit the uncertainty. The result of the legal proceedings upset the committee's strategy, but not until well after the election.

Big Contributors

The three largest contributors in 1972 gave a total of $4 million, the bulk of it to the presidential campaigns. The largest single contributor was again W. Clement Stone of Chicago, who donated $2,141,655.94. Stone contributed $2 million of the total to the Nixon reelection campaign in the pre-April period and $51,643.45 after disclosure became mandatory. The second largest 1972 contributor was Richard Mellon Scaife, heir to the Mellon oil (Gulf), aluminum (Alcoa), and banking fortune, who gave the Republicans $1,068,000, most of it—$1 million—as a contribution to the Nixon campaign. The third largest contributor, Stewart R. Mott, heir to a General Motors fortune, was a McGovern supporter. Mott gave $822,592 in 1972 (not including some $25,200 in investment-loss deductions) to liberal candidates and causes, particularly those opposed to the administration's policies in Vietnam. Most of Mott's contributions went to the Democrats. Nearly half ($400,000) went to McGovern.

Missing from the list of top givers in 1972, with the exception of Richard Mellon Scaife, are the names of the owners of the great American fortunes—the Fords, Rockefellers, Whitneys, and Astors, whose support had been crucial in earlier political campaigns, particularly those of Republicans. In 1972 those families were displaced by donors such as Stone, John A. Mulcahy, Anthony Rossi, and Abe Plough. All of the latter could boast of Horatio Alger success stories. Mulcahy, a poor Irish immigrant in the 1920s, rose to the presidency of a steel industry equipment supplier and then, through a corporate merger, became a major stockholder in Pfizer, the drug company. Rossi, a former bricklayer and tomato farmer and a native of Sicily, built Tropicana Products into a major company. Plough, chairman of Schering-Plough Corporation, maker of St. Joseph's aspirin, began his career in 1908 as a door-to-door medicine oil salesman. Like Stone, all three were major backers of Nixon, with Mulcahy's $625,000 topping their gifts.

Along with Mott on the Democratic side, the biggest contributors were Max Palevsky, at one time the largest stockholder in the Xerox Corporation; Martin Peretz of the Harvard faculty and his wife Anne, a Singer Company heiress; and Dr. Alejandro Zaffaroni, the Uruguayan-born president of Alza Corporation, a California drug research firm. All of these were among George McGovern's top contributors, replacing the traditional Democratic supporters such as the Lehmans, the Harrimans, and others of earlier years.

Several of the largest 1972 contributors gave to both Republican and Democratic presidential campaigns. One so-called "split contributor," Meshulam Riklis, chairman of the board of Rapid-American Corporation, contributed $188,000 to Nixon, $125,000 to Humphrey, and $100,000 to Democratic senator Henry M. Jackson. Riklis also lent Humphrey $550,000, most of which was not repaid. Leon Hess, chairman of the board of Amerada Hess Oil Company, gave Nixon $250,000 and Jackson $225,000. These contributors gave to favored Democratic candidates for nomination, then to Nixon in the general election when McGovern became the Democratic nominee.

Public Funding

In 1976 and 1980 candidates for the presidential nomination and for the presidency itself received government funds to subsidize their campaigns. The federal subsidies were intended in part to make up for the monies candidates no longer could seek from wealthy donors, because the 1974 FECA Amendments limited the amount of money individuals and groups could contribute.

During the prenomination campaigns, matching funds were provided for qualified presidential candidates. The U.S. Treasury contributed $23.7 million to the 1976 prenomination campaigns of 15 candidates (13 Democrats and 2 Republicans), and $31.3 million to the 1980 prenomination campaigns of 10 candidates (6 Republicans and 4 Democrats). The Treasury provided $21.8 million each to the 1976 general election campaigns of Jimmy Carter and Gerald Ford and $29.4 million each to the 1980 general election campaigns of Carter and Ronald Reagan.[24]

In 1976 federal funding accounted for about 33 percent of the money spent by the principal campaign committees of the prenomination candidates qualified to receive matching funds. Of the $275 million spent to elect a president in 1980, about 34 percent came from public funds.

Other Sources of Funds

The 1974 FECA Amendments limited contributions by an individual to a candidate for federal office to $1,000 for each primary, runoff, and general election and to an aggregate contribution of $25,000 for all federal candidates annually. Faced with this restriction, many wealthy donors continued to contribute to federal campaigns but only in the smaller amounts permitted by the new laws.

To make up for the revenue lost because of restrictions placed on large donors, presidential candidates now fund their prenomination campaigns in a variety of ways. Some enlist the volunteer services of rock music groups and other entertainers to hold benefit concerts for their campaigns. Some use direct mail appeals to solicit small contributions from large numbers of donors. The use of direct mail in presidential and other election campaigns is considered later in the chapter. In many campaigns the role once filled by large contributors is now filled by "elite solicitors," well-connected individuals who can persuade a large number of people to contribute the $1,000 maximum. Political action committees generally do not play an important role in presidential campaign fund raising. In 1980, for example, PAC contributions to presidential candidates accounted for about $1.6 million, only 1.4 percent of the total prenomination campaign net receipts. Those contributions are not matchable under the FECA's public funding provisions. PAC money, as Chapter 4 indicates, is directed mainly to congressional campaigns.

Independent Expenditures

In 1976 independent expenditures—those made by individuals or groups without consultation with a candidate's campaign organization—played a role of little importance in the prenomination or general election campaigns. In the entire 1975-1976 election cycle, less than $800,000 was spent independently by individuals and political committees for or against presidential and congressional candidates.[25] In 1980, as individuals and groups became more familiar with the law, the importance of independent expenditures increased significantly as a means of circumventing the contribution limits and of supplementing candidate spending in early primary states with low spending ceilings or in later primary states when candidates might approach the national spending limit. During the 1980 presidential prenomination campaigns, independent expenditures advocating or opposing the election of clearly identified candidates totaled about $2.7 million.

Although political committees accounted for the greater share of the independent expenditures, significant independent spending also was reported by several individuals. Texas industrialist and real estate investor Cecil R. Haden reported spending $184,000 on behalf of John Connally and $32,000 to assist Ronald Reagan's campaign for nomination. Stewart Mott reported independent expenditures of $110,000 during the prenomination campaign: $90,000 on behalf of John Anderson and $20,000 to aid Edward Kennedy. Television producer Norman Lear spent $106,000 on Anderson's behalf. Theo N. Law reported spending $66,000 on Connally's behalf, and former Texas state legislator Henry C. Grover reported spending $29,000, also to assist Connally.

General Election Campaigns

As we saw in Chapter 2, the Supreme Court upheld the FECA ban on direct contributions to the major party nominees after the conventions, if those candidates accepted public funding. Because both Carter and Ford accepted the federal grants in 1976, individuals and groups were barred from contributing directly to their campaigns in the general election. Unions, as well as corporations, however, were free to spend unlimited amounts on political communications directed toward their own members or employees and their families. Unions reported spending more than $2 million on such communications to help Carter. In addition, it is estimated that unions spent $11 million on other political activity, such as general political communication, voter registration, and get-out-the-vote activities, that also benefited the Democratic nominee. Corporations and other business-related groups, on the other hand, did little spending on political activity during the presidential general election campaign.

In 1980 greater familiarity with the law, as well as some provisions of the 1979 Amendments, allowed individuals and groups seeking direct financial participation in the presidential general election campaigns to spend their funds to influence the election outcome. Labor organizations continued to spend on behalf of the Democratic ticket—probably about $15 million in all, including $1.3 million in reported communications costs. This spending was more than offset by pro-Republican independent spending of about $10.6 million and about $15 million spent by state and local Republican party committees on behalf of the presidential ticket in the general election period. Included in the independent expenditure total are large outlays by some individuals, including $381,151 by Cecil Haden and $70,575 and $68,453 by Richard DeVos and Jay Van Andel respectively, cofounders of Amway Corporation. Included among the state and local party expenditures is some $9 million from individuals and corporations coordinated by the Republican National Committee and directed to state and local party committees in states where such contributions to these committees were permitted and where spending for the volunteer-oriented voter-identification and -turnout drives encouraged by the 1979 Amendments would have the greatest benefit.[26]

Ambassadorships for Big Donors

The common practice of rewarding large contributors with federal jobs became the focus of one set of investigations by the special Watergate prosecutor following the 1972 election. After his landslide reelection, President Nixon appointed 319 persons to high-level federal positions (including ambassadorships), and all won Senate confirmation. Fifty-two of these appointees, or 17 percent, were recorded as having contributed $100 or more to the Republicans; their gifts totaled $772,224, with $703,654 of that going to the Nixon campaign.

The appointment of Ruth Farkas, a sociologist and a director of Alexander's, a New York department store, as ambassador to Luxembourg generated by far the most controversy of any of Nixon's ambassadorial appointments. According to testimony during the Watergate hearings, Farkas reportedly had balked at an offer of an ambassadorship to Costa Rica, saying, "Isn't $250,000 an awful lot of money for Costa Rica?"[27] Farkas actually gave a total of $300,000 to Nixon's campaign, making her the largest single donor in the group.

Several individuals felt the repercussions of the Farkas affair. Herbert W. Kalmbach, President Nixon's personal lawyer, was imprisoned for fund-raising activities relating in part to "ambassadorial auctions"; promise of a federal job in return for financial support is a violation of federal law.

Peter Flanigan, who as a White House aide had figured in the Farkas discussions, asked President Ford not to renew his nomination as ambassador to Spain.

Carter's Pledge

During his 1976 campaign, Jimmy Carter declared that he would take the selection of envoys out of the realm of politics. Unfortunately, an analysis of the campaign contributions of the ambassadors he appointed is not possible because the FEC did not compile full lists of contributors for 1976, and limits on allowable donations make their analysis less revealing than in previous election years.

Some of Carter's nominations met with criticism. The American Foreign Service Association (AFSA) opposed the nominations of Anne Chambers Cox and Philip H. Alston, Jr., who were named ambassadors to Belgium and Australia, respectively. The AFSA charged that both had been major contributors to Carter's past political campaigns and that neither was qualified. The appointment of Marvin L. Warner, an Ohio real estate developer, to Switzerland also was controversial. Warner, a large contributor to Carter's campaign, also had been an Ohio fund-raiser for Carter, arranging one breakfast netting $20,000. Cleveland businessman Milton Wolfe, named ambassador to Austria, was a former Jackson supporter who switched to Carter and is credited with helping to raise $80,000 in one evening from Cleveland businessmen. On the other hand, some observers complained that Carter's appointments to ambassadorial and other posts were not sufficiently political. These critics included the DNC, which adopted a resolution opposing the new president's approach to patronage.

Reagan Appointees

The Reagan administration also was criticized by the AFSA, which claimed that the "vast majority" of Reagan's appointees to foreign service posts were "relatively undistinguished as public figures." [28] Retired career foreign service officer Malcolm Toon was critical particularly of four of Reagan's appointments: Hollywood actor John Gavin as ambassador to Mexico, Johnson's Wax heir and Republican contributor John Lewis as ambassador to Great Britain, financier Evan Griffin Galbraith as ambassador to France, and banker-lawyer Maxwell Raab as ambassador to Italy. The Reagan administration, said Toon, former U.S. ambassador to the Soviet Union, used diplomatic posts as "a dumping ground for defeated politicians and Republican financial backers." [29]

Late in 1981 Sen. Charles McC. Mathias, R-Md., introduced a bill that would limit the number of noncareer ambassadors to 15 percent. "Ambassadorial posts have often been granted in exchange for political support or campaign contributions," said Mathias. "Our national security is too important to be subordinated to the patronage requirements of partisan politics." [30] Mathias's bill was not enacted into law.

Direct Mail Appeals

The direct mail approach to raising campaign funds—essentially an appeal for a great many individual contributions, however modest—had been used before in politics, but it was raised to a high art form in 1972.

McGovern's 1972 Campaign

The use of direct mail made a financial success of George McGovern's campaign, even though the Democratic senator from South Dakota lost badly to Nixon in the general election. Direct mail also contributed to McGovern's political success in the prenomination period.

The Democratic presidential nominee's campaign, launched with a reported $280,000 debt, was the party's first to end with a surplus since the campaigns of FDR. In part, this financial success was due to McGovern's appeal to a clear-cut segment of the voting population. Like Barry Goldwater in 1964 and George Wallace in 1968, McGovern was considered a factional or fringe candidate. All three succeeded in getting financial support from large numbers of small contributors, though, in the end, they failed to win their contests.

McGovern attracted at least 600,000 donors to his campaign, starting with a massive direct mail drive in early 1971, more than a year before he won the nomination. During that year, when McGovern was the choice of fewer than 10 percent of Democrats responding to the national opinion polls, $600,000 was raised by this means. Between the New Hampshire primary in March 1972 and the convention in the summer, an additional $2.4 million was raised through direct mail; that spring, some three million pieces were mailed. Thus, McGovern raised some $3 million in the prenomination period, at a cost of about $1 million. Most of the money was received in contributions of $100 or less. In the general election campaign, $12 million was brought in through direct mail, with 15 million pieces mailed, at a cost of about $3.5 million to the national headquarters.

McGovern's use of direct mail had its beginnings in South Dakota politics. A compulsive list-keeper as he crisscrossed the traditionally

Republican state, McGovern added to his lists when he moved into the national spotlight with anti-Vietnam War activities in 1970. He obtained still more names that year from a massive national direct mail appeal for some of his fellow Democratic senators.

In January 1971, three days before McGovern formally announced he was seeking the presidency, 300,000 letters went into the mail, timed to arrive on the day he announced. The seven-page letter had been drafted in consultation with Morris Dees, a millionaire civil rights lawyer and direct mail expert, and Thomas Collins of Rapp and Collins, a New York advertising firm. The letter discussed McGovern's reasons for seeking the nomination and appealed for funds to help. The combination announcement and appeal letter brought in about $300,000 from 16,000 contributors at a cost of about $40,000. A major appeal of McGovern's fund-raisers was for loans from wealthy persons to serve as "seed money" for the direct mail drive. This money made it possible to reach out continually to the thousands of potential small contributors, whose gifts, in turn, helped repay the loans. This practice of lending large sums of money is no longer possible because the FECA's $1,000 individual contribution limit also limits loans to that same amount.

McGovern invariably appealed for funds at the conclusion of his television broadcasts; some five-minute broadcasts were designed essentially as fund-raisers. Such appeals brought in an estimated $3 million. Broadcasts were timed to coincide with direct mail appeals that were already on their way. The McGovern campaign direct mail strategy proved to be the most successful effort using this approach in American political history to that date. It more than tripled the Goldwater direct mail effort of 1964, which raised some $5.8 million from about 661,000 donors.

There were several reasons for McGovern's direct mail fund-raising success. In addition to the expert help and advice received from Dees and Collins, he got an early start, giving him the lead time he needed to build up a list of proven contributors. His lists of names were continually replenished, often through telvision appeals. And as the war in Vietnam dragged on, his letters triggered an emotional response. Candidates who do not enjoy similar fund-raising circumstances of a salient issue combined with productive mailing lists cannot expect to emulate McGovern's direct mail success.

Nixon's 1972 Campaign

Although direct mail was not as important to the 1972 Nixon campaign as it was to McGovern's, the Nixon organization did make use of it. Before July 1972 the appeals to small contributors were conducted chiefly by the Republican National Committee. In the months before Nixon's renomination, the RNC raised $5.3 million, largely through direct mail appeals for its National Sustaining Fund. After Nixon's renomination, direct mail programs conducted jointly by the RNC and the Committee for the Reelection of the President brought in about $9 million from mailings of 30 million appeals. The total cost for the RNC and Nixon direct mail programs was about $5.5 million. Direct mail drives conducted by the RNC alone and conducted jointly with the CRP after Nixon's renomination brought in $14.3 million. Combined telephone drives raised $2.5 million.

About 250,000 persons contributed to the RNC. About 600,000 contributors were claimed by national and state affiliates of the CRP. Eliminating duplications and repeat contributors, probably 600,000 persons contributed to the RNC in its annual program or to the Nixon campaign.

1976 Primaries

Most major candidates who entered the presidential primary contests in 1976 used direct mail fund raising, at least to some extent. When Morris Dees, who helped engineer McGovern's 1972 direct mail fund drive, became Jimmy Carter's national finance chairman in 1975, the role of direct mail in Carter's campaign was assured. Dees felt that direct mail would not be so productive for a centrist candidate like Carter as it had been for the more liberal McGovern. Consequently Carter did not rely so heavily on direct mail as McGovern had. Nevertheless, by May 1976, according to Dees, about one-third of all private contributions—more than $2.5 million—came in response to direct mail.

Other Democratic candidates relied in varying degrees on direct mail fund raising. One of Rep. Morris Udall's campaign managers called direct mail the "heart and soul" of his campaign fund raising. As in his previous presidential campaigns, George Wallace used direct mail to great advantage, raising most of the $6.8 million he received through mail appeals. Sen. Henry Jackson was less dependent on direct mail, but he successfully reached selected groups, such as members of the Jewish segment of the population, many of whom supported his outspoken pro-Israel posture.

On the Republican side, both Gerald Ford and Ronald Reagan benefited from direct mail. In all, the President Ford Committee mailed nearly 2.6 million appeals and raised $2.5 million. Reagan also had some success with direct mail, but he started his direct mail program too late to enjoy its full advantages. Reagan found televised appeals more effective.

1980 Primaries

Some of the 1980 prenomination candidates also used direct mail appeals as part of their fund-raising strategies. This time, among Republicans, Reagan used the approach the most successfully, in part because his campaign had available a mailing list of proven contributors developed by Citizens for the Republic, a PAC the candidate had formed in 1977 to launch his 1980 presidential bid. According to the Reagan campaign treasurer, through late April 1980, 45 to 50 percent of Reagan's campaign funds had come as a result of direct mail drives.[31] George Bush's campaign generally shunned the mass-mailing approach, sometimes successful for candidates with clear ideological positions, and concentrated with good results on small mailings of highly personalized letters to carefully selected lists. John Anderson's direct mail program got off to a disappointing start, but after the candidate established himself as a somewhat unconventional Republican, direct mail results improved dramatically. By mid-April 1980 Anderson had attracted nearly 80,000 contributors, whose contributions averaged $30. Howard Baker's campaign received about $1.4 million from 40,000 individuals who responded to its direct mail appeals. In addition almost $900,000 was raised by direct mail to help retire Baker's prenomination campaign debt.

On the Democratic side, direct mail solicitations enjoyed only limited success. About $800,000 of the more than $13 million the Carter campaign raised in private contributions was donated in reponse to direct mail appeals. Most of Edward Kennedy's contributors were identified through means other than direct mail, although the Kennedy campaign used mail appeals to resolicit donors once they had made initial contributions.

Other Candidates and Committees

Some candidates for other federal offices as well as a variety of political action committees have come to rely on direct mail to raise needed funds. In 1978, for example, Sen. Jesse Helms, R-N.C., raised some $6.9 million for his reelection campaign. A large portion of that money was contributed in response to direct mail appeals. Direct mail fund raising, however, is too costly for many Senate and House candidates and often requires more lead time than many House candidates in particular have. It generally is more effective for candidates for prominent national offices, for candidates identified with issues that arouse the emotions of large numbers of potential contributors, or for candidates to the left or the right on the political spectrum. Finally, increased competition for funds from those likely to respond to direct mail appeals may dilute its effectiveness for individual candidates.

A number of political action committees also make extensive use of direct mail to raise money, including the National Committee for an Effective Congress, Independent Action, and ProPAC on the liberal side and the National Conservative Political Action Committee (NCPAC) and the National Congressional Club on the conservative side. The latter two groups have raised substantial funds through direct mail but have been criticized for contributing only small amounts to candidates. According to one analysis, only about 2 percent of the $12.3 million the two groups raised in 1980 was contributed to candidates, and about 77 percent was spent on operating expenses, independent expenditures, and direct mail fund raising.[32]

Political Party Committees

The Republican National Committee has relied on direct mail appeals for a substantial portion of its funds since 1962 when it undertook its first national sustaining fund membership drive and collected $700,000. The effort met with increasing success in each passing year, yielding particularly large amounts in presidential election years, including $10.1 million in 1976, a $4.1 million increase over the previous year.

In 1977 the committee stepped up its fund-raising activities, depending on direct mail solicitations to raise most of its money. By year's end the RNC had added 100,000 names to its contributor file, bringing it to 350,000 names, and netted $7.3 million. In 1978, 510,000 donors gave the committee $10.1 million after fund-raising costs had been paid. A 1978 law allowing national party committees to mail at the nonprofit rate of 3.1 cents rather than the commercial bulk rate of 8.4 cents enabled the RNC to expand its direct mail program. In the following year the committee mailed 18 million fund-raising letters and netted $12 million from 550,000 contributors.

In 1980 the RNC reported having raised almost $26.5 million from small donors—those giving less than $500. Most of those donations, which averaged $25, came in response to direct mail appeals. The committee's direct mail success continued in 1981 when the RNC received $26.7 million in response to mail and telephone solicitations.

The two other national level Republican party committees—the National Republican Congressional Committee and the National Republican Senatorial Committee—also have been remarkably proficient in the use

71

of direct mail. National Democratic party committees, on the other hand, have not enjoyed the same level of success. From 1976 through 1980, for example, the Democratic National Committee raised about $8.3 million through direct mail, less than one-third the amount the RNC received in response to mail and telephone solicitations in 1980 alone. Following the 1980 elections, the DNC redoubled its direct mail efforts, but because the start-up costs involved in developing a contributor list are considerable, the fruits of the committee's efforts are not reflected in the 1981 direct mail receipts. In the postelection year, the DNC collected $1.7 million in response to direct mail appeals to previous donors, at a cost of about $820,000, and $1 million from responses to mailings to potential donors—prospect mailings—at a cost of almost $1.1 million.

The overall fund-raising success of the Republican party committees gives party candidates a decided financial advantage over their Democratic opponents. In 1981-1982, for example, Republican party committees contributed $5.6 million directly to party candidates and made $14.3 million in coordinated expenditures on their behalf. Democratic party committees were able to contribute only $1.7 million to their candidates and to spend only $3.3 million on their behalf. The Republican committees were able to spend money in other ways that benefited party candidates: on media advertising to promote Republican policies, on congressional reapportionment battles, and on communications systems to allow party leaders around the country to confer and party operatives and candidates to participate in seminars.

Patterns In Political Giving

Despite the widely reported post-Watergate disillusionment with elective politics among large segments of the electorate, in 1980 the proportion of the population contributing money to political candidates and causes increased significantly. The development of sophisticated fund-raising methods aimed at garnering large numbers of small contributors, particularly by the national Republican party committees and ideological political committees, probably is responsible in great part for the increase in political giving in the most recent presidential election year.

Surveys taken between 1952 and 1976 indicate that from 4 to 12 percent of the total adult population contributed to politics at some level in presidential election years, with the figure standing at 9 percent in 1976. But a survey by the Center for Political Studies at the University of Michigan indicates that 13.4 percent of the adult population gave to candidates and causes during the 1980 presidential election year.[33] Survey data suggest that the increase in 1980 is due to the larger number of persons giving to interest groups. Of those surveyed, 6.8 percent gave to candidates, 3.8 percent gave to parties, and 6.8 percent gave to interest groups. Because those three figures add up to well over 13.4 percent, it is obvious that a significant number of those contributing gave in two or all three categories.

Although only 3.8 percent gave to parties, nearly half of those contributors did so at the federal level, with 29.8 percent giving to local parties, 22.1 percent giving to state parties, and 48.1 percent giving to national parties. In addition to those contributing directly to candidates and committees, some 25 to 30 percent of federal income taxpayers consistently show a willingness to earmark $1 of their tax liability for the presidential campaign fund through the checkoff procedure.

Survey results compiled by the Gallup Poll and the Survey Research Center over the last quarter-century also show a surge in the number of political contributors during the 1950s (Table 3-1). As shown below, the number remained relatively steady in 1960 and 1964, fell off in 1968, and in 1972 climbed back to about the level of eight years earlier. This number increased slightly in 1976 before rising by nearly five million in 1980. Applying survey percentages to the adult, noninstitutionalized, civilian population suggests the following number of contributors in each presidential election year listed:

3 million in 1952	8.7 million in 1968
8 million in 1956	11.7 million in 1972
10 million in 1960	12.2 million in 1976
12 million in 1964	17.1 million in 1980

Furthermore, survey findings spanning more than four decades indicate that despite the increase, a reservoir of untapped potential for campaign funds continues to exist. From time to time the Gallup Poll has asked people whether they would contribute $5 to a party campaign if they were solicited. Throughout the 1940s and 1950s, approximately one-third of those surveyed said they would be willing to contribute; in the 1960s this segment increased to more than 40 percent. A June 1981 Gallup Poll indicated that 39 percent of those surveyed expressed a desire to join one or more special interest groups.[34] Even with the enormous costs of today's presidential elections, only a small portion of such potential would have to be tapped to eliminate many of the financial problems of candidates and parties.

Table 3-1 Percentage of National Adult Population Solicited and Making Political Contributions, 1952-1980

Year	Polling Organization	Solicited by: Rep.	Dem.	Total[1]	Contributed to: Rep.	Dem.	Total[1]
1952	SRC				3	1	4
1956	Gallup	8	11	19	3	6	9
1956	SRC				5	5	10
1960	Gallup	9	8	15	4	4	9
1960	Gallup						12
1960	SRC				7	4	11
1964	Gallup				6	4	12
1964	SRC	8	4	15	6	4	11
1968	SRC	9	7	23[2]	4	4	9[3]
1972	SRC				4	5	10[4]
1974	SRC				3	3	8[5]
1976	Gallup				3	3	8[6]
1976	SRC				4	4	9[7]
1980	CPS[8]				7	3	13.4[9]

[1] The total percentage may add to a total different from the total of Democrats and Republicans because of individuals solicited by or contributing to both major parties, nonparty groups, or combinations of these.

[2] Includes 4 percent who were solicited by both major parties and 1.4 percent who were solicited by Wallace's American Independent Party (AIP).

[3] Includes .7 percent who contributed to AIP.

[4] Includes contributors to AIP.

[5] Includes .7 percent who contributed to both parties and .8 percent who contributed to minor parties.

[6] Includes 1 percent to another party and 1 percent Do Not Know or No Answer.

[7] Republican and Democratic figures are rounded. The total includes .6 percent who gave to both parties, .4 percent to other, and .3 percent Do Not Know.

[8] The Center for Political Studies (CPS), located at the University of Michigan, is the successor to the Survey Research Center (SRC).

[9] Includes persons giving to special interest groups. Because some 6.8 percent of all those surveyed fell into this category, it appears that many persons contributed in two or all three categories.

SOURCE: Survey Research Center (SRC), University of Michigan; data direct from center or from Angus Campbell, Philip E. Converse, Warren E. Miller, Donald E. Stokes, *The American Voter* (New York: John Wiley and Sons, 1960), 91; 1980 data from Ruth S. Jones, Center for Political Studies, University of Michigan; Gallup data direct or from Roper Opinion Research Center, Williams College, and from American Institute of Public Opinion (Gallup Poll).

The Importance of Individual Donors

Extraordinary publicity has been given in recent years to the growing importance of political contributions from groups, specifically from political action committees. Nevertheless, direct gifts from individuals remain the most important source of campaign funds. In the 1980 presidential prenomination campaigns, for example, individuals contributed $73.6

million directly to the candidates, almost 68 percent of net campaign receipts. PACs, as noted, accounted for only 1.4 percent of campaign receipts, and federal matching funds accounted for the remainder. Of course, individuals are the ultimate source of money for both PACs, parties, and the Presidential Election Campaign Fund.

Likewise, in the 1979-1980 election cycle, individuals accounted for 67 percent of all funds contributed to major party House general election candidates and 78 percent of the funds contributed to Senate general election candidates. Although the percentage of funds contributed by PACs has increased steadily since 1972, direct individual contributions also have increased proportionately to help meet growing campaign costs. It is political party contributions to candidates that have *decreased* as a percentage of total contributions. The decrease has occurred despite both national parties' efforts to solicit more widely and some subsequent success, especially by the Republican party.

Individuals contribute to candidates, parties, and PACs for a variety of reasons. Concern for government policy espoused by a candidate or party may motivate some to contribute while personal identification with a candidate, party, or PAC may move others. Some contributors may seek favorable treatment from—or at least access to—government officials or from those who solicit contributions. Some may decide to contribute simply out of a sense of civic duty. Most often a contributor's motivation is mixed— no single purpose or goal explains why he or she contributes.[35]

A recent study of the role of individual contributors concluded that those who donate money also participate more than noncontributors in other ways in the political process.[36] Their additional participation often includes not only voting but also trying to persuade others to support a par- ticular candidate or party, publicizing a candidate or campaign, volunteer- ing, and attending rallies and fund-raisers. Further, the study confirmed what good sense seems to dictate: that contributing is positively correlated with income, the desire to help one's own party, a willingness to support the political system, interest in campaign and electoral outcomes, and belief in one's ability to influence politics.

In conclusion, despite much warranted concern about levels of public confidence in the electoral processes, there is evidence of the changing nature of participation in politics as illustrated by individual contributions to PACs, parties, and candidates. Moreover, while tax checkoff rates have leveled off, they have done so at percentages easily able to provide public funding needs and leave surpluses every four years.

Notes

1. Jasper B. Shannon, *Money in Politics* (New York: Random House, 1959), 14.
2. Louise Overacker, *Money in Elections* (New York: Macmillan, 1932), 102.
3. Shannon, *Money and Politics*, 21.
4. Wilfred E. Binkley, *American Political Parties*, 4th ed. (New York: Alfred A. Knopf, 1962), 279.
5. Edwin P. Hoyt, Jr., *Jumbos and Jackasses, A Popular History of the Political Wars* (Garden City: Doubleday & Co., 1960), 77.
6. Alexander Heard, *The Costs of Democracy* (Chapel Hill, N.C.: University of North Carolina Press, 1960), 233.
7. Herbert E. Alexander, "Financing Presidential Elections," in *History of American Presidential Elections 1789-1968,* vol. 4, ed. Arthur M. Schlesinger and Fred L. Israel (New York: Chelsea House), 3884.
8. Quoted in Shannon, *Money and Politics*, 26.
9. Eugene H. Roseboom, *A History of Presidential Elections* (New York: Macmillan, 1957), 242.
10. Shannon, *Money and Politics,* 27.
11. Hoyt, *Jumbos and Jackasses,* 189.
12. Roseboom, *Presidential Elections,* 304.
13. Shannon, *Money and Politics,* 33.
14. Roseboom, *Presidential Elections,* 316.
15. Quoted in M. R. Werner, *Bryan* (New York: Harcourt, Brace & Co., 1929), 101.
16. Quoted in Shannon, *Money and Politics,* 35.
17. Ibid.
18. Ibid.
19. Ibid.
20. Overacker, *Money in Elections,* 180.
21. Arthur M. Schlesinger, Jr., *The Politics of Upheaval* ("The Age of Roosevelt," vol. 3, 1960 [Boston: Houghton Mifflin Co.]), 594-595.
22. CRF Listing of: *Political Contributors and Lenders of $10,000 or More in 1972* (Princeton, N.J.: Citizens' Research Foundation, 1975).
23. CRF Listing of: *Political Contributors of $500 or More Voluntarily Disclosed by 1972 Presidential Candidates* (Princeton, N.J.: Citizens' Research Foundation, 1972), Introduction, unpaged.
24. Figures cited for the primary and general election campaigns do not take into account repayments of public funds required for various reasons by the FEC after postelection audits of the candidates had been completed.
25. See Joseph E. Cantor, "The Evolution and Issues Surrounding Independent Expenditures" (Washington, D.C.: Congressional Research Service, May 5, 1982), 20-21.
26. See Elizabeth Drew, A Reporter at Large, "Politics and Money - II," *New Yorker,* December 13, 1982, 64.
27. *Final Report of the Senate Select Committee on Presidential Campaign Activities,* 93d Cong., 2d sess. (Washington, D.C.: Government Printing Office, 1974), 904.

28. Quoted in Jack Nelson, "Reagan to Name More Political Ambassadors," *Los Angeles Times,* April 8, 1982.
29. Ibid.
30. Quoted in "Envoy Nominations Faulted," *Washington Post,* November 25, 1981.
31. E. J. Dionne, "Small Donors Gave Reagan Primary Aid," *New York Times,* July 2, 1980.
32. Robert D. Shaw, Jr., "Direct Mail Pleas Raise Thousands for Fundraisers, Little for Causes," *Miami Herald,* March 30, 1981.
33. This figure was obtained directly from Ruth S. Jones, Center for Political Studies, University of Michigan.
34. Gallup Poll, "Participation in Interest Groups High," *Gallup Report,* August 1981, 45.
35. See Heard, *The Costs of Democracy,* 68-74.
36. Ruth S. Jones and Warren E. Miller, "Financing Campaigns: Modes of Individual Contribution." (Paper delivered at the annual meeting of the Midwest Political Science Association, Chicago, April 21-23, 1983).

Sources of Funds: Groups 4

An overriding purpose of the campaign financing reforms of the 1970s has been to relocate some political power, taking it from monied interests and broadening financial constituencies. Thus the new laws include restrictions aimed at reducing the political power of large contributors and of large corporations, labor unions, and other so-called "special-interest" groups in American society.

Public policy, however, seldom evolves precisely the way reformers hope it will. The Federal Election Campaign Act Amendments of 1974 have reduced effectively the influence of large contributors by limiting to $1,000 the amount an individual may contribute to any federal candidate in one primary or election. But the 1974 Amendments also allow a committee of a business, a labor union, or another organized group (usually called a political action committee, or PAC) to contribute, under the right conditions, as much as $5,000 per candidate per election.[1] This provision gives new emphasis to the roles of business, labor, and other special interests in the electoral process.

Unlike individuals, who sometimes have to be cajoled to make political contributions, special interests often are eager to support promising candidates they feel would be friendly to their causes. Consequently, they often object to laws and regulations designed to prevent them from using their resources to exert influence on elections.

Corporations

Although corporate contributions to federal election campaigns have been prohibited since 1907, traditionally there have been a number of ways by which corporate funds could percolate into partisan politics. Some companies have gotten around the prohibition by giving employees pay raises or bonuses with the understanding that the employee would make political contributions with the extra money. That was the device used by the American Ship Building Co. in 1972 to raise $25,000 as a Nixon gift. The company chairman, George Steinbrenner III, an owner of the New York Yankees, later was found guilty and fined for his role.

Another way to get around the federal prohibitions has been to provide free use of company goods, services, and equipment, ranging from furniture and typewriters to airplanes or office suites or storefronts. Complimentary travel in company autos and airplanes has been common even when no campaigns were going on. Corporations also have kept executives and their secretaries on the payroll while they were working full time in a campaign. In the aftermath of the abuses brought to light in Watergate-related investigations, the laws against such corporate practices are now being more vigorously enforced, and corporations generally are far more cautious. The definition of "contribution" is now very broad, including "anything of value," and the value of goods and services, if offered, cannot exceed the $1,000 contribution limit and must be disclosed as "in-kind" contributions.

Earlier, payments to public relations firms, lawyers, and advertising agencies had been used by companies to charge off to "business-as-usual" what are really political contributions. During the last year of the Johnson administration and the first year of the Nixon administration—1968 and 1969—there was a series of federal prosecutions of corporations for illegal practices. The Justice Department obtained 15 indictments and 14 convictions of businesses, many of them in southern California, for deducting, as legitimate business expenses, payments that were in effect political contributions; the cases had been uncovered initially by the Internal Revenue Service.

Institutional advertising also can serve as a means of using corporate funds to convey a political message. For example, oil company ads in newspapers and news magazines, such as those placed by Mobil and other corporations, frequently seek to influence public opinion and public policy on energy and related issues; but these are not considered political contributions.

In 1980 corporations exploited a provision of the 1979 FECA Amendments. The change in federal election law allowed state and local party committees to spend unlimited amounts on volunteer-oriented activities on behalf of presidential candidates. As described in Chapter 5, a number of corporations contributed funds to party committees in many of the states where such contributions are permitted, thus adding to the success of the 1980 Republican presidential ticket, on behalf of which the party committees spent the money.

Paying for Political Conventions

In 1936 the Democratic party found a way to help corporations circumvent the ban on direct corporate contributions. At their national nominating convention, the Democrats produced a *Book of the Democratic Convention of 1936.* It contained pictures of the Democratic leaders, articles about various branches of the national government written by party figures, and other information. Advertising space was sold to national corporations. The book was sold in various editions, ranging in price from $2.50 to a $100 deluxe edition that was bound in leather and autographed by President Franklin D. Roosevelt. Sales and advertising revenue from the book raised $250,000 for the campaign.[2]

Convention program books became more and more elaborate, and the advertising rates went up accordingly, but after 1936 the money was used to pay for convention costs, not campaign costs. At the local level, however, program books often were used to raise money for party organizations.

The major parties continued to publish the convention books every four years, with ads costing about $5,000 a page, until 1964. That year, the Democrats published their convention book as a memorial to President John F. Kennedy. Ads cost $15,000 a page and produced an estimated profit of $1 million. The success prompted the Republicans to publish a program in 1965 called *Congress: The Heartbeat of Government,* which charged $10,000 a page for ads and raised about $250,000. Not to be outdone, the Democrats came back in late 1965 with *Toward an Age of Greatness.* Ads again cost $15,000 a page and produced a profit of at least $600,000. This edition had been prepared for distribution at fund-raising movie premieres for Democratic congressional candidates in 1966.

Reaction in Congress and the press was hostile. The result was an amendment in 1966 that required the Internal Revenue Service to disallow corporate tax deductions for advertisements in political program books, which previously had been construed as legitimate business expenses. Congress backed off a bit in 1968, however, changing the law to permit such tax deductions, but only in connection with the national nominating conventions.

Besides buying ads in program books, businesses directly helped host cities pay the costs of nominating conventions. For many years hotels, restaurants, and transportation lines servicing the host city made contributions— considered as legitimate business expenses—to nonpartisan committees established to guarantee bids for bringing the convention to the city. Such funds helped the host city provide the extra services required by a national political convention. The reported pledge of the International Telephone and Telegraph Company (ITT) of $100,000 or more to help San Diego finance the 1972 Republican convention was one example of that practice. The subsequent uproar, which caused the Republicans to relocate the convention, was not so much about the propriety of the pledge itself as about an alleged connection between the pledge and the terms of the government's settlement of an antitrust suit against ITT.

In addition to money for bid guarantees, many companies provided free goods or services, forms of indirect contributions, to the national conventions—car dealers provided fleets of autos, soft drink companies gave away drinks. Many such practices, however, became illegal for the 1976 and future national conventions under new guidelines set down by the Federal Election Commission in the process of administering the FECA.

Public Funds for Political Conventions

The 1974 Amendments established for the first time an option for public financing of party conventions. Both major parties exercised that option for their 1976 national conventions, although the Republicans did so with reluctance. Each party was entitled to $2,182,000 of convention money from the presidential checkoff fund. Neither party, however, used the full amount. Ostensibly, public funding replaced the traditional mode of convention financing. The 1974 Amendments eliminated any income tax benefit for advertising in convention program books. Also absent in 1976 were the contributions in kind formerly provided by many businesses. Nevertheless, private and host city money still played a role in the 1976 convention, albeit a limited and newly regulated one.

Prompted by complaints from the Republican and Democratic national committees that a narrowly defined subsidy of $2.2 million would be unrealistically low, the FEC ruled that state and local governments could provide certain services and facilities such as convention halls, transportation, and security assistance, the cost of which would not count against the expenditure limits tied to the subsidy. The FEC also permitted the parties to accept free hotel rooms and conference facilities in return for booking a certain number of room reservations, so long as other conventions of similar size and duration received similar benefits. In addition the commission allowed nonprofit host committees to collect contributions, under specified conditions, from businesses based in the convention city and from national corporations having local operations there. By sanctioning certain spending in addition to federal grants, the FEC facilitated a partial return to traditional convention finance.

The 1979 Amendments raised to $3 million, plus Consumer Price Index adjustments, the amount that each major political party could receive for the nominating conventions of 1980 and thereafter. When indexed to account for the rise in the cost of living, the federal subsidy amounted to $4.4 million in 1980. Both parties accepted the subsidy; the Republican National Committee spent all but $15,000 of that amount, and the Democratic National Committee spent $3.7 million, returning the remainder to the U.S. Treasury. In addition the federal Law Enforcement Assistance Administration provided separate grants of $3.5 million to each host city—Detroit for the Republican convention and New York for the Democratic convention— to help pay the costs of convention security.

Labor Unions

Labor union funds became significant in national politics in 1936 and ever since have provided an important resource to the Democratic party. With a great infusion of labor support in 1968, Hubert Humphrey nearly defeated Richard Nixon. Labor was badly divided in 1972 when presidential nominee George McGovern went down to the worst Democratic defeat in history. Jimmy Carter defeated an incumbent Republican president with the help of significant labor expenditures on internal communication with members and their families, on voter registration, and on getting out the vote in 1976.

In their early years, unions were not important political contributors. Union funds were used only for expenses such as postage, leaflets, and speakers and were not contributed directly to candidates. In 1936, however, unions were estimated to have contributed $770,000 to help reelect Roosevelt. The biggest contributor was the United Mine Workers, which gave $469,000.[3] John L. Lewis, the union president, wanted to show up at the White House during the campaign with a check for $250,000 and a photographer, but Roosevelt vetoed the idea.[4]

In 1943, when resentment had mounted against wartime strikes and labor's successful organizing drives of the 1930s, the restrictions imposed in 1907 on corporate giving were extended temporarily to labor unions. Under the Smith-Connally Act, which Congress passed by overriding the president's veto, labor contributions to federal election campaigns were barred for the duration of World War II. In 1947 the Taft-Hartley Act made the ban permanent. The act extended the prohibition to include corporate and labor contributions and expenditures for primary elections and nominating conventions as well as for general elections.

Like corporations, unions learned ways to get around the law against direct contributions. They formed political auxiliaries, such as the AFL-CIO's Committee on Political Education (COPE), that collect voluntary contributions from union members for political purposes. In 1944, the first year in which there was a union-affiliated political committee, more than $1.4 million was raised.[5] That was the campaign in which the Republicans charged that everything the Democrats did had to be "cleared with Sidney"—referring to Sidney Hillman, then head of the CIO.[6]

Although members are not required to contribute, a strong union may use various means, not the least of which is simple social pressure, to persuade them to "volunteer." The funds thus gathered can be used legally for direct assistance to candidates.

Besides these voluntary funds, there are three other channels by which labor money can flow into campaigns:

1. Nonfederal Contributions. These are sums spent where state laws permit contributions by labor unions to election campaigns for state and local office. As will be seen in Chapter 7, more states prohibit or limit corporate contributions than labor contributions. Studies have shown that labor consistently provides 10 to 20 percent of the funds of major Democratic candidates in some states and often is the largest single organized group in Democratic circles.

2. 'Educational' Expenditures. Funds taken directly from union treasuries to be used for ostensibly nonpartisan purposes such as registration drives, get-out-the-vote campaigns, or the printing of voting records of legislators are considered "educational" expenditures. Labor's registration drives may be of more value to Democratic candidates than direct money contributions. In recent presidential election years, COPE has spent more than $1 million on registration drives, carried out selectively in heavily Democratic areas.

3. Public Service Activities. Union newspapers, radio programs, and the like, financed directly from union treasuries, express a sharply partisan, prolabor point of view. Such expressions of opinion are, of course, constitutionally protected, but in the matter of partisan communications, such as candidate endorsements, the law restricts unions to communicating with members and their families as it restricts corporations to communicating with executive and administrative personnel, stockholders, and their families.

In recent elections labor has spent considerable sums on behalf of candidates it supported. Although labor was split badly over the McGovern candidacy in 1972, the unions reported gross disbursements at the federal level of $8.5 million. In 1976 public funding prevented the presidential candidates from accepting any private contributions to further their campaigns. Nevertheless labor is estimated to have spent some $11 million for nonreportable items such as registration, get-out-the-vote drives, candidate logistical support, and general political education—all citizenship activities of great benefit to the presidential ticket and other labor-backed candidates.[7] This sum was in addition to the $17.5 million labor reported spending; $8.6 million of that represents direct contributions to candidates by labor union PACs.

In 1980, due at least in part to inflation, labor's spending on behalf of Carter-Mondale reached about $15 million. Included in that total is $1.3 million that 40 labor organizations reported spending on communications costs. The rest was spent on nonreportable activities, such as voter registration and turnout.

Many political observers contend that labor's true strength lies not in its campaign war chests but in the volunteers it can muster to handle the strenuous precinct work, with all the drudgery of registering voters and getting them to the polls. In 1968, for example, when the labor effort almost put Humphrey over the top in the closing weeks of the campaign (he had been trailing Nixon in the polls), unions registered 4.6 million voters and printed and distributed more than 100 million pamphlets and leaflets from Washington, D.C. Local chapters deployed nearly 100,000 telephone callers or house-to-house canvassers and, on election day, put 94,457 volunteers to work as poll watchers and telephone callers, and in other jobs designed to get "their people" to the polls.[8]

The money limits set by the 1974 legislation placed an even greater value on the ability of labor to mobilize large numbers of volunteers. There are no limitations on the use of "person power," and labor has an enormous pool of people who can be recruited. A similar advantage accrues to any other organization that can draw on the services of large numbers of people.

Illegal Contributions

One of the disturbing aspects of election financing, brought to light by Watergate-related investigations, was the string of illegal contributions made by a number of the most prestigious U.S. companies in 1972 and earlier. That some businesses had engaged in such practices in the past was suspected; what was particularly startling about the roster of illegal corporate contributors in 1972 was its "blue chip" quality and the amounts involved. Moreover, these disclosures opened the window on a multitude of unethical practices by American industry, both within the country and abroad.

The story began in the fall of 1973 when the Watergate special prosecutor filed suit in U.S. District Court in the District of Columbia against American Airlines, Goodyear Tire and Rubber Company, and Minnesota Mining and Manufacturing Company, alleging violations of federal laws in making illegal contributions of corporate funds to Nixon and other presidential candidates in the 1972 campaign. Over the next two years, 21 companies pleaded guilty to this charge.

In all, the 21 companies were charged with contributing almost $968,000 illegally, with the bulk of it, $842,500, going to the Nixon campaign. Democrats receiving illegal corporate contributions included McGovern, Humphrey, Henry M. Jackson, Wilbur D. Mills, and Edmund S. Muskie.

'Laundered' Money

The phrase "laundering money" entered the American political lexicon in 1972. It described the process by which corporations sought to hide the fact that the contributions had originated in their company treasuries and were thus illegal. The laundering took many forms. American Airlines, for example, sent money from one U.S. bank to an agent in Lebanon for supposed purchase of aircraft; it came back to a second U.S. bank and then on to the Finance Committee for the Reelection of the President. Other firms drew on secret slush funds, sold bogus airline tickets, or created fictitious bonus schemes for employees. The employees then contributed the bonus to a campaign.

Although there had been sporadic federal prosecutions of corporate political practices in past elections, the picture that unfolded from 1973 to 1975 suggested illegal corporate giving on a scale unlike anything previously imagined. Many of the convicted corporate officials said they had contributed illegally because the fund raising had been carried on by high officials such as Maurice Stans, former secretary of commerce, and by persons close to the president, such as Herbert Kalmbach, Nixon's personal attorney. They claimed they gave not to obtain favors but to avoid possible government retaliation against them. Some said that the Nixon fund-raising effort differed from earlier campaign fund raising in the amounts of money involved and the unquestioning acceptance of cash. In the words of the Senate Select Watergate Committee, "... there is no evidence that any fund-raiser who was involved in these contributions sought or obtained assurances that the contribution was legal at the time it was made." [9]

Certain companies reportedly flatly refused when they were asked for large amounts. Among them were American Motors Corporation,[10] Union Oil Company, and Allied Chemical Corporation.[11]

Most of the prime defense contractors, a *New York Times* survey disclosed, had been solicited by fund-raisers from the Finance Committee for the Reelection of the President. The customary amount suggested for the major corporations was $100,000; requests were scaled down for the smaller companies. The survey uncovered a distinct pattern of high-pressure solicitation.[12] As reports of the pressures put on potential corporate contributors were published, the conventional image of the greedy business executive as the corrupter, seeking to buy favors from politicians, underwent a change. Instead, the businesses became the victims, not the perpetrators, of what some saw as extortion. George Spater, chief executive officer of American Airlines, told the Senate Watergate Committee that he was motivated by "fear of the unknown," likening his state of mind to "those medieval maps that show the known world and then around it, Terra Incognita, with fierce animals."

Gulf's Claude Wild said he decided to arrange the contribution so that his company "would not be on a blacklist or at the bottom of the totem pole" and so that somebody in Washington would answer his telephone calls.[13] How much of this was rationalization on the part of corporate executives, remains for the reader to determine.

The Finance Committee for the Reelection of the President maintained that it never solicited corporate contributions—that it only asked corporate executives to take responsibility to raise money from among their colleagues. Target amounts were proposed, it was admitted, but no quotas imposed. Yet targets, by their very nature, suggest quotas that, if unmet, pose problems for those not complying. And because the Nixon campaign represented an incumbent administration, requests for funds were taken seriously. The pattern of pressure was reported by so many corporate executives that the abuses could not be attributed merely to the overzealousness of some fund-raisers operating on behalf of an incumbent with his implied power.

The uncovered illegal practices led to a widening circle of investigations that, by mid-1975, were being conducted by four government agencies and one Senate subcommittee. The focus shifted from the relatively limited area of illegal contributions to U.S. politicians, to the issue of multimillion-dollar expenditures by corporations seeking to obtain contracts or influence abroad. In perspective, $100,000 to a presidential campaign was not much compared with millions of dollars given in Italy, Korea, and other countries by certain American multinational corporations. The practice of spreading money around foreign countries was common among multinational businesses and considered a necessary evil to allow American business to catch up to and compete with foreign companies.

Foreign Money

Under federal law in 1972, it was a felony to solicit, accept, or receive a political contribution from a foreign principal or an agent of a foreign principal.[14] The law also prohibited an agent of a foreign principal from making a political contribution on behalf of his principal or in his capacity as agent of the principal. The legality of political contributions by foreign nationals hinged on the definition of the term "foreign principal." A direct contribution from a foreign national, without an agent or other connection with a "foreign principal," was considered legal—even though that had the effect of permitting political contributions from individuals who neither resided in the United States nor had the right to vote in U.S. elections.

Watergate investigators uncovered several sizable gifts to the Nixon campaign from foreign nationals associated with interests that would benefit from favorable U.S. policy decisions, including $25,000 from a representative for Philippine sugar interests[15] and $27,500 from the head of a Greek company chosen to supply fuel to the U.S. Sixth Fleet.[16] Following such revelations the FECA Amendments of 1974 revised the law to apply directly to foreign nationals. Under the 1974 Amendments, any individual who is not a U.S. citizen and who is not lawfully admitted for permanent residence (as defined in the Foreign Agents Registration Act of 1938) is prohibited from contributing.

Corporate and Labor PACs

The reforms of the 1970s sought, among other things, to tighten restrictions on the kind of illegal contributions uncovered by Watergate-related investigations and to diminish the influence of special interest groups and wealthy contributors in the electoral process. While reducing the role of the large individual contributor, the changes, particularly the 1974 Amendments, have served to increase—or at least to make more visible—the roles played by special interests by sanctioning the establishment of political action committees.

A PAC normally is organized by a business, labor, professional, agrarian, ideological, or issue group to raise political funds on a voluntary basis from members, stockholders, or employees for the purpose of aggregating numerous smaller contributions into larger, more meaningful amounts that are then contributed to favored candidates or political party committees. A PAC can contribute up to $5,000 per candidate per election (that is, $5,000 in a primary and another $5,000 in the general election) provided the committee has been registered with the Federal Election Commission for at least six months, has more than 50 contributors, and has supported five or more candidates for federal office.

As noted, by the time the reform legislation was passed, labor unions already had significant experience in the formation and use of political action committees. Although unions had long been prohibited from using dues to make contributions or expenditures in support of any federal candidate, the voluntary contributions the union committees collected from union members could be used legally for direct assistance to candidates. In addition, for many years the prowess of labor unions in organizing political activity, such as voter registration and turnout drives, was envied by business. In the reforms of the 1970s, labor unions, ironically, supported the legislation that triggered establishment of many corporate and business PACs that now rival the labor committees in political influence.

1971 Legislation

For years labor officials pushed for legislation allowing unions and corporations to establish and operate PACs, finally succeeding with passage of the 1971 FECA. The new legislation did not change the longstanding— but heretofore ill-enforced—prohibitions against the use of corporate or union funds in federal elections. But it did officially sanction corporations and unions to use corporate treasury funds and union dues to set up and administer PACs and solicit voluntary contributions. It also permitted use of such funds to pay the costs of partisan communications with stockholders and members and their families, as well as the costs of nonpartisan registration and get-out-the-vote drives aimed at those persons.

Labor, following an adverse Supreme Court decision, sought to forestall a Justice Department challenge to its use of dues money to administer its political action committees. It included corporations in the proposed legislation to gain Republican support. Labor officials, however, were confident that corporations could not fully exercise their rights in this area, since the old law barring federal contractors from "directly or indirectly" contributing remained intact. Using corporate funds to administer a PAC could be considered an indirect contribution, thus precluding direct political activity by companies that were government contractors, which included most of the nation's largest corporations.

Although the restrictions on government contractors did inhibit somewhat the growth of corporate-related PACs, the 1971 laws sanctioned direct and open participation by labor and corporate organizations wanting to play a prominent role in partisan politics. Even with the restrictions, almost 90 corporate-related PACs were in existence during the 1972 election, many sprouting after enactment of the 1971 law. (Corporate PACs were permissible before that law was passed, but the use of corporate money to support them was not legally sanctioned.)

1974 Legislation

The 1972 elections brought new pressures for additional election reforms, culminating in the 1974 Amendments. One provision had a significant impact on the use of PACs by corporations as a main vehicle for political giving. The provision revised the law to permit corporations and labor unions holding government contracts to create PACs. Again, ironically, labor worked to have the prohibition lifted. Having secured government contracts to train workers, a few labor unions were concerned that their maintenance of PACs might be threatened unless the law was changed. The 1974 Amendments not only protected those unions but also permitted corporations that held large defense and other government contracts to use corporate funds for establishing and administering their PACs and for fund-raising purposes. Many of the largest corporations in the United States have since done so.

SunPAC Advisory

Despite the 1974 Amendments, many companies with government contracts remained reluctant to establish PACs. It was not until the FEC had issued an advisory opinion in November 1975, in response to a request by the Sun Oil Company regarding the establishment of a political action committee, that corporations were assured about the validity of such political activities. In a 4-to-2 decision, the FEC voted to permit corporations to support the election campaigns of candidates for president, vice president, the Senate, and the House, provided the money came from voluntary contributions from stockholders and employees. The commission cautioned corporations that there was potential for coercion in soliciting employees, however, and established guidelines for solicitation.

Following the SunPAC decision, the business community began to realize the potential of PACs as a means of competing with labor unions for political influence. In the six months following the decision, corporate PACs more than doubled in number.

1976 Legislation

Having recognized its strategic errors in supporting changes in the original FECA and concerned about the rapid growth of corporate PACs, labor sought legislative remedies. The 1976 Amendments placed new restrictions on the range of corporate, trade association, and labor PAC solicitation. Corporate PACs may seek contributions only from stockholders and executive or administrative personnel and their families. Labor union PACs may solicit contributions only from union members and their families. Twice a year, however, corporate and union PACs are permitted to seek contributions, by mail only, from all employees not otherwise available to them for solicitation. A trade association or its PAC can solicit contributions from stockholders and executive or administrative personnel of any of the association's member corporations if such solicitation is approved separately and specifically by the corporation. No corporation, however, can approve any such solicitation by more than one trade association in any calendar year.

The 1976 Amendments also imposed on political action committees reporting requirements in addition to those enacted in 1971 and 1974. Under the 1976 law, corporations, unions, and membership organizations must report expenditures that are directly attributable to a communication expressly advocating the election or defeat of a clearly identified candidate if the costs exceed $2,000 an election. This provision does not apply if the communication, such as a union or company magazine or newspaper, is devoted to general news of interest to the employees or membership and is not sent primarily to help elect or defeat a clearly identified candidate.

The law imposed a $5,000 ceiling on individual contributions to a political committee in a calendar year. The 1976 Amendments also restricted the proliferation of membership organizations and corporate and union political action committees. All PACs established by a company, union, or any other organization are treated as a single committee for contribution purposes. Finally, and most important, the 1976 legislation allowed corporate, union, and association officials to determine, within the limitations of the law, how the money collected should be used. The AFL-CIO Committee on Political Education (COPE), for example, distributes its funds to candidates selected by vote at state labor conventions or by bodies designated by the conventions.

Republicans and the business community generally were unhappy with the 1976 law but have managed to use it to their advantage. Despite the added restrictions, corporate and trade association committees have demonstrated their ability to increase the number of PACs they sponsor and the amounts raised and contributed to candidates.

PAC Solicitation Practices

A survey of corporate political action committees undertaken in 1981 by Civic Service, a private political research organization, provides some useful information about corporate PAC solicitation practices and results.[17] According to the survey, to which 275 corporate PACs responded with information about their activities during the 1979-1980 election cycle, few corporate PACs took advantage of the right to solicit stockholders, and fewer still of the twice-yearly opportunity to solicit employees otherwise not available to them for solicitation. Only about 17 percent reported seeking contributions from stockholders, and fewer than 10 percent reported soliciting nonexecutive employees under the twice-yearly provision of the law. Instead corporate PACs concentrate their solicitation on their sponsors' executive and administrative personnel. Some 63 percent of such personnel were solicited by all the PACs responding to the survey, and about 33 percent of the solicited employees made contributions.

According to the survey the average number of donors was 388 per PAC, and the average contribution during the two-year period was $161. About 72 percent of the PACs use payroll withholding plans for their eligible personnel to make contributions. Methods of solicitation generally used by corporate PACs include mail, personal contacts, group presentations, and combinations of the three methods.

Almost 97 percent of the PACs responding to the survey said they had some type of committee or board that determined who was to receive contributions. Only about 25 percent allowed contributors to earmark their donations for specific candidates or parties. Almost 88 percent communicated regularly with their members—through meetings, newsletters, annual reports, and other means—and about 80 percent made known to their employees and stockholders who made PAC contribution decisions and how such decisions were made.

Less information is available about labor PAC solicitation practices. Companies using payroll withholding for executive contributions must make the same service available at cost for a union to collect contributions from its members who work for the companies. But, according to the Civic Service survey, only about 15 percent of the PACs responding indicated that the unions in their companies had asked for payroll deductions for their PACs, and only about 45 percent of those unions actually were using payroll deductions. Generally a union business agent or steward solicits members in person or in a group on an annual basis.

Although precise information is not available, contributors to union PACs far outnumber those to corporate PACs, but corporate PACs receive much larger average donations. There are some indications, however, that in the wake of the 1980 elections, unions have begun to turn increasingly to payroll deduction or checkoff plans to close or at least narrow the growing gap in money raised between labor and business-related PACs. While permitted by law to have contributions deducted from employees' pay, the unions still must negotiate for the privilege in their contracts. The AFL-CIO now is urging its affiliated unions in the private sector to negotiate contract provisions in which the employer agrees to have a set amount, authorized by individual employees, deducted regularly from their paychecks for political contributions. In the public sector, unions are being encouraged to negotiate checkoffs or seek legislation to permit them.

The Civic Service survey indicated that nearly nine corporate PACs in ten bar trade associations from soliciting their employees. Nor are the corporations any less possessive about their shareholders. One corporation executive said he would be surprised "if 3 percent of the companies are willing to let an association PAC work their shareholders." [18] Many corporations belong to several trade associations, each reflecting a different facet of the company and representing a different constituency within the company. This can make the choice of which association will be allowed to solicit an awkward one. Consequently, successful associations often are not those with company members but those with individual members, such as real estate agents, or with professional members, such as doctors, who can be solicited directly.

A nationwide survey of the political contribution activities of the mass public in 1980 found that most of those in the sample of 3,000 who contributed to PACs rather than to parties or candidate organizations came from the middle-income bracket—$15,000-$35,000—and that nearly half were under 35 years old.[19] Forty-two percent of those PAC contributors came from union households. Fifty-four percent identified themselves as Democrats, 36 percent as Republicans, and 10 percent as independents. Thirty-one percent identified themselves as liberals; 37 percent were self-identified conservatives; 18 percent were self-identified moderates; and the remainder did not place themselves on the liberal-conservative spectrum. Finally, in comparison with individuals who contributed to parties or candidate organizations rather than to PACs, the PAC contributors were less likely to engage in campaign discussions or in traditional campaign activities such as wearing a campaign button, working for a party, or attending a rally or fund-raiser. They also were somewhat less likely to vote than those in the other two categories of contributors.

Growth of PACs

Despite the solicitation restrictions imposed by the 1976 Amendments, corporate and trade association PACs in particular have grown at a remarkable rate. The data in Table 4-1 compare the growth in numbers of the various categories of PACs on file with the FEC from 1974 through 1982. Corporate PACs grew from 89 in 1974 to 1,467 in 1982;

Table 4-1 Number of Registered PACs, 1974-1982[1]

Category	1974	1975	1976	1977	1978	1979	1980	1981	1982
Corp.	89	139	433	550	784	949	1,204	1,327	1,467
Labor	201	226	224	234	217	240	297	318	380
Trade/ Memb./ Health[2]	318	357	489	438	451	512	574	608	628
Nonconn.				110	165	250	378	539	746
Coop.				8	12	17	42	41	47
Corp. w/o stock				20	24	32	56	68	103
Total	608	722	1,146	1,360	1,653	2,000	2,551	2,901	3,371

[1] Data as of December 31 for all years except 1975 (November 24).
[2] Includes all noncorporate and nonlabor PACs through December 31, 1977.

SOURCES: For 1974-1981 data, Federal Election Commission, "PACs Increase at Declining Rate," press release, January 17, 1982; for 1982 data, Federal Election Commission, "1981-82 PAC Giving Up 51%," press release, April 29, 1983.

trade/membership/health PACs grew from 318 in 1974 to 628 in 1982, and labor PACs, which have less potentital for growth than the other two categories, increased from 201 in 1974 to 380 in 1982. Nonconnected PACs, which include ideological and issue groups, also demonstrated notable growth during this period.

The solicitation practices and political strategies of such committees are described below. Not all PACs registered with the FEC actually contribute to candidates. In 1981 and 1982, for example, of the 3,727 active PACs, only 2,651 made contributions to federal candidates. In addition, a study of the 1,349 PACs that were active in the 1979-1980 election cycle and that gave at least $5,000 to federal candidates during the period from January 1, 1977, through December 31, 1980, indicates most PAC operations are relatively modest.[20] The study found that 37 percent of the PACs made total direct contributions of $10,000 or less, and only 2 percent made contributions of $300,000 or more.

The data in Table 4-2 show that the adjusted expenditures of all PACs rose from $19.2 million in 1972 to $190.4 million in 1982—an 892

Table 4-2   Financial Activity of PACs, 1972-1982

Election Cycle[1]	*Adjusted Receipts*[2]	*Adjusted Expenditures*	*Contributions to Congressional Candidates*
1972	n.a.	$ 19,168,000	$ 8,500,000[3]
1974	n.a.	25,000,000[4]	12,526,586
1976	$ 54,045,588	52,894,630	22,571,912
1978	79,956,291	77,412,860	35,187,215
1980	137,728,528	131,153,384	55,217,291
1982	199,250,455	190,360,900	87,316,285

[1] The periods covered by the election cycles vary. Data for 1972 is limited for the period prior to April 7, 1972, the effective date for disclosure under the 1971 FECA. The 1974 data covers September 1, 1973, to December 31, 1974. The 1976 data covers January 1, 1975, to December 31, 1976. The 1978 data covers January 1, 1977, to February 22, 1980. The 1980 data covers January 1, 1977, to February 22, 1980. The 1980 data covers January 1, 1979, to December 31, 1980.
[2] Adjusted receipts and expenditures exclude funds transferred between affiliated committees and are thus more representative of levels of financial activity.
[3] This figure excludes contributions to candidates defeated in primaries.
[4] This figure is a rough estimate.

SOURCES: For 1972-1980 data, Joseph E. Cantor, *Political Action Committees: Their·Evolution and Growth and Their Implications for the Political System* (Washington, D.C.: Congressional Research Service, May 7, 1982), 67. For 1982 data, Federal Election Commission, "1981-82 PAC Giving Up 51%," press release, April 29, 1983.

Table 4-3   Adjusted Expenditures of PACs by Category, 1972-1982[1]

Type of PAC	1972	1974	1976	1978	1980	1982
Labor	$ 8.5	$11.0	$17.5	$18.6	$ 25.1	$ 35.0
Business-oriented[2]	8.0	8.1	—	—	—	—
Corporate	—	—	5.8	15.2	31.4	43.2
Trade/Membership/Health	—	—	—	23.8	32.0	41.7
Nonconnected[3]	2.6	.8	—	17.4	38.6	64.6
Other[4]	—	1.1	29.6	2.4	4.0	5.8
Total	$19.2	$20.9	$52.9	$77.4	$131.2	$190.4

[1] Figures are in millions of dollars, rounded to the nearest tenth.

[2] This category is based on the assumption that the majority of PACs within it have a pro-business orientation. It is roughly comparable to the combined corporate and trade/membership/health categories listed in 1978-82.

[3] For 1972 and 1974, this represents spending by ideological PACs; after 1976 it corresponds directly to the FEC's nonconnected grouping.

[4] Totals in this category are comparable only for 1978-82; included are PACs sponsored by cooperatives and corporations without stock.

SOURCES: For 1972-1980 data, Joseph E. Cantor, *Political Action Committees: Their Evolution and Growth and Their Implications for the Political System* (Washington, D.C.: Congressional Research Service, May 7, 1982), 83-84. For 1982 data, Federal Election Commission, "1981-82 PAC Giving Up 51%," press release, April 29, 1983.

percent increase—and that PAC contributions to congressional candidates during the same period rose from $8.5 million to $83.1 million—an 877 percent increase.

Table 4-3 provides a breakdown of the adjusted expenditure total for each election year from 1972 through 1982 according to PAC categories. Table 4-4 compares amounts contributed to congressional candidates by each category of PAC in the same election years. Although changes in categorization of PACs by the FEC prevent actual comparisons, it is clear that corporate and other business-related PAC contributions to congressional candidates have increased at a significantly greater rate than labor contributions to those candidates.

Presidential prenomination campaigns are financed primarily with individual contributions and public matching funds for those individual contributions of $250 or less. No contributions from private sources are permitted to publicly funded general election campaigns, except to defray compliance costs. Consequently most PAC contributions go to congressional campaigns. And because House candidates are far more numerous than Senate candidates, between two-thirds and three-fourths of all PAC congressional contributions in each election cycle have been made to House campaigns.

Although corporate PACs outnumber other types of PACs and, in the last two election cycles, have contributed more in the aggregate than any other category of PAC, individual corporate PACs are rarely found among the top ten PACs measured by contributions to candidates. In 1981-1982, for example, five of the top ten PAC contributors to candidates were sponsored by trade/membership/health organizations, four by unions, and one by a cooperative:

1. Realtors Political Action Committee, $2,115,135
2. American Medical Political Action Committee, $1,737,090
3. UAW-V-CAP (United Auto Workers), $1,623,947
4. Machinists Non-Partisan Political League, $1,444,959
5. National Education Association PAC, $1,183,215
6. Build Political Action Committee of the National Association of Home Builders, $1,005,628
7. Committee for Thorough Agricultural Political Education of Associated Milk Producers, $962,450
8. American Bankers Association BANKPAC, $947,460
9. Automobile and Truck Dealers Election Action Committee, $917,295
10. AFL-CIO COPE Political Contributions Committee, $906,425.

Assessing the PAC Phenomenon

Despite their obvious popularity—or in part because of it—PACs have generated lively controversy. According to a nationwide survey published in 1982, most citizens, including a majority of those in the "executive, professional class," have negative attitudes toward PACs because they believe PACs have too much influence on electoral outcomes.[21] Corporate and other business-related PACs often have been singled out for criticism, at least in part because of past misuse of corporate funds to gain political influence or to forestall political reprisals.

Nationalization of Fund Raising. Some PAC critics maintain that congressional candidates increasingly raise funds from out-of-state sources, particularly from Washington-based PACs, and that this development works to divorce officeholders from their constituents. It is true that PAC funds as a percentage of total congressional campaign receipts have increased steadily since 1972 but, as noted in Chapter 3, not at the expense of private contributions. Contributions from individuals, including the candidates themselves, remain by far the most important source of

Table 4-4 Contributions to Congressional Candidates of PACs by Category, 1972-1982[1]

Type of PAC	1972	1974	1976	1978	1980	1982
Labor	$3.6	$ 6.3	$ 8.2	$10.3	$13.2	$20.2
Business-related[2]	2.7	4.4	10.0	—	—	—
Corporate	—	—	—	9.8	19.2	27.4
Trade/Membership/Health	—	—	—	11.3	15.9	21.7
Nonconnected[3]	—	.7	1.5	2.8	4.9	10.7
Other[4]	2.2	1.0	2.8	1.0	2.0	3.1
Total	$8.5	$12.5	$22.6	$35.2	$55.4	$83.1

[1] Figures are in millions of dollars, rounded to the nearest tenth.
[2] This encompasses the categories for business, health, and, in 1976, lawyers.
[3] For 1974 and 1976, this represents contributions by ideological PACs. Beginning with 1978, it corresponds directly to the FEC's nonconnected grouping.
[4] Totals in this category are comparable only for 1978-1982; included are PACs sponsored by cooperatives and corporations without stock.

SOURCES: For 1972-1980 data, Joseph E. Cantor, *Political Action Committees: Their Evolution and Growth and Their Implications for the Political System* (Washington, D.C.: Congressional Research Service, May 7, 1982), 87-88. For 1982 data, Federal Election Commission, "1981-82 PAC Giving Up 51%," press release, April 29, 1983.

congressional campaign funds. In the 1979-1980 election cycle, for example, private individuals accounted for 67 percent of all funds contributed to major party House general election candidates and 78 percent of the funds contributed to Senate general election candidates. PACs provided 29 percent of the funds contributed to those House candidates and only 21 percent of the money contributed to the Senate general election candidates. PACs, then, do not appear to be the dominant element in congressional campaign fund raising they are sometimes portrayed to be. Of course, these percentages do not take into account independent expenditures.

A study of the contribution patterns of PACs active in the 1979-1980 election cycle that contributed at least $5,000 to federal candidates during the period January 1, 1977, through December 31, 1980, showed the existence of "many large PACs that centralize and rationalize small individual contributions." The study noted that in addition to national PACs there are small local PACs, sometimes acting as adjuncts to local party organizations, which reward or punish local incumbents on the basis of one or another litmus test. The study concluded, "For better or worse, much of what is going on at the local level may not be too different from the pre-PAC era." [22]

A certain degree of nationalization in congressional campaign fund raising is both desirable and inevitable. Senators and representatives have national interests to consider as well as local ones. And to the degree that public policy affecting interest groups is formulated in Washington rather than in state and local communities, a trend toward out-of-state campaign fund raising is to be expected. Finally, it is important to recognize that candidates often take the initiative in seeking campaign funds from out-of-state or Washington-based PACs sympathetic to their positions because they are persuaded they cannot raise sufficient funds at home to carry on competitive campaigns. The rising costs of federal election campaigns and the federal law limiting the size of individual contributions combine to make some degree of reliance on out-of-state funding a necessity for many candidates, thus serving to nationalize our politics.

PACs and Parties. Although they are extra-constitutional entities, American political parties often have functioned as the primary coalition-builders among competing political factions. The decline of the political parties in recent years has been widely reported and amply discussed.[23] Some PAC critics hold that PACs are in good part responsible for party decline. They say that by making substantial sums of campaign money available to political candidates and providing other useful services, PACs have decreased the reliance of candidates on the parties.[24]

In fact, the decline of the parties was well under way before political action committees achieved their current level of popularity. The replacement of party-controlled patronage of civil service; the ascendancy of television as a means of reaching voters directly; the development of effective but expensive campaign technologies; the proliferation of presidential primaries; the rise of a better educated electorate interested in issues—all these factors have contributed to party decline.

The decline of the parties also is, in part, a consequence of the election campaign finance reforms. The reform laws, which were intended to increase citizen participation in election campaigns and decrease so-called special-interest influence, actually have had the largely unforeseen consequence of reinforcing candidate-centered politics to the detriment of the parties and the purposes they once served.

The FECA of 1971 made federal candidates self-contained units for purposes of disclosure of monies received and spent. The 1971 Revenue Act had the same effect on presidential candidates for purposes of public financing. Thus, to avoid difficult allocation problems, many candidates shun joint appearances with other candidates on the party ticket.

The 1974 Amendments imposed limits on the amount of money national and state party organizations may contribute to federal election campaigns. (Some limits on state and local party group financial activity in presidential campaigns subsequently were lifted by the 1979 Amendments.) The 1976 Amendments imposed an annual limit on the amount an individual may contribute to the national committee of a political party.

The 1971 Revenue Act, as amended in 1978, permits tax credits for contributions to candidates and parties. Because the law makes no distinction between the two types of contributions, parties have been forced to compete with candidates for available campaign money.

Formerly parties exercised some adjudicating influence among competing interest groups. As the parties have proven less able to do so, interest groups and their PACs have become correspondingly more visible in their efforts to promote their claims. Some PACs have even assumed a number of the functions once served only by parties, including recruiting and endorsing candidates and conducting voter registration and get-out-the-vote drives.

Moreover, in recent years Congress has taken steps that make greater interest-group involvement in legislative decision making inevitable. The seniority system has been overturned, the number of congressional employees and committee staffs has increased enormously, and semi-autonomous subcommittees have proliferated. Members of Congress function more than ever as independent issue leaders, and interest groups are able to take their cases directly to those members who have influence in areas of specific concern to the groups. Interest group PACs are able to channel their contributions to those members who can do the most for the PAC interests.

Finally, the revival of the Republican party since its post-Watergate nadir and the efforts of the Democratic party to recover its former position of influence after the 1980 election suggest there is room in the political system for both parties and PACs. In the 1981-1982 election cycle the Republican party was notably successful not only in providing funds directly to its candidates from party committee treasuries and in spending additional sums on behalf of candidates but also in steering PAC contributions to selected party candidates. In many cases the party has been able to use its ability to provide money and its access to PAC funds to unify Republican members of Congress.[25]

Access. PACs do not contribute to candidates for the sheer pleasure of it, and it is undoubtedly true, as some critics hold, that some PACs contribute in the hope of gaining access to elected candidates. But access should not be confused with buying votes. Individuals or groups that gain access have not thereby ensured that officeholders will agree with their goals or positions. It simply means that those individuals and groups have an opportunity to get a hearing, to state their case.

Giving money to a candidate, of course, does not guarantee access to a legislator, nor is money the only factor that may affect access. Other contributions to electoral success, such as a PAC's perceived influence among voters, may be as effective in gaining the official's attention. In fact, because PACs often are sponsored by corporations employing thousands of workers, their representatives probably would have access to officeholders without making a campaign contribution.

Not all PACs are interested primarily in access. Some are ideologically motivated and work to elect like-minded candidates. They seek to tip the balance of thinking in Congress in favor of a pro-business or pro-labor or liberal or conservative point of view. Other PACs make contributions to show their appreciation for past support rather than to gain future access. In many cases, all three types of motivation—desire for future access, hope of an ideological return, and the inclination to reward past support—influence PAC contribution decisions.

Legislative Influence. Some critics argue that PACs often join forces and, through contributions to members of Congress and related lobbying, exert undue influence on legislative decisions. But the ability of PACs to achieve their political goals may be overstated. What is offered as evidence of the power of PACs in legislative politics often is anecdotal and frequently is based on simple correlations between PAC spending and legislative outcomes—correlations that are incapable of determining the true cause and effect.

PAC critics, for example, publicized widely the fact that maritime unions contributed heavily to some members of the House Merchant Marine Committee who favored a cargo preference bill introduced in 1977 and supported by the unions. They implied that the committee members were influenced by the contributions to report out a favorable bill. They gave little attention, however, to the committee members' other sources of funds. The American Medical Political Action Committee, for example, contributed to every incumbent on the House committee, but AMPAC and its supporters had no vested interest in the cargo preference bill or in any other legislation considered by the committee. Nor did PAC critics publicize the fact that the two committee members who received the greatest financial support from the unions represented districts with significant maritime interests.

A study of PACs active in the 1979-1980 election cycle concluded that PAC influence on legislative decisions frequently is overrated. "Compared to the other influences on congressional voting—ideology, party, constituency interests—the effect of PAC spending is small indeed." [26] The study found PAC strategies remarkably unsophisticated. "Instead of targeting their resources for maximum legislative effect (for example, giving to a member of Congress who is uncommitted on the PAC's favored bill), political action committees tend to reward the best behavior of congressmen who were positively predisposed toward the interest group's legislation to begin with," it stated. "This is the crudest and least effective of all 'exchange' strategies." [27]

The inability of business-related PACs to alter the Clean Air Act may be a case in point. This pervasive regulatory law, often criticized by business as unduly burdensome and counterproductive, expired in fiscal 1982. Despite considerable spending and lobbying by business to temper it, shortly before the 97th Congress concluded, Congress reauthorized the act with no substantive alterations.

An examination of the political influence of various organized interest groups during the course of the last several decades suggests that the political marketplace of ideas has remarkable powers of self-regulation. At different times groups representing diverse interests such as consumer or environmental protection, civil rights, labor, and business have had a significant effect on the course of legislation. No groups representing any one of those areas of concern have remained in ascendancy for long. Challenges from groups representing competing interests and shifts in the public mood have caused the pendulum to swing first to one side, then the other. Although organized business interests seemed to be especially influential during the first two years of the Reagan administration, for example, the results of the mid-term 1982 elections suggested that the pendulum was swinging away from business interests and in favor of competing interest groups. In the 1982 general elections, labor's overall win record was 64 percent; labor-endorsed candidates won overwhelmingly in the House and won half of the Senate and gubernatorial seats contested.[28] In comparison, many business-backed candidates lost. Only 45 percent of congressional candidates endorsed by the U.S. Chamber of Commerce won their races in 1982, down from 70 percent in 1980 and 60 percent in 1978.[29]

Incumbency. That incumbency is an advantage in congressional election campaigns is seldom questioned by knowledgeable political observ-

Table 4-5   PAC Contributions by Category to Incumbents, Challengers, and Open Seat Races (All Congressional Candidates), 1978-1982 (millions and percentages)

Year	PAC Category	Incumbent	Challenger	Open Seat
1982	Corporate	$19.8/73%	$3.6/13%	$3.9/14%
1980		10.9/57%	5.9/31%	2.4/12%
1978		5.8/59%	2.0/20%	2.0/20%
1982	Labor	$11.5/57%	$5.6/28%	$3.1/15%
1980		9.4/71%	2.2/17%	1.6/12%
1978		6.1/59%	2.2/21%	2.0/19%
1982	Trade/Member/Health	$16.0/74%	$2.8/13%	$2.8/13%
1980		10.2/64%	3.7/23%	2.0/13%
1978		6.7/58%	2.3/20%	2.5/22%
1982	Nonconnected	$4.9/46%	$3.7/34%	$2.1/20%
1980		1.6/32%	2.5/50%	.9/19%
1978		.7/28%	1.1/44%	.7/28%
1982	Corp. w/o Stock	$ .8/81%	$ .09/9%	$ .1/10%
1980		.4/70%	.1/19%	.07/11%
1978		.1/100%	——	——
1982	Cooperative	$1.7/82%	$ .14/7%	$ .23/11%
1980		1.1/81%	.1/7%	.2/13%
1978		.6/67%	.1/11%	.2/22%
1982	Total	$54.8/66%	$16.0/19%	$12.3/15%
1980	Total	33.5/61%	14.5/26%	7.2/13%
1978	Total	19.9/57%	7.7/22%	7.4/21%

SOURCES: For 1982, Federal Election Commission, "1981-82 PAC Giving Up 51%," press release, April 29, 1983; for 1980, Federal Election Commission "FEC Release Final PAC Report for 1979-80 Election Cycle," February 21, 1982, 3; for 1978, Federal Election Commission, "FEC Release Year-End 1978 Report on 1977-78 Financial Activity of Non-Party and Party Politicial Committees," press release, May 10, 1979, 3.

ers. PAC critics often complain that PAC contribution practices increase the built-in advantages of incumbency and thereby decrease the possibility of competitive election campaigns.

PAC contributions generally do favor incumbents, as shown in Table 4-5, but so do contributions from individuals. Historically a far larger percentage of incumbents than challengers are successful in each general election. Because few contributors, whether individuals or organized groups, are interested in giving money to candidates who appear to have little chance of winning, incumbents garner a disproportionate percentage of campaign funds from all sources.

Even among those PACs that generally have favored incumbents over challengers, the mere fact of incumbency is not enough to guarantee a PAC contribution. Other factors also figure in the decisions of PACs whether to contribute: party affiliation, candidate need, the location of a corporate facility or union local in the district or state, and the competitiveness of the race. In fact, challengers in competitive election campaigns often have received more in PAC funds than the incumbents.[30] According to a study of PACs active in the 1979-1980 election cycle, some 471 (16.9 percent) of the 2,785 committees registered with the FEC spent 50 percent or more of their congressional contribution budgets on challengers. Another 1,217 (43.7 percent) spent 50 percent or less on incumbents, with the remainder going for challengers and open-seat candidates. The rest of the PACs gave primarily to incumbents.[31] The study also drew some conclusions about the characteristics of PACs that are incumbent-oriented. With the exception of nonconnected PACs, which are discussed below, Washington-based PACs tend to favor incumbents more than PACs headquartered elsewhere. Among corporate PACs, those representing industries that are targets or beneficiaries of federal government economic regulation—banking, transportation, tobacco, communication, and utilities industries—tend to give to incumbents, whereas those that are targets of "social regulation" and other federal government economic policies—oil and gas, construction, chemicals, rubber, plastics, paper, and marketing—give more to nonincumbents.

Partisanship. Perhaps because corporate and other business-related PACs have been singled out for criticism, PACs in general are portrayed as pro-Republican. But, as shown in Table 4-6, in the 1981-1982 election cycle, Democrats received 54 percent of all PAC funds contributed to congressional candidates, and Republicans received 46 percent. This result repeats a pattern demonstrated in previous election cycles.

There has been a decidedly Republican preference among corporate and business-related PACs—a predictable phenomenon because the Republican party historically has been considered more favorable to business interests than the Democratic party. In 1981-1982 corporate-sponsored PACs gave about 66 percent of their congressional contributions to Republicans and about 34 percent to Democrats. The preference among trade/membership/health PACs, many of which are business-related, was about 57 percent for Republicans and about 44 percent for Democrats.

Table 4-6   PAC Contributions by Category to Democrats and Republicans (All Congressional Candidates), 1978-1982 (millions and percentages)

Year	PAC Category	Total Contribution	Democrat	Republican
1982	Corporate	$27.4	$9.4/34%	$18/66%
1980		19.2	6.9/36%	12.3/64%
1978		9.8	3.6/37%	6.1/62%
1982	Labor	$20.2	$19.1/95%	$1.1/5%
1980		13.2	12.4/94%	.8/6%
1978		10.3	9.7/94%	.6/6%
1982	Trade/Member/Health	$21.7	$9.3/43%	$12.4/57%
1980		15.9	7.0/44%	8.9/56%
1978		11.5	5.0/43%	6.5/57%
1982	Nonconnected	$10.7	$5.4/51%	$5.2/49%
1980		4.9	1.5/30%	3.4/70%
1978		2.5	.7/28%	1.9/76%
1982	Cooperative	$2.1	$1.3/62%	$.8/38%
1980		1.4	.9/65%	.5/35%
1978		.9	.6/67%	.2/22%
1982	Corp. w/o Stock	$1.0	$.6/59%	$.4/41%
1980		.6	.33/52%	.3/48%
1978		.1	.1/96%	.04/4%
1982	Total	$83.1	$45.1/54%	$38/46%
1980	Total	55.2	28.9/52%	26.2/48%
1978	Total	35.1	19.7/56%	15.3/44%

SOURCES: For 1982, Federal Election Commission, "1981-82 PAC Giving Up 51%," press release, April 29, 1983; for 1980, Federal Election Commission "FEC Release Final PAC Report for 1979-80 Election Cycle," February 21, 1982, 3; for 1978, Federal Election Commission, "FEC Releases Year-End 1978 Report on 1977-78 Financial Activity of Non-Party and Party Politicial Committees," press release, May 10, 1979, 3.

The degree of preference for Republicans among corporate PACs, however, varies significantly. A study of PACs sponsored by *Fortune*-ranked companies in the 1979-1980 election cycle, for example, found that utilities divided their contributions to congressional candidates almost equally between Republicans and Democrats; transportation firms preferred Democrats to Republicans by a 60-to-40 margin; and leading oil producers heavily favored Republicans by more than a 70-to-30 margin.[32] Although there are exceptions, there is generally a greater degree of preference for Republican candidates among smaller *Fortune*-ranked companies, whereas larger corporations are likely to be somewhat more even-handed in their contributions.

Labor PACs have been the most partisan in their giving. In 1981-1982, labor committees preferred Democrats to Republicans by a 95-to-5 percent margin. In addition to their financial contributions to Democratic candidates through their PACs, labor unions, more cohesive and unified in their political objectives than the nation's corporations, provide Democratic candidates with favorable communications and voter mobilization programs.

Legislative Proposals

Some critics of political action committees—including election reform groups such as Common Cause—have proposed reducing or eliminating the perceived influence of PACs by extending public financing to congressional campaigns. Many labor unions, apprehensive about the potential growth of corporate PACs, have supported this proposal. Efforts to enact such legislation, however, have encountered strong opposition.

Other critics propose to diminish PAC influence by lowering the amount the committees may contribute to federal candidates, now $5,000 per candidate per election, and placing an aggregate limit on the amounts candidates may receive from all PACs. One such measure, introduced in 1979 by Rep. David Obey, D-Wis., and Rep. Tom Railsback, R-Ill., actually was passed in the House but, threatened with a filibuster, languished without action in the Senate and died when the 96th Congress adjourned. Under the Obey-Railsback proposal, which would have applied only to House candidates, PACs would be allowed to contribute a maximum of $6,000 to a candidate for a primary and a general election combined, instead of the $10,000 currently allowed. In addition, candidates would be allowed to accept from all PACs no more than $70,000 during a two-year election cycle. Currently there is no overall limit on the amount candidates may accept from PACs. Despite the proposal's lack of success in the 96th Congress, a number of similar bills was introduced in the 97th Congress, but none received action.

Unintended Consequences. Legislation to limit PAC contributions further—particularly legislation limiting the aggregate amount candidates may accept from PACs—might cause more problems than it would solve.

In the face of rising campaign costs and the unlikely prospect that a budget-conscious Congress would enact compensatory legislation providing for public funding as an alternative source of money, such legislation would make it more difficult for candidates, especially challengers, to conduct competitive campaigns. Recent research has found that any increase in campaign funds generally helps challengers more than incumbents.[33] To limit PAC giving would make it more difficult for challengers to mount effective campaigns and would increase the power of incumbents, who begin their reelection campaigns with notable advantages: the ability to command greater media attention than most challengers and allowances for salary, staff, travel, office, and communications worth about $1 million over a two-year term. And it would disadvantage candidates running against wealthy opponents spending large amounts of their own funds.

Reducing the amount PACs may contribute to candidates or the amount candidates may accept from PACs in the aggregate probably would not reduce PAC influence on the campaign process. Rather it would cause PACs to intensify their efforts to be heard through direct and indirect lobbying. A study of the effects of the FECA undertaken by the Institute of Politics at Harvard University's John F. Kennedy School of Government concluded that such a legislative change probably would lead to a proliferation of PACs and a resulting diffusion of accountability in the electoral process; would encourage coordination of giving among like-minded PACs; and would increase the use of independent expenditures by PACs—a controversial tactic thus far used primarily by ideological group PACs, as described below.

Alternative Proposals. Other means of offsetting the development of PACs without risking the problems that could result from limiting their contributions also have been proposed. One idea is to raise the $1,000 individual contribution limit. A $1,000 contribution to a federal candidate in mid-1983 was worth only about $500 when compared with the buying power of $1,000 when the contribution limit was enacted. While the value of the dollar has decreased, campaign expenses have increased dramatically. Raising the individual limit, rather than limiting PAC contributions, would make some needed funding available to underfinanced campaigns and at the same time would respect the values of diversity and increased participation that PACs bring to the political system.

Another means proposed to offset PACs without unduly restricting them is to strengthen the role of the political parties. Although the campaign finance reforms of the early 1970s are by no means the major cause of the decline of the parties, some proposals to strengthen the parties include suggestions to amend the FECA. Among these proposals are the following:

● Eliminate limits on party committee spending on behalf of candidates or increase substantially those limits.

● Eliminate all limits on contributions to parties and on the amount parties may contribute to candidate committees or substantially increase those limits.

● Extend to party committees at the federal level the permission state and local party committees now have to spend unlimited amounts on volunteer-oriented activity on behalf of candidates.

● Provide a separate tax credit for small contributions to political parties or provide a separate tax checkoff for political party funding.

Advocates of such party-strengthening measures maintain that parties with more funds to help candidates—through direct contributions, services, and campaign technology—might well earn the respect, even the loyalty, of party candidates. Stronger parties, they hold, might again fulfill the coalition-building function they once served, thereby strengthening the entire political system.

Other Special Interests

Like corporate, labor union, and trade/membership/health PACs, those designated by the FEC as "nonconnected" PACs have shown growth in the amounts of money raised and spent. Among nonconnected PACs, two types are particularly notable: ideological committees and committees formed by presidential hopefuls. The activity of the presidential PACs is described in Chapter 5.

Ideological Committees

Nonconnected PACs described as ideological committees are groups that espouse the ideas and relatively broad agendas identified with political liberals or conservatives. They also include single-issue groups, such as gun lobbies, environmentalists, and women's groups.

Some ideological PACs active in recent elections are longstanding organizations such as the liberal National Committee for an Effective Congress and the American Conservative Union. Many of the most active conservative PACs are relative newcomers, including the National Conservative Political Action Committee (NCPAC), the National Congressional Club, the Fund for a Conservative Majority, and the Committee for the

Survival of a Free Congress. Those groups are prominent in the New Right—a loosely knit coalition of politically conservative individuals, PACs, think tanks, and publications intent on gaining political influence to promote their conservative agenda and moral orthodoxy. In response to the highly publicized activity of such groups in the 1978 and 1980 elections, several ideologically liberal PACs were formed to take part in the 1982 elections, including the Progressive Political Action Committee (ProPAC), Democrats for the '80s, Independent Action, and two liberal presidential PACs to be described in Chapter 5.

Tables 4-1, 4-3, and 4-4 show the dramatic increase in the number of PACs and their financial role in federal election campaigns since 1972. In the 1981-1982 election cycle, nonconnected PACs, many of which are ideological committees, reported spending almost $65 million, more than any other kind of PAC and about $22 million more than corporate PACs.

In the 1981-1982 election cycle, six of the ten leading money raisers among PACs and five of the ten leading spenders were ideological groups. No ideological PACs, however, were included among the ten leading *contributors* to federal candidates. Ideological PACs have been criticized for contributing only a small portion of their total receipts directly to candidates, as low as 2 percent in some cases. These groups must spend large amounts on operating expenses and fund-raising costs because, unlike corporate, union, and trade/membership/health PACs, ideological PACs have no sponsors to pay these expenses with treasury or dues money.

The relatively small amount of money left to donate to candidates also is due to the tactics the groups employ. Leaders of many New Right PACs maintain they prefer to spend large amounts to finance candidate-training schools, polls, and consultants, all of which show up on disclosure reports as operating expenses, not contributions. A number of those committees also spend substantial amounts in independent expenditures: funds used to advocate the election or defeat of specific candidates but spent without consulting or coordinating with the candidates or their campaigns. In 1980 the independent expenditures of conservative PACs, particularly NCPAC, to defeat a number of prominent liberal Democrats in Congress received considerable publicity. Although it is not possible to determine how influential the expenditures were, some targeted officeholders were defeated in their reelection campaigns: Birch Bayh of Indiana, Frank Church of Idaho, John Culver of Iowa, and George McGovern of South Dakota.

In the 1979-1980 election cycle, independent committees spent about $960,000 advocating the election of certain House and Senate candidates and $1.4 million advocating the defeat of others. The committees spent even more substantial amounts in the presidential prenomination and general election campaigns, as described in Chapter 5. In the 1981-1982 cycle, independent committees spent about $352,000 *for* candidates and almost $4.1 million *against* candidates.

Following the 1980 elections, critics of independent expenditures insisted that such spending decreased accountability in the electoral process by diverting money from the control of candidates and their campaigns. In particular they denounced the strident, negative campaigns some committees undertook against candidates they sought to defeat. Nevertheless, some independent committees, particularly NCPAC, continued the tactic in the 1981-1982 election cycle (Chapter 6). ProPAC, one of the new liberal PACs formed after the 1980 elections, announced plans to adopt the negative campaign tactics characteristic of NCPAC, but found little support for the plan among its potential backers.

A study of PACs presented in 1983 characterized the fund raising and spending of nonconnected PACs as "entrepreneurial" and contrasted it with the more "participatory" style of connected committees.[34] The latter committees, the study said, tended more than the former to support incumbents and to spend in ways that suggest their donors have some influence on spending decisions. "The decision-makers for non-connected PACs," it concluded, "have no responsibility—not even nominal responsibility—to any cohesive group of donors who share a profession or workplace. Thus the leaders are free to pursue ideological, challenger-oriented strategies or to spend independently of any candidate organization." [35]

Notes

1. The conditions under which PACs may contribute up to $5,000 are described later in this chapter in the section on corporate and labor PACs.
2. Louise Overacker, *Presidential Campaign Funds* (Boston: Boston University Press, 1946), 29.
3. Overacker, *Presidential Campaign Funds*, 50.
4. Jasper B. Shannon, *Money and Politics* (New York: Random House, 1959), 54.
5. Eugene H. Roseboom, *A History of Presidential Elections* (New York: The Macmillan Co., 1957), 487.
6. Overacker, *Presidential Campaign Funds*, 49.
7. Michael J. Malbin, "Neither a Mountain nor a Molehill," *Regulation*, May/June 1979, 43.

8. Theodore H. White, *The Making of the President 1968* (New York: Atheneum, 1969), 365.
9. *Final Report of the Senate Select Committee on Presidential Campaign Activities*, 93d Cong., 2d sess. (Washington, D.C.: Government Printing Office, 1974), 446-447.
10. Morton Mintz and Nick Kotz, "Automen Rejected Nixon Fund Bid," *Washington Post*, November 17, 1972.
11. Michael C. Jensen, "The Corporate Political Squeeze," *New York Times*, September 16, 1973.
12. Ben A. Franklin, "Inquiries Into Nixon's Re-election Funds Turning Up a Pattern of High Pressure," *New York Times*, July 15, 1973.
13. *Final Report*, 470.
14. 18 U.S.C. § 613.
15. James R. Polk, "Philippine Cash Surfaces," "Sugar Envoy Mum on Donation," and "Nixon Donation From Second Filipino Revealed," *Washington Star*, June 11, 12, and 13, 1973.
16. Rowland Evans and Robert Novak, "Greek Gifts for President," *Washington Post*, July 20, 1972; and Seth Kantor, "Jaworski Eyes Probing Foreign '72 Gifts," *Washington Post*, January 25, 1974.
17. Untitled study of corporate PAC activity conducted by Civic Service, Inc., St. Louis, Missouri, 1981. The survey was commissioned jointly by the Business-Industry PAC, the National Association of Business PACs, the National Association of Manufacturers, and the Public Affairs Council.
18. "Percentage of Corporate PACs Soliciting Shareholders May Increase," *Campaigning Reports*, July 11, 1979, 9.
19. Ruth S. Jones and Warren E. Miller, "Financing Campaigns: Modes of Individual Contribution." (Paper delivered at the annual meeting of the Midwest Political Science Association, Chicago, April 21-23, 1983).
20. Theodore J. Eismeier and Philip A. Pollock III, "Political Action Committees: Varieties of Organization and Strategy." (Paper delivered at the annual meeting of the Midwest Political Science Association, Chicago, April 21-23, 1983).
21. Sethi S. Prakush and Nobuaki Namiki, "Public Perception of and Attitudes Toward Political Action Committees (PACs): An Empirical Analysis of Nationwide Survey Data—Some Strategic Implications for the Corporate Community." (Paper prepared for the Center for Research in Business and Social Policy, University of Texas-Dallas, 1982).
22. Eismeier and Pollock, "Political Action Committees," 29.
23. See, for example, Jeane Jordan Kirkpatrick, *Dismantling the Parties: Reflections on Party Reform and Party Decomposition* (Washington, D.C.: American Enterprise Institute for Public Policy Research, 1979); James W. Ceasar, *Reforming the Reforms* (Cambridge, Mass.: Ballinger, 1982); Edward C. Banfield, "Party 'Reform' in Retrospect," in *Political Parties in the Eighties*, Robert A. Goldwin, ed. (Washington, D.C.: American Enterprise Institute for Public Policy Research, 1980); David S. Broder, *The Party's Over: The Failure of Politics in America* (New York: Harper & Row, 1972); Nelson W.

Polsby, *Consequences of Party Reform* (Oxford: Oxford University Press, 1983).

24. See Elizabeth Drew, A Reporter at Large, "Politics and Money - I," *New Yorker,* December 6, 1982, 68-71.

25. Ibid., 101-106.

26. Eismeier and Pollock, "Political Action Committees," 3.

27. Ibid.

28. Julia Malone, "PAC Election Money Wasn't All for Nought," *Christian Science Monitor,* November 15, 1982.

29. Ibid.

30. Gary Jacobson, *Money in Congressional Elections* (New Haven: Yale University Press, 1980), 88, 90-91.

31. Eismeier and Pollock,"Political Action Committees," 33.

32. Edwin M. Epstein, "PACs and the Modern Political Process," unpublished paper, October 1982.

33. Jacobson, *Money in Congressional Elections,* 36-45.

34. Eismeier and Pollock, "Political Action Committees," 9.

35. Ibid.

The 1980 Election: Public Funding Revisited 5

The 1980 presidential election was the second to be conducted under the basic campaign finance laws enacted and upheld in the 1970s. The 1976 and 1980 contests provide sufficient experience from which to draw some conclusions about the impact of the laws and to determine whether they have had their intended effects.[1] In general, it appears that the laws have accomplished some of their aims, but also that they have had some unintended, and not always salutary, consequences. The degree to which the laws have failed to achieve their intended effects, however, may testify at least as much to the intractability of problems connected with election campaign finance and to the inventiveness of political actors in circumventing the laws as to their deficiencies.

The Prenomination Campaigns

Under the FECA, candidates for the 1980 presidential nomination who accepted public matching funds were permitted to spend no more than $14.7 million plus 20 percent ($2.9 million) for fund raising. The prenomination period is the time from the establishment of the campaign committee (normally in advance of the candidate's announcement) through the party convention—often a period of 18 or so months. In addition, the 1974 FECA Amendments limited candidate spending in each state to the greater of $200,000 or 16 cents per eligible voter, plus a cost-of-living increase. Candidates who did not accept public funding were not bound by the overall or individual state limits. Payments made by the candidates for legal and accounting services to comply with the campaign law were exempted from the law's spending limits, but candidates were required to report such payments.

All candidates were bound by the FECA's contribution limits. No candidate was permitted to accept more than $1,000 from an individual contributor or $5,000 from a multicandidate committee. Candidates who accepted public funding were allowed to contribute no more than $50,000 to their own campaigns. That limit included the candidates' families.

As in 1976, to qualify for public matching funds available under the FECA, candidates were required to raise $5,000 in private contributions of $250 or less in at least 20 states. The federal government matched each contribution to qualified candidates up to $250, although the federal subsidies could not exceed $7.35 million, half of the $14.7 million prenomination campaign spending limit.

The money for the matching funds was provided by the income tax checkoff procedure described in Chapter 2. Of approximately $175.6 million available for the 1980 payout, about $31.3 million originally was certified in matching funds to 10 qualified major party prenomination candidates, some 33 percent of the money spent by the principal campaign committee of those candidates.[2]

The Impact of the FECA

The basic provisions of the FECA had a significant impact on the conduct of the 1980 presidential prenomination campaigns. According to a number of campaign participants, the expenditure and contribution led to many challenging problems for the campaigns.[3]

The Overall Spending Limit. The 1980 national spending limit of $17.7 million ($14,720,000 plus a 20 percent fund-raising overage) for candidates accepting federal matching funds required candidates who had a realistic chance of remaining in the race until the convention to plan carefully when to spend the money they had available. Ronald Reagan's campaign, for example, invested large sums at the outset, spending about 75 percent of the maximum allowed by March 31, 1980, when only 11 of the 36 primary contests had been held. The strategy proved successful, although it laid Reagan open to the possibility of a well-financed challenge by former president Gerald R. Ford, who did not decide until mid-March to forgo another run for the nomination.

George Bush's campaign, on the other hand, husbanded its funds carefully, allowing Bush to outspend Reagan by as much as 5-to-1 in later primaries in delegate-rich states such as Pennsylvania, Michigan, and Texas. Nevertheless, the recognition and support Reagan had solidified early in the prenomination campaign proved unbeatable.

Throughout the prenomination period, candidates and campaign officers complained that the $17.7 million overall spending limit was set too low. Although the limit was adjusted to account for inflation, campaign costs had increased at a rate far exceeding that of inflation. In some markets, for example, television advertising costs had doubled since 1976. Faced with rising costs and what was perceived as a low spending limit—as well as with a larger-than-ever number of primary contests—many campaigns adopted a strategy that also had been chosen by a number of campaigns in 1976. They sacrificed grass-roots campaigning and the paraphernalia that goes with it—buttons, bumper stickers, and banners—and put substantial amounts into television advertising. The Bush, Carter, and Reagan campaigns each reported spending $3 million or more on television advertising, and the Connally and Kennedy campaigns almost $2 million each. Campaigns organized their activities to draw maximum media attention so that candidates' messages would be transmitted to the public at no direct cost to the candidates. Before the primaries began, one newspaper editorial writer observed that some candidates would "end up spending more time in television stations than chatting with live voters." [4]

State Limits. Like the overall spending limit, the boundaries established by the FECA for spending in individual states called for strategic prenomination campaign decisions, particularly in the early primary contests. Candidates, of course, felt the need to do well in the early prenomination contests, which customarily are assigned more importance by the news media than the number of delegates at stake would warrant. The spending ceilings in early contests in less populous states such as Iowa ($489,882) and New Hampshire ($294,400) forced candidates to budget tightly; these amounts contrasted with New York's $3 million limit and California's $3.9 million limit. Often the national campaign organizations maintained control of expenditures in each state. Before the FECA, said one campaign veteran, "we had some (local) control over the format and content. Now it's all run from Washington." [5]

Campaigns also resorted to a variety of subterfuges in an attempt to get around low state spending ceilings. Staffers, for example, sometimes stayed overnight in a state bordering on the state where they were working on a campaign so that the costs of accommodations could be counted against the other state's limit. Prior to the New Hampshire primary, campaigns purchased television time in cities such as Boston, whose media market includes southern New Hampshire, and charged the costs against the Massachusetts limit.

John Connally became the first major candidate to reject public funding since the matching system was first used in the 1976 election. He was convinced that the only way he could overtake Ronald Reagan was to outspend him in key states, something he would not have been able to do if he had accepted matching funds and the state spending limits that went with them. But Connally's strategy failed. Despite spending $12.6 million, he succeeded in winning only a single convention delegate.

Contribution Limit. The contribution limit also helped shape prenomination campaign strategy. Although the expenditure limit was adjusted upward to account for a 35 percent rise in the cost of living since 1976 and the number of primary election contests increased from 30 to 37 overall, the individual contribution limit remained the same: $1,000 per candidate.

In 1980, as in 1976, the limit achieved its intended effect of eliminating large gifts from "fat-cat" contributors. But by prohibiting candidates from gathering seed money for their campaigns from a handful of wealthy contributors, the contribution limit gave an advantage to well-known politicians and forced lesser-known candidates to begin the public side of their campaigns earlier than ever.

The limit also altered fund-raising patterns in sometimes unforeseen ways. The role once filled by large contributors was now filled by well-connected individuals who could persuade a large number of persons to contribute the $1,000 maximum amount. Candidates also were forced to rely more often on costly direct mail solicitations—in many instances the most effective way of reaching large numbers of small contributors—and on the direct mail specialists who have emerged as important forces in many political campaigns. Entertainers, whose services were volunteered and hence not subject to the $1,000 limitation, were enlisted to hold benefit concerts for candidates; artists, whose time and efforts on behalf of candidates were exempt from the contribution limit, were prevailed upon— at least by the Kennedy campaign—to donate artwork to be offered as inducements to potential contributors. In a sense, the campaign law has had the effect of replacing one type of solicitation mechanism with several others.

Circumventing the Limits. The spending and contribution limits also were responsible in large part for the development of three methods of circumventing the limits: independent expenditures, draft committees, and "presidential PACs." In its 1976 *Buckley* decision, the Supreme Court ruled that individuals and groups could spend unlimited amounts in communications advocating the election or defeat of clearly identified candidates provided the expenditures were independent—that is, made without consultation or collaboration with the candidates or their campaigns. In 1976 relatively few individuals or groups resorted to independent spending, in part, no doubt, because of a lack of familiarity with the new election laws.

In 1980 the use of independent expenditures increased significantly, allowing individuals and groups to circumvent the contribution limits and to supplement candidate spending in early primary states with low spending ceilings and later when the candidates approached the national spending limit. During the 1980 prenomination campaigns, independent expenditures made to advocate or oppose the election of clearly indentified presidential candidates totaled $2.7 million, almost 3.5 times the total spending for or against presidential and congressional candidates during the entire 1975-1976 election cycle. Ronald Reagan was the major beneficiary of such spending; some $1.6 million was spent on his behalf, most of it reported by ideologically conservative political committees. In the midst of the general election campaign, both the legality and the constitutionality of independent expenditures was challenged in the courts.

Groups working independently without authorization by a potential candidate to draft that individual also are not bound by the contribution and spending limits that apply to candidate committees. In 1980 a large number of committees organized to draft Sen. Edward M. Kennedy as a Democratic candidate. Because Kennedy officially disavowed their activities, each committee was permitted to accept individual donations of up to $5,000 ($4,000 more than authorized candidate committees could accept) and to spend unlimited amounts seeking to draft Kennedy. These expenditures did not count against individual state spending limits or the overall national limit when Kennedy finally declared his candidacy. More than 70 draft-Kennedy committees, operating in 38 states, reported spending some $550,000. In a ruling in a suit initiated by the Federal Election Commission (FEC) over the activity of some draft-Kennedy committees, a U.S. appeals court ruled that draft groups do not qualify as political committees under the Supreme Court's *Buckley* decision. The appeals court held that because draft committees do not support a "candidate" as defined by the law, they cannot be bound by the contribution and spending limits that apply to candidate committees.[6]

Finally, long before they announced their candidacies, four Republican presidential hopefuls—Reagan, Bush, Connally, and Sen. Robert Dole of

Kansas—formed political action committees ostensibly to raise and spend money on behalf of favored candidates and party committees. The four PACs no doubt helped the candidates who received their direct or in-kind contributions, but they also were helpful to the prospective presidential candidates who sponsored them. The PACs allowed their sponsors to gain the favor and support of federal, state, and local candidates and of state and local party organizations through the direct and in-kind contributions the PACs made—$590,000 worth during the 1977-1978 election cycle in the case of Reagan's PAC, Citizens for the Republic (CFR).[7] They also allowed the sponsors to travel extensively throughout the country, attracting media attention and increasing their name recognition among party activists and the electorate, without having the costs count against future spending limits that would apply once they declared their candidacies and accepted federal matching funds. The appeal of this method of circumventing the campaign finance laws is indicated by the establishment of similar PACs in 1981 by former vice president Walter Mondale and Senator Kennedy, both looking at that time to the 1984 presidential campaign.

Matching Funds. In 1976 federal matching funds provided eligible but little-known outsiders the opportunity to compete effectively in the primary campaign. One of these outsiders, Jimmy Carter, won his party's nomination. In 1980 public money similarly helped candidates such as George Bush and Rep. John Anderson of Illinois, who were not well known and could not raise large amounts of private money without first achieving greater name recognition. Matching funds helped Bush establish himself as front-runner Reagan's major competitor and stay the course of the primaries and caucuses. Public funds helped Anderson become an influential factor in some early Republican primaries. More significantly, the public money helped him begin building the name recognition and national organization he needed to mount his independent candidacy for the presidency.[8] In these cases the FECA opened up the electoral process to some candidates who otherwise might not have had an opportunity in that process.

Presidential Fund Raising and Spending

Despite the strictures of the FECA's spending and contribution limits, a significant amount of money was raised and spent by candidates for their parties' 1980 presidential nominations. The 16 presidential candidates whose financial activity exceeded $100,000 raised $108.6 million (including matching funds) and spent $106.6 million.[9] In 1976 the 17 presidential prenomination candidates who reported expenditures of more than $100,000 spent only $67.2 million.[10] The 1980 prenomination campaign expenditures represent a 58 percent increase over the corresponding 1976 figure, while the Consumer Price Index rose only 37 percent for the four-year period.

The relatively high expenditures for the 1980 prenomination campaigns may be credited to several factors, some of which were described in Chapter 1: early announcements and thus early campaigning by a number of candidates from the party not in control of the White House; a larger number of primaries plus other costly prenomination contests such as caucuses and straw polls in which candidates felt obliged to participate; a strong challenge to an incumbent president by a member of his own party; a relatively large field of out-party candidates capable of raising large amounts of money; and skyrocketing costs for items and services, such as television advertising and air travel.[11]

Republicans. In August 1978, nearly two years before the Republican nominating convention, Rep. Philip M. Crane of Illinois became the first major candidate to declare his candidacy for the 1980 presidential nomination. With his announcement, Crane continued a trend toward increasingly early formal entry into the presidential prenomination contest by little-known candidates from the party not in control of the White House. These early birds are seeking name recognition and a head start in fund raising and campaign staff organization.

In time Crane was joined by six other Republicans who remained in serious contention at least through the early stages of the primary season: Reagan, Bush, Connally, Anderson, Dole, and Sen. Howard Baker of Tennessee. In addition, two other Republican officeholders, Sen. Lowell P. Weicker, Jr. of Connecticut and Sen. Larry Pressler of South Dakota, made brief forays into the Republican prenomination contest. Businessman Benjamin Fernandez and perennial candidate Harold Stassen also made runs for the Republican nomination, but they never were influential factors in the race. Finally, in March 1980 a national Draft Ford Committee was formed to persuade former president Ford to run again, but he, after considerable press speculation, declined.

Although Reagan did not announce his candidacy until November 13, 1979, his strong challenge to Ford in the 1976 prenomination contest and his continuing activity on behalf of Republican candidates and organizations as chairman of CFR made him the front-runner from the start. Reagan campaign fund raising in 1979 was second only to that of the Connally campaign; direct mail drives using mailing lists developed by CFR and larger contributions, particularly from his home state of California, brought in $7.2 million, less than the campaign had anticipated but a substantial sum nonetheless. The campaign also spent heavily in the preelection year, particularly on fund raising and campaign staff, reporting indebtedness of $1.5 million at year's end.

Initial campaign strategy called for Reagan to enter all of the prenomination contests but to remain above the fray by ignoring his Republican rivals and focusing criticism on Carter's record. That strategy was abandoned after Reagan lost the first major prenomination contest, the January 21 Iowa caucuses, to George Bush. Reagan had campaigned sparingly in Iowa and declined to participate in public debates and joint appearances with other Republican candidates, while Bush had begun campaigning in the state early in 1979 and had spent long hours developing a campaign organization and cultivating potential caucus participants.

The Reagan campaign regained momentum with a February 26 primary victory in New Hampshire, after which the candidate dismissed his campaign director, John Sears, who had devised the initial strategy, and replaced him with lawyer William Casey, former head of the Securities and Exchange Commission. By the time of the New Hampshire primary, the campaign had spent close to two-thirds of the overall spending limit. Casey's main responsibility was to get a grip on spending. He ordered extensive cutbacks in campaign staff, media advertising, and candidate travel, yet Reagan continued to enjoy success at the polls, gaining momentum as the front-runner. Primary losses in Massachusetts, Connecticut, Pennsylvania, and Michigan were only temporary setbacks on the road to the nomination.

As Reagan's nomination became more certain, his financial support grew. And the funds his campaign raised from private sources triggered federal matching grants that gave him a decided advantage over his opponents. Ironically, although Reagan had accepted public funds for his 1976 prenomination campaign, late in 1979 he voiced opposition to public funding, saying he preferred to see candidates raise their own money. But after researching the pros and cons of matching funds, his campaign staff concluded that the candidate could not run successfully in the large number of primaries scheduled if he had to rely solely on funds from private sources with an individual contribution limit as low as $1,000.

By the conclusion of the primary season, all of Reagan's challengers had dropped out, and the candidate had captured more than enough

Table 5-1 Total Spending on Behalf of Republican Presidential Candidates in 1980 Campaigns (millions)

Reagan		
Prenomination (including compliance costs)		$ 19.8
General election		
candidate committee	$29.2[1]	
national committee (RNC)	4.5	
		$ 33.7
Compliance costs (general election)		1.5
Transition planning		.5
Total spending controlled by candidate		$ 55.5
General election spending in support of		
Reagan-Bush		
State and local party	$15.0	
Labor, corporate, and association	3.0	
Total coordinated spending		$ 18.0
Unauthorized delegates, independent expenditures,		
and communication costs, primary and general		
election		12.9
Total Reagan		$ 86.4
Other Republican candidates		
Prenomination candidate committees	$49.9	
Unauthorized delegates, independent expenditures,		
and communication costs	1.4	
Total other candidates		$ 51.3
RNC and affiliates		$ 48.5[2]
Republican National Convention		
RNC convention committee	$ 4.4	
Host committee	.7	
		$ 5.1
Republican total		$191.3

[1] The Reagan campaign was required to return to the U.S. Treasury $251,122, the value of interest earned on its investment of a portion of the $29.44 million in public money it received.
[2] Includes administrative and fund-raising costs.

SOURCE: Citizens' Research Foundation

convention delegates to win the nomination on the first ballot. At the close of convention, the Reagan campaign had spent $19.8 million, making it the most expensive of the prenomination campaigns (Table 5-1).

Democrats. In the 1976 prenomination period, an incumbent president met with a strong challenge from a member of his own party. The unusual character of this phenomenon, however, was tempered by the fact that the incumbent, Gerald Ford, had never been elected to the presidency but had assumed the office in 1974 after the resignation of Richard Nixon. Neither had Ford been elected to the vice presidency; rather he had been appointed by Nixon to complete the term of Spiro T. Agnew, who had resigned under pressure in 1973. By the time the 1976 presidential campaigns were getting under way, Ford had been in office only a short time and did not enjoy the usual advantages of incumbency.

In the 1980 presidential prenomination campaign, an incumbent president once again met with a strong challenge from a member of his own party. But this time the incumbent, Jimmy Carter, had been elected to the office and had occupied it for nearly three years when Senator Kennedy formally announced his candidacy. Carter also was challenged by California governor Edmund G. Brown, Jr., whose last-minute campaign in 1976 had stirred some excitement among the electorate and brought Brown five primary victories. Lyndon LaRouche, U.S. Labor Party founder, and Cliff Finch, former governor of Mississippi, also ran as candidates for the Democratic nomination, but neither was a factor in the outcome of any of the prenomination contests.

Despite his low standing in public opinion polls throughout most of 1979, there never was any serious doubt that President Carter would seek renomination, no matter who chose to run against him. And although campaign strategy called for Carter to remain a noncandidate as long as possible, relying on the tools at an incumbent's disposal to gain favor among opinion leaders and the electorate, there were indications that, when the time came, the president would campaign actively and directly for the nomination. On November 6, prior to his formal announcement, he even had agreed to debate his Democratic opponents, with a first meeting scheduled to take place in Iowa early in January.

Events outside the control of the Carter administration intervened to alter whatever campaign strategies had been devised. On November 4, the U.S. Embassy and its personnel in the Iranian capital of Tehran were seized. On December 27 Soviet troops invaded Afghanistan. These two international crises rallied support around the incumbent. Carter's standing in the polls improved markedly, and on December 28 the president announced he was withdrawing from the scheduled debate and would not campaign outside the White House to give the crises his undivided attention.

Carter's decision to withdraw from direct campaigning became an issue throughout the prenomination campaign, but it apparently did not hurt his chances for reelection. In his first major prenomination contest, the

Table 5-2 Total Spending on Behalf of Democratic Presidential Candidates in 1980 Campaigns (millions)

Carter		
Prenomination (including compliance costs)		$ 18.5
Debts		.6
General election		
candidate committee	$29.4[1]	
national committee (DNC)	4.0	
		$ 33.4
Compliance costs (general election)		1.5
Total spending controlled by candidate		$ 54.0
General election spending in support of		
Carter-Mondale		
State and local party	$ 4.0	
Labor, registration, and get-out-the-vote	15.0	
Total coordinated spending		$ 19.0
Unauthorized delegates, independent expenditure, and communication costs, primary and general election		1.7
Total Carter		$ 74.7
Other Democratic candidates		
Prenomination candidate committees	$17.2	
Draft committees, unauthorized delegates, independent expenditures, and communication costs.	1.7	
Total other candidates		$ 18.9[2]
DNC and affiliates		$ 10.00
DNC convention committee	$ 3.7	
Host committee	.5	
		$ 4.2
Democratic total		$107.8

[1] The Carter campaign was required to repay to the U.S. Treasury $87,232, the value of interest earned on its investment of a portion of the $29.44 million in public money it received. The campaign also was required to repay $929 it had received in improper contributions and $1,270 in non-qualified campaign expenses.
[2] Includes administrative and fund-raising costs.

SOURCE: Citizens' Research Foundation

January 21 Iowa caucuses, Carter overwhelmed Kennedy, and he followed that with a convincing win in the influential New Hampshire primary five weeks later. Kennedy rebounded, as expected, by winning his home state primary in Massachusetts in the following week, but Carter took some of the gloss off that victory by crushing his opponent in Vermont's primary on the same day. The president then put together a string of victories in southern primaries, where he was expected to do well, followed by a win in Illinois, which some thought would knock Kennedy out of the race. The challenger, however, won both the New York and Connecticut primaries in late March and decided to continue despite increasing odds against him.

The first two months of the primary season established a pattern for the remainder of the contest: Carter's victories were punctuated by enough Kennedy victories to keep the challenger in the race and to escalate the cost of the Democratic prenomination campaigns. Throughout the primaries and caucuses, the Carter campaign maintained its financial advantage. Carter forces were far more successful in raising funds, particularly from donors of $500 to $1,000, and the Kennedy campaign suffered from extravagant early spending. Because the president maintained his resolve to stay in the White House as long as the crises in Iran and Afghanistan were not concluded, the campaign depended heavily on Carter surrogates as the main attractions at fund-raising dinners and events. Rosalynn Carter, Vice President Mondale, and campaign chairman Robert Strauss were the candidate's chief stand-ins.

Kennedy finished with a flourish, winning five of eight primaries on June 3, including two of the three largest states contested. But Carter won enough delegates on that final primary day to assure him of a first-ballot nomination at the Democratic convention. In all Carter won 51 percent of the Democratic primary votes cast to Kennedy's 38 percent; he won 24 of the 34 primaries he entered and 20 of the 25 state and territorial caucuses. A last-ditch effort by Kennedy to wrest the nomination from the incumbent by engineering a convention rules change failed, and the challenger finally withdrew on the first night of the nominating convention. Carter's long and hard-fought campaign cost $18.5 million, the most expensive Democratic campaign and the second most expensive among all contestants, after Reagan, in 1980 (Table 5-2).

The General Election Campaigns

In 1980, as in 1976, both major party presidential candidates accepted public funding and were prohibited from taking any further private donations. But the candidates' publicly funded activities comprised only one fact of the election. When we consider the money spent to influence the outcome of the election, we see that three different but parallel campaigns, distinguished by who was in control of the spending, actually were conducted either by the candidates or on their behalf (Table 5-3).

Table 5-3   Candidate Sources of Funds, 1980 General Election[1]

	Sources of Funds	Reagan	Carter
Limited campaign Candidate-controlled	(Federal Grant	$29.4	$29.4
	(National Party	4.6	4.0
Unlimited campaigns	(State and Local Party	15.0	4.0
Candidate may coordinate	(Labor[2]	1.5	15.0
	(Corporate/Association[2]	1.5	0
	(Compliance	1.5	1.5
Independent of candidate	Independent Expenditures[3]	10.6	.03
	TOTAL	$64.1	$53.9

[1] Figures in millions.
[2] Components of these amounts include internal communications costs (both those reported, in excess of $2,000, as required by law, and those unreported, of $2,000 or less), registration and voter turnout drives, overhead, and related costs.
[3] Does not include amounts spent independently against Carter ($209,781) or Reagan ($47,868).

SOURCE: Citizens' Research Foundation

The *first* campaign, publicly financed and legally limited, was within the control of the major party nominees and their campaign organizations. This campaign was supplemented by funds raised privately by each of the major national parties for spending on behalf of its presidential ticket. According to the 1974 FECA Amendments, the national party spending limit is based on the voting-age population of the nation.

The *second* campaign, in which spending was permitted but not limited under the law, was in part under the direct control of the candidates and their organizations and in part outside their control. While the funds could be coordinated with the candidates' spending, that did not always happen. This campaign was financed partly by funds each candidate's campaign organization raised from private contributions to pay legal and accounting costs incurred in complying with the stipulations of the law. This second campaign also was financed by funds raised by state and local party committees that were allowed under the 1979 FECA Amendments to spend unlimited amounts on volunteer-oriented activity on behalf of the parties' presidential tickets.

Some sources outside federal restraints—individuals, unions, and corporations—were willing to have their contributions channeled to states where state law allowed party committees to use such contributions for volunteer-oriented voter registration, get-out-the-vote drives, and similar activities. This type of fund raising, which results in what has been called "soft money," was allowed under the 1979 Amendments. This spending was coordinated by the national party committees in consultation with the candidates' organizations. Finally, this second campaign was financed in part by money spent on behalf of the candidates by labor unions, corporations, trade associations, and membership groups on partisan communications within their own constituencies and on nominally nonpartisan activities directed to the general public. Such spending could be coordinated with the candidates' organizations, but efforts at coordination were not always successful.

The *third* campaign, in which spending also was allowed but not limited under the law, was funded by independent expenditures and controlled by independent groups. As noted, according to the Supreme Court's *Buckley* ruling, individuals and groups are allowed to spend unlimited amounts for or against candidates, provided the expenditures are made without consultation or collaboration with candidates or their campaigns.

These three parallel campaigns were supplemented by less direct, more subtle efforts to influence the electoral outcome. Each of these efforts either cost their sponsors money or provided the candidates with benefits whose financial value, though difficult to calculate, was substantial. They included an expensive, Republican party-sponsored media campaign designed to benefit all Republican candidates; nominally nonpartisan organized group activities focusing on issues closely related to the campaigns; and a number of uses of incumbency to benefit Jimmy Carter.

Public and National Party Funds

Because major party nominees Carter and Reagan each received $29.4 million in public funds, spending in the first campaign was largely equalized. There was a slight imbalance in favor of Reagan, however. The RNC easily raised the $4.6 million it was permitted to disburse for the Republican presidential ticket and spent $4.5 million of it to supplement the Reagan-Bush committee's own expenditures. The DNC encountered difficulties in raising its funds and was able to spend only about $4 million for Carter-Mondale; some $600,000 of it was spent after the campaign had concluded to pay off debts.

Reagan campaign strategy called for money from public funds to be spent primarily on media advertising, candidate travel, and campaign committee headquarters expenses. In fact, the lion's share of the public funds received by the Reagan-Bush committee was devoted to media advertising, particularly television. In all the committee spent $16.8 million on media advertising and production, including about $10.8 million on television time, $1.5 million on radio time, $2.2 million on newspaper and magazine space, and $2.3 million on production costs.

RNC funds were to be spent in part on organizing and supervising state and local party activities to benefit the presidential ticket. Most of this money, however, was spent to supplement the Reagan-Bush committee's own expenditures for items and services, such as campaign-related travel and newspaper advertising. But the RNC also was able to spend substantial amounts to benefit the party's presidential ticket without having the expenditures count against the party committee's permissible spending limit. Thus the committee spent $1 million of nonallocable funds on voter registration, an additional $1 million on voter turnout, and about $4.2 million during the general election campaign on the media program noted above, urging viewers to "vote Republican for a change."

The Carter campaign planned to concentrate its public funds on paying for media advertising, candidate travel, state campaign coordinators' expenses, and polling. Unlike the Reagan campaign, however, the Carter campaign did not enjoy a high level of financial support from party committees. Further, labor spending for Carter, although significant in dollar terms, came late and sometimes without the wholehearted support of union leaders. Consequently the campaign organization was forced to use some of its public grant for services and items the Republicans could count on their party committees to purchase or fund. The Carter campaign's flexibility was reduced and strict controls had to be exercised over campaign committee spending.

The campaign spent $15.8 million to purchase television broadcast time, $2.6 million to broadcast radio advertisements, and $2.1 million more on print advertising and media production costs. The campaign spent additional large amounts on candidate travel, polling, voter registration, and campaign staff and consultants. The DNC was able to spend only about $3.4 million on presidential campaign support during the campaign itself, large portions of it for media advertising, polling, voter registration, and turnout drives. After the election the committee agreed to assume about $600,000 in obligations incurred by the Carter-Mondale committee, which had reached its legal spending limit.

Both campaigns raised and spent about $1.5 million for compliance costs. But the Reagan-Bush committee and the RNC were much more successful than their Democratic counterparts in ensuring that state and local party committees could take full advantage of the 1979 FECA Amendments provisions that were designed to bring back the grass-roots political activity missing from the 1976 general election campaigns. The Reagan campaign encouraged potential contributors to its compliance fund to give instead to state and local party committees, and Reagan and Bush took part in fund-raising events intended to fill state and local party committee coffers.

Other Sources of Funds

Total spending in the second campaign also was largely equivalent, but the sources of money differed markedly. In general, Reagan enjoyed an advantage here because most of the money spent for him could be coordinated more effectively with his own campaign organization than could money spent on behalf of the Carter campaign.

More significantly, the RNC successfully exploited fund-raising options made possible by the 1979 Amendments—options not foreseen by those who formulated the law. Under RNC auspices, some $9 million was raised from individuals and corporations and channeled into those states where such contributions to party committees were permitted and where spending for voter identification and turnout drives would have the greatest benefit.[12] Those contributions were free from federal restraints and were subject only to applicable state laws, which often are less restrictive than federal law. At least 26 states, including populous states such as New York and California, for example, permit direct corporate contributions to political campaigns. Several others allow at least some types of corporations to contribute, and 41 states permit labor organization contributions. Twenty-five states place no limits on the amount individuals may contribute. Thus, for example, corporate money raised in Texas, which did not allow corporate contributions, could be funneled into Missouri, where corporate money was permissible. And money from individual contributors, which could be collected in large amounts in Missouri, was sent to Texas. This kind of spending was free from federal limits and not subject to federal reporting. It not only supported activities beneficial to the presidential ticket, such as registration drives among likely Republican voters but also freed the Reagan-Bush organization's own funds for use on other activities, such as media advertising and candidate travel.

When money raised for the presidential ticket by state and local parties is combined with the money raised nationally and channeled to the individual states, the total spent by state and local party committees on behalf of Reagan-Bush reaches $15 million. Democratic state and local party organizations were able to spend only about $4 million on activities intended to benefit their presidential ticket. About $1.3 million was raised at the national level from unions and individuals and channeled to state and local party committees in states that permitted such contributions, and the remainder was raised by state and local committees from their own sources, sometimes with the aid of appearances by the candidates.[13]

The $15 million spent by Republican state and local party organizations was matched by a roughly equal amount that labor organizations spent on communications and activities intended to benefit Carter-Mondale. The Reagan-Bush campaign had only about $3 million spent on such activities and communications on its behalf by corporations, trade associations, membership groups, and some labor organizations. Because labor's spending for the Democratic ticket came late in the campaign and was not well coordinated with the Carter-Mondale campaign, it failed to have as much impact as RNC-supported state and local party spending.

Independent Spending

The third parallel campaign conducted during the general election period was funded entirely by money raised and spent independently. The Reagan campaign attracted a substantial amount of independent spending, some $10.6 million, most of it coming from five ideologically conservative political action committees. The Carter campaign officially discouraged such expenditures on its behalf; less than $30,000 was reported in independent spending favoring Carter-Mondale.

The independent spending on behalf of Reagan-Bush was the subject of considerable litigation. Lawsuits alleged that the spending actually was conducted in concert with the Reagan campaign. One suit maintained the scale of the outlays violated a provision of the Internal Revenue Code that prohibited organized political committees from spending more than $1,000 to support a candidate who was eligible to receive public funds. The Supreme Court had not directly considered the issue in *Buckley v. Valeo*, and the provision was left untouched when Congress subsequently rewrote the election law in 1976 to conform to the Court's ruling. The courts found in favor of the committees conducting the independent campaigns, but debate regarding such spending continues. Opponents argue that the growth of independent committees could frustrate congressional efforts to limit the influence of large sums of money on presidential elections.

Supporters counter that independent spending is protected by the First Amendment and is a predictable result of the FECA's ban on private contributions to publicly funded campaigns.

Anderson Campaign

The FECA had a significant impact on John Anderson's independent campaign, but one far different from its impact on the campaigns of the major party candidates. Anderson was able to build on the name recognition and the organizational network he had developed—in part with the help of federal matching funds—as a Republican candidate during the prenomination period. But the election laws also worked to his disadvantage. Unlike the major party candidates, Anderson received no federal grant in advance of his campaign. Further, when he undertook his independent candidacy late in April 1980, there was no explicit provision in the law—as there was for third-party candidates—that would allow him to receive federal money retroactively, if he achieved a stipulated measure of electoral success. He was required to fund his campaign entirely from private contributions raised according to the FECA's individual and political action committee contribution limits. He was obliged to comply with the law's disclosure requirements, but money raised to pay compliance-related costs was subject to the same set of contribution limits. Thus potential contributors were not permitted to donate $1,000 to further the campaign and an additional sum to help pay compliance costs. Finally, Anderson had no national or state party organization working for him, providing volunteer services, or spending money other than that raised by his own campaign organization.

An innovative FEC decision in September 1980 declared Anderson eligible for retroactive public funds, if he received 5 percent or more of the general election vote. The commission found his independent candidacy the functional equivalent of a minor party campaign. Another FEC ruling in October, that bank loans to the campaign would not violate federal law, appeared to give Anderson's fund raising a boost. But the candidate's organization, unable to arrange commercial loans, instead sought loans from its 200,000 individual contributors who had been identified and solicited through a direct mail drive. The appeal yielded about $1.8 million for use in the campaign's closing days. Altogether, including money received from such loans and $4.2 million received in postelection federal funds, the Anderson campaign raised $17.1 million, about half the amount the major party candidates had directly under their control and a much smaller percentage of the totals those candidates had spent for them.

Fund-raising costs of $3.4 million and ballot access costs of $2 million made up more than one-third the campaign's net operating expenditures. Other significant costs included media advertising, $2.3 million; candidate travel, $2 million; and personnel, $1.7 million.

Consequences of Reform

The experience of two presidential election cycles indicates that the FECA has achieved mixed results. In the prenomination period, public funding has improved access to the presidential contest by supplementing the treasuries of candidates who attain only a modest degree of private funding. The law's contribution limit has diminished the potential influence of wealthy donors. Its disclosure provisions have resulted in more campaign finance information than ever before being available to the public, and its compliance requirements have caused campaigns to place greater emphasis on money management and accountability.

These results have been achieved at some cost, however. Low expenditure limits have encouraged candidates to favor mass media advertising (as the most economical way to reach large numbers of potential voters) over grass-roots campaigning and to nationalize control of their campaigns at the expense of local authority and initiative. They also have led candidates to resort to a variety of subterfuges to circumvent the limits or, as in the case of John Connally, to refuse public matching funds in order to avoid the limits.

The low individual contribution limit has worked to the advantage of well-known candidates capable of raising money quickly and lengthened the campaign season by forcing lesser-known candidates to begin their fund raising earlier than ever. It has replaced wealthy contributors with a variety of other fund raisers upon whom candidates have become dependent. And it has reduced flexibility and rigidified the election campaign process. Ford decided not to enter the nomination contest in March 1980 in part because, under the contribution limit, it would have been extremely difficult at that late date to raise sufficient funds to conduct a competitive campaign.

The low contribution and expenditure limits have encouraged development of methods to frustrate the intent of the limits; two of them—draft committees and independent expenditures—are outside the control of the candidates and not directly accountable to the electorate. Moreover, the complexities of the law's compliance requirements have contributed to the professionalization of campaigns, possibly chilling enthusiasm for volunteer citizen participation in politics.

In the general election campaign, public funding, combined with a ban on private contributions to those eligible candidates who accept the public money—except to defray compliance costs—was intended to equalize spending between major party candidates and to eliminate the possibility of large individual or interest group contributions influencing election outcomes. In 1976 those purposes appeared to be achieved, with some exceptions, but in 1980, because of increased familiarity with the law's provisions and some changes in the law, political partisans discovered a variety of ways to upset the balance and to reintroduce substantial amounts of private money into the campaigns.

As in the prenomination period, the law's disclosure provisions have led to far greater public information about sources and uses of political money, and its compliance requirements have forced campaigns to adopt more effective and efficient practices. Those same compliance requirements, however, have contributed to increased centralization of campaign operations and decisions and increased professionalization of campaign staffs, with important consequences for the voluntarism that should animate politics in a democracy. Finally, the experience of the 1980 general election campaigns makes clear that the FECA works to the advantage of major party candidates over independents.

Congressional Spending

During the 1980 election cycle, U.S. House and Senate candidates spent a record $239 million, an increase of 21 percent over the 1978 congressional elections and $114 million more than in the 1976 congressional elections, an increase of 90 percent.[14] The impact of inflation and the fact that 379 more candidates ran in this election than in 1978 were major factors in spending growth. A record 2,288 candidates were entered at some stage of the primary and general election campaigns.

As in previous elections, incumbents spent more than challengers, $103.6 million to $91 million, but the margin narrowed substantially compared with prior years. Open seat candidates spent $44.4 million and primary losers $47.4 million. Democratic and Republican candidates were almost equal in their spending, with the Democrats spending $121.4 million and the Republicans $116 million. Because of the disparity in the number of candidates between the House (1,944) and the Senate (344), the House candidates, as usual, spent considerably more—$136 million to $103 million—but again, the margin, compared with previous years, narrowed significantly.

Senate

Senatorial candidates spent $103 million in the 1980 elections, of which $74.9 million (73 percent) was disbursed by general election candidates.[15] Democratic general election candidates outspent their Republican opponents by $39.9 million to $35 million. This was a switch from the 1978 senatorial elections when the Republicans spent $38 million compared with $27 million by the Democrats. More Democratic seats were at stake, however, and more were lost, despite the overall Democratic advantage in spending. In the 1976 election cycle, spending for Senate campaigns totaled $46 million; hence the 1980 total represents an increase of 124 percent.

Of the $103 million spent by Senate candidates in primary and general election campaigns, Democrats spent $53.6 million, Republicans $48.9 million, and all other candidates $439,000. In addition, the national party senatorial campaign committees and other party-identified committees spent $23.5 million on the 1980 Senate campaigns. That figure includes the administrative and fund-raising costs of the national committees as well as their coordinated expenditures on behalf of Senate candidates. Here Republican candidates enjoyed a decided financial advantage. The National Republican Senatorial Committee spent $21.2 million on such items, but the Democratic Senatorial Campaign Committee spent only $1.6 million. Finally, independent expenditures and communication costs for or against candidates totaled about $2 million.

House

A record 1,944 contestants sought nomination or election to the House of Representatives in 1980. They raised $144 million and spent $136 million. Total spending by party was almost equal: $67.8 million by Democrats and $67.1 million by Republicans. Third-party and independent candidates spent an additional $1.1 million. General election candidates spent $116.9 million of the $136 million total, but that amount includes their primary campaign expenditures as well. Democratic and Republican spending was virtually equal in the general election also: $57.2 million to $58.6 million. Primary losers spent a record $19.1 million.

In addition to the $136 million spent by House candidates, the national party congressional campaign committees and other party-identified congressional committees spent $32.3 million on administrative and fund-raising costs and coordinated expenditures on behalf of House candidates. The National Republican Congressional Committee spent $26 million on those items, and the Democratic Congressional Campaign

Committee spent only $2 million. About $1.6 million was reported in independent expenditures and communication costs on behalf of or opposing congressional candidates.

The extent of independent expenditures on behalf of and opposing candidates for the House and the Senate in 1980 was described in Chapter 4. That chapter also contains information on how much political action committees contributed to Senate and House campaigns.

Rising Costs

Like presidential election campaign costs, the costs of Senate and House campaigns have been rising steadily. For congressional races, however, there are no public funding programs or expenditure limits to halt the pattern of increase. In fact, expenditure limits in publicly funded presidential campaigns and the ban on private contributions to publicly funded presidential general election campaigns have served to divert some contributions to congressional campaigns, thereby raising the ante for all candidates. The data in Table 6-1 in Chapter 6 show total congressional spending for the years 1972-1982.

Republican candidates were notably successful in the 1980 congressional elections; the party picked up 12 seats in the Senate and 33 in the House. Political scientist Gary Jacobson argues against the temptation to conclude that Democratic candidates simply were repudiated for the perceived failings of the Carter administration, reflected among other ways in high inflation and high unemployment.[16] Rather, Jacobson maintains, Republican success was due primarily to the large number of strong challenges mounted by individual Republican candidates. Those challenges, in turn, were made possible by the commitment of time and money, particularly to Senate campaigns, made by Republican activists—party leaders, PACs, and others who recruit candidates and supply campaign resources—early in the election campaign process. To the degree that the congressional activists were encouraged by national forces to mount an offensive strategy designed to take seats from the opposition, says Jacobson, those forces, including economic conditions and public reactions to presidential candidates, were instrumental in 1980 election results. Nevertheless, he argues, "Individual candidacies still dominate the process; few Republicans who did not thoroughly prepare the ground were swept into office."[17]

Notes

1. For a thorough analysis of the impact of the FECA of 1971 and its amendments of 1974, 1976, and 1979 on the conduct of the 1976 and 1980 campaigns, see Herbert E. Alexander, *Financing the 1976 Election* (Washington, D.C.: CQ Press, 1979); and *Financing the 1980 Election* (Lexington, Massachusetts: D. C. Heath, 1983).

2. The $31.3 million figure cited does not take into account repayments of public funds required for various reasons by the FEC after postelection audits of the candidates had been completed. By March 1982 repayments had reduced the total prenomination campaign payout to $29.7 million.

3. See, for example, Herbert E. Alexander and Brian A. Haggerty, *The Federal Election Campaign Act: After a Decade of Political Reform* (Los Angeles: Citizens' Research Foundation, 1981).

4. "Media Politicking," *Washington Post,* January 2, 1980.

5. John P. Kenny, quoted in "On Tuesday, the Candidates Will Learn How Their Campaigns Played in Peoria," William J. Lanouette, *National Journal,* March 15, 1980, 439.

6. *Federal Election Commission v. Machinists Non-Partisan Political League,* 655 F. 2d 380 (D.C. Circuit 1981); and *Federal Election Commission v. Citizens for Democratic Alternatives in 1980,* 655 F. 2d 397 (D.C. Circuit 1981).

7. Because federal law does not require itemization of all expenses on behalf of nonfederal candidates, such as travel costs for fund-raising appearances, the contribution figure reported to the FEC probably is less than what actually was donated outright or in-kind.

8. See Joel Goldstein, "Impact of Federal Financing on the Electoral Process," (Paper delivered at the 1981 Kentucky Political Science Association annual meeting, February 27-28, 1981, Bowling Green, Kentucky.)

9. Federal Election Commission, "FEC Releases Final Report on 1980 Presidential Primary Activity," news release, November 15, 1981.

10. Ibid.

11. See, for example, Adam Clymer, "Inflation and a Limit on Contributions Strain Presidential Hopeful Budgets," *New York Times,* February 4, 1980; see also, "Inflation Runs Wild on the Campaign Trail," *U.S. News & World Report,* March 31, 1980, 33-34; and Maxwell Glen, "It's More Expensive to Run for President as Inflation Takes to the Campaign Trails," *National Journal,* February 23, 1980, 311-313.

12. See Elizabeth Drew, A Reporter at Large, "Politics and Money-II," *New Yorker,* December 13, 1982, 64.

13. Ibid., 75.

14. This section is derived in part from "FEC Releases Final Statistics on 1979-80 Congressional Races," news release, March 7, 1982; and *FEC Reports on Financial Activity, 1979-1980: U.S. House and Senate Campaigns* (Washington, D.C.: Federal Election Commission, January 1982).

15. As used by the FEC, spending by a general election candidate means total spending, primary and general election combined, by a candidate running in

the general election. This formulation omits primary losers.
16. See Gary C. Jacobson, *The Politics of Congressional Elections* (Boston: Little, Brown & Co., 1983), 150-156; and Jacobson and Samuel Kernell, *Strategy and Choice in Congressional Elections* (New Haven: Yale University Press, 1981).
17. Jacobson, *The Politics of Congressional Elections,* 156.

The 1982 Election: Money, Strategy, and Organization 6

The 1982 midterm elections were conducted under the intense scrutiny of the media and academia. Representatives of both groups had several objectives: observing the election as a referendum on the Reagan administration; noting the effects of a House reapportionment that shifted some 17 seats away from the Snow Belt; gauging the influence of the New Right, which had been particularly active in 1980, and the countervailing influence of the liberal independent committees that arose to combat it; and monitoring the continued increase in the number and wealth of political action committees.

Money played a major role, although the battle that some observers predicted between the New Right and liberal PACs did not materialize. PACs helped push total congressional campaign spending to $343.9 million in 1982, up about 44 percent from the 1980 total of $239 million.[1] The data in Table 6-1 compare 1982 congressional costs with previous election years back to 1972. PACs were a major factor in the increase, contributing $83.1 million to House and Senate campaigns, up from $55.2 million in 1980. In addition, the Republican party proved to be a potent source of assistance to its candidates in 1982, far surpassing the Democratic party in candidate support. For the 1981-1982 election cycle, the three major Republican committees—the Republican National Committee, the National Republican Senatorial Committee, and the National Republican Congressional Committee—raised $190.5 million and spent $189 million. The three corresponding Democratic committees—the Democratic National Committee, the Democratic Senatorial Campaign Committee, and the Democratic Congressional Campaign Committee—raised $28.4 million and spent $28.5 million.

Moreover, money played a major role in a number of races in which wealthy candidates spent large amounts of their own money. There are

Table 6-1 Congressional Campaign Expenditures, 1972-1982

Year	Total	Senate	House
1972	$ 66.4 million	$ 26.4 million	$ 40.0 million
1974	73.9	28.9	45.0
1976	125.5	46.3	79.2
1978	197.3	86.7	110.6
1980	238.9	102.9	136.0
1982[1]	343.9	139.3	204.6

[1] 1982 figures are inflated because they double amounts transferred between all committees within a campaign.

SOURCE: Citizens' Research Foundation compilation based on FEC and other data.

several reasons for this. First, the Supreme Court in *Buckley v. Valeo* declared unconstitutional the limits on what candidates for Congress could donate to their own campaigns. Second, with contribution limits on individuals, PACs, and parties upheld, self-contributions by wealthy candidates became a major means by which some could have large amounts of early "seed money." Third, with the cost of campaigns exploding, quick infusions of large sums of money have made the difference between successful and unsuccessful nonincumbent campaigns.

Despite high levels of Republican party support for its candidates, the Democrats gained 26 seats in the House, and the two parties fought to a standoff in the Senate. The House results represent an average loss for the first midterm election of a new president during the post-World War II period. The standoff in the Senate may be seen as both a Democratic and a Republican victory: for the Republicans because they maintained control of the Senate and for the Democrats because they did not lose ground in an election in which 20 of the 33 contested seats were held by Democrats.

Congressional Spending

In 1982 more money again went to incumbents and winners. During the election cycle, incumbents spent $157,593,717; challengers spent $100,655,370; and open-seat candidates spent $85,668,483. Incumbents received 66 percent of the PAC contributions, challengers 19 percent, and open-seat candidates 15 percent. In the Senate the winners' average spending was almost $2.1 million; their major party opponents' spending averaged about $1.5 million. House winners averaged more than $266,000;

major party losers spent slightly more than $137,000. Democrats received the larger share of PAC receipts, 54 percent. PACs supplied Democratic House general election candidates with 34.1 percent of their net receipts and their Republican counterparts with 28.1 percent; many more Democratic House incumbents were running. Republican Senate general election candidates received 19.9 percent of their funds from PACs, outpacing their Democratic opponents who received 17.3 percent from PACs.

The relative stinginess that PACs exhibited toward congressional challengers in 1982 has been well documented. The *Baron Report* noted in late August 1982, for example, that "at least 20 Democratic congressional candidates . . . have so far failed to raise the minimal funds necessary to wage viable campaigns." [2] The newsletter went on to note specific cases of potentially strong Democratic candidates who were unable to mount effective challenges because of lack of funds, even though they were running against vulnerable Republican incumbents. Later reports noted the same pattern.

Furthermore, despite its well-publicized success at raising money, the Republican party was unable to provide adequate financing for GOP challengers running against Democratic incumbents. According to a *New York Times* report, the Republican party and its major contributors set as their top 1982 priority protection of the 52 Republicans who were newly elected in 1980. Their second priority was assisting GOP contenders for 58 open-seat races. Republican challengers running against incumbent Democrats were to receive assistance only when the first two types of candidates had been adequately supported. According to William Greener, communications director of the RNC, "It's easier to protect what you've got than go after something else." [3]

Congressional campaigns in 1982 required unprecedented amounts of money, in part because of the increasing use of broadcast advertising and computerized campaign techniques. According to the Television Bureau of Advertising, political advertising costs on television in 1982 rose to a record $117 million, surpassing the 1980 presidential election year total by 29 percent. Most of this amount went for regional or local television, where the bulk of political advertising takes place. Such expenditures were expected to rise to at least $180 million in the presidential election year of 1984, with some $40 million of that amount to be allotted to network television. [4]

The increasing technical sophistication of political campaigns is another factor that has driven the cost of elections up. The Republicans have taken the initiative in high-tech campaigning, leading to a description of the GOP as the "electronic party," emphasizing computers and broadcasting over precinct organizing and patronage in congressional and presidential campaigns alike.[5] Computers have helped campaigns reach likely voters and contributors, personalizing their messages to suit the recipient's concerns.

Computer data banks also are being used increasingly to store negative information about opposition candidates, particularly pertaining to legislative votes and other public positions on issues.[6] In addition, the California Republican party has had success in using computer technology to send the state's registered Republicans absentee ballot applications—completely filled out except for the voter's signature. Use of absentee ballots, sent by the millions, provided George Deukmejian with his margin of victory in the 1982 gubernatorial campaign.[7]

The losses the Republicans experienced in the House could have been much greater, considering the relatively high unemployment rate at the time of the 1982 midterm election. The Republican edge in fund raising, however, acted as an insulator against heavy losses. Political scientists Gary Jacobson and Samuel Kernell argue that the Republicans used their financial resources to "counteract rather than reinforce" unfavorable national conditions, thus protecting more Republican incumbents than otherwise would have been possible.[8] In 1980, for example, the RNC ran an $8 million institutional advertising program urging voters to "vote Republican for a change." [9] The party spent an additional $6 million to $7 million on advertising in 1982.[10] Moreover, the Republicans' fund-raising efforts have stressed broad-based direct mail campaigns targeting the business and professional communities and other supporters, making the flow of money steady and somewhat immune to fluctuations in the political and economic environments. This large and relatively stable source of money has allowed the Republicans to recruit and train candidates as well as to help finance their campaigns. According to Joe Gaylord, campaign director of the National Republican Congressional Committee, finding "high-quality candidates" was the committee's top priority in 1981. Much of its recruiting success was based on the optimism that characterized the Republican party in 1981 after President Reagan's economic plans won acceptance in Congress. At that time, in fact, some Republicans were talking about taking control of the House in 1982.[11]

Jacobson and Kernell believe that both the Democrats and the Republicans fielded top-rated challengers in 1982, but for different reasons. Strong Democratic challengers were drawn in by their belief that the nation's economic problems, reflected in high interest rates and growing unemployment despite Reagan's economic programs, would make 1982 a promising year for the Democrats. The Republicans, on the other hand, stressed their advantages in money and organization and concluded that they had the resources to reverse the usual cycle.[12] But simply having good challengers does not by itself ensure victory. According to one Democratic strategist, "You need twice as many strong challengers as the number of seats you hope to gain." [13]

Furthermore, there were some House races in 1982 that depended on the personal wealth of the candidates. In the Republican primary in California's 43d Congressional District, for example, trailer tycoon Johnnie Crean contributed $304,000 to his own campaign, health spa owner Deborah Szekely gave $200,988 to her own cause, and former football star Bill McColl put in $192,500 of his own money.[14] Unlimited use of personal wealth in one's own campaign for office was deemed part of an individual's First Amendment free speech rights by the Supreme Court in 1976 in *Buckley v. Valeo,* so long as public funding is not provided, or, if provided, is not accepted by a candidate. If the candidates accept public funding, limits can be imposed on personal spending. Because there is no public funding in congressional campaigns, candidates can spend unlimited personal funds. Both challengers and incumbents try to build up large "war chests" early in the campaign to frighten off potential rivals.[15] But it also is important to have a great deal of money for the closing days of a campaign. According to one RNC survey, about one-third of all voters in 1980 made their choice during the last three days of the campaign.[16] In 1982 U.S. Senate races, a number of candidates spent particularly large sums of money— both their own and others'.

California

The senatorial race in California between Pete Wilson and Edmund G. "Jerry" Brown, Jr. was an example of a high-spending race marked by the use of other people's money. It also illustrates other trends in contemporary campaign financing. Brown, whose job approval rating as California's governor dropped perilously low during his second term, mounted an all-out early fund-raising drive, apparently to discourage potential challengers. This strategy probably was intended to deter not only potential Democratic challengers in the primary but also Republican challengers to Sen. S. I. Hayakawa, considered by many political observers to be vulnerable to a Brown challenge. Although he faced no strong opponents in the Democratic primary, Brown managed to amass more than $1 million through June 30, 1981, and nearly $3.2 million through June 30, 1982—more than any other Senate candidate except Sen. Lloyd Bentsen, D-Texas. Furthermore, Brown managed to receive considerable media exposure while holding primary expenditures to a minimum by appearing as a guest on radio talk shows around the state. The invitations stopped after Republican candidate Ted Bruinsma complained to the Federal Election Commission.[17]

In the meantime, a number of potentially strong candidates challenged Hayakawa for the Republican nomination, including Wilson, the mayor of San Diego; Rep. Barry Goldwater, Jr., who made extensive use of nationwide fund-raising lists distilled from his father's Senate campaigns; Rep. Robert Dornan, who had strong appeal in New Right circles; Rep. Pete McCloskey, who had substantial name recognition from his 1972 prenomination challenge to Richard Nixon and who appealed to moderate and liberal Republicans; and Maureen Reagan, the president's daughter.[18] The result was a costly Republican primary contest that concluded with Wilson's victory on June 8. McCloskey and Goldwater spent more than $2 million each; Wilson spent more than $1.8 million; and Dornan, who was never a serious contender, spent nearly $1 million. Together, Republican prenomination candidates raised nearly $8 million and spent almost $7.8 million. Candidates of both parties raised more than $12.5 million through June 30, 1982; total spending by Republicans and Democrats amounted to more than $9.8 million.

The general election contest also involved heavy spending. In particular it demonstrated the financial resources strong Republican candidates can command from individual contributors, PACs, and the party. As of June 30, 1982, Democrat Brown reported cash on hand totaling nearly $2.5 million following his virtually uncontested primary victory. The Wilson campaign reported it had incurred a debt of almost $100,000 following the hard-fought Republican primary.[19] But money flowed into the Wilson campaign following his primary victory. According to one analysis, the Wilson campaign received more than $3.7 million between July 1, 1982, and October 13, 1982, with about half coming from "major business interests." By the end of the campaign, PAC contributions to Wilson reached nearly $1.2 million, more than any other U.S. Senate candidate received from PACs in 1982. Brown, meanwhile, raised more than $1.5 million during the July 1-October 13 period with about a third coming from business.[20] Brown's fund-raising lead diminished during the general election campaign, and by the end of the year Wilson had outraised Brown by $7.2 million to $5.5 million overall, and $5.3 million to $2.3 million after June 30. Brown's total PAC receipts amounted to $241,000, largely from labor PACs.

Wilson's fund-raising prospects were enhanced following a declaration that his election—or, more precisely, Brown's defeat—was the White House's top priority in the 1982 elections. Wilson's one-day fund-raising trip to Washington at the beginning of July netted more than $80,000;[21] President Reagan appeared at a $1,000-a-plate western-style fund-raiser at 20th Century Fox studios that netted approximately $1 million;[22] an October fund-raiser in Las Vegas featuring entertainer Wayne Newton brought in another $100,000; and a $100-a-plate dinner with former secretary of state Henry Kissinger as the featured speaker raised about $60,000.[23] Much of the frenzied financial activity reflected the antipathy business felt toward Brown, whose eight-year tenure as governor was marked by increasing regulation of business, particularly in regard to environmental matters.[24]

Added to all this was the assistance offered by the Republican party. In Wilson's case, the Republican National Committee and the National Republican Senatorial Committee combined to contribute $19,743 to his campaign. But the big party money came in the form of coordinated expenditures, a category under which both the state and national party committees may spend two cents for each person in the state's voting-age population, plus cost-of-living increases. In California the state and national party committees together were allowed to spend $1,311,748. By agency agreement—a process whereby a state party committee may agree to assign its expenditure limit to a national committee that has money available to make such expenditures—the National Republican Senatorial Committee made $1,311,272 in coordinated expenditures to pay off costs incurred by the Wilson campaign. By contrast, the Democratic Senatorial Campaign Committee could muster only $128,716 in coordinated expenditures in support of Brown. In addition, the DSCC contributed $17,500 to the Democratic candidate. By the end of the primary and general election campaigns, major party candidates in California had raised $20.1 million and spent $19.7 million. With coordinated party expenditures included, the aggregate spending total was $21.2 million.

Campaigns in California are notably expensive. The state includes three sprawling media markets—Los Angeles-Orange County, San Francisco-Oakland-San Jose, and San Diego—in addition to numerous smaller markets. A 30-second spot on "60 Minutes" in Los Angeles, for example, cost the Wilson campaign as much as $30,000. Despite its large fund-raising total, the Wilson campaign claimed to be short of funds as late as October 1982 when 300,000 letters were sent out to California Republicans in an appeal for "emergency contributions." [25]

Minnesota

The 1982 Senate race in Minnesota provides an interesting counterpoint to the California contest. In California the incumbent Republican senator, Hayakawa, was considered so vulnerable that he was only sixth best among his state's candidates of his own party in fund raising and never ranked high in the polls. In Minnesota the incumbent Republican senator was considered one of the most skilled and popular politicians in the state, and he won renomination virtually unopposed. But the larger difference between the two races, in this context at least, is that in California the candidates raised their large sums through contributions by individuals, parties, and PACs; in Minnesota, the greater part of the Democratic campaign money came from nominee Mark Dayton's deep pockets. Republican incumbent David Durenberger received significant PAC support.

Dayton, principal heir to the Dayton-Hudson retail chain and husband of the former Alida Rockefeller, West Virginia governor Rockefeller's sister, is the classic case of a wealthy candidate. Although he had never held elective office and was only 35 years old at the time, Dayton, whose wealth has been estimated as high as $30 million, was able to begin filling his campaign chest with his own money late in 1980. By the end of 1981 he had given or lent more than $1.1 million to his campaign. A wealthy candidate like Dayton has a number of advantages. First, because he does not have to rise through the ranks of political office, he has no embarrassing political past (and no experience, his opponents will say). Second, with generous spending he can hire a media consultant to create an image tailored to fit the electorate's current mood. Third, he need not divert himself from the campaign trail to attend fund-raisers. Fourth, a rich candidate is likely to discourage potential challengers. And last, money automatically makes the rich office seeker a "serious" candidate. In Dayton's case, the Minnesota Democratic-Farmer-Labor party recognized the candidate's advantages and gave him the preprimary endorsement in June 1982 over former senator Eugene McCarthy.

Dayton dipped into his personal fortune to finance a television advertising campaign so extensive that, according to the *New York Times,* his campaign commercials were seen more often than those for McDonald's hamburgers in Minnesota during part of 1982.[26] By October 1982 he had paid New York media consultant David Garth more than $600,000 to plan his campaign against Durenberger.

But the power of Dayton's wealth cut two ways. On the one hand, it enabled a political novice—save for short stints as a Mondale staffer and as a state economic development commissioner—to win his party's nomination and become a strong contender for a U.S. Senate seat. On the other hand, Dayton's wealth itself became an issue—perhaps the overriding issue—in the campaign. Durenberger repeatedly asked his audiences, "How much is he [Dayton] spending?"[27] He accused his opponent of being a spoiled rich kid trying to buy a U.S. Senate seat. Dayton, a liberal Democrat, was able to neutralize some of the negative sentiment aroused by his opponent's criticism by advocating a tax system that would close tax loopholes for the rich. Durenberger, meanwhile, was able to offset the wealth of his opponent by drawing more than $1 million in PAC contributions—a total second only to Pete Wilson's—and raising more than $4.1 million overall. In postelection testimony before the Senate Committee on Rules and Administration, Durenberger indicated that the current political financing system, which places tight limits on individual contributions but sets no limits on how much a candidate can raise, strikes a delicate balance between keeping federal candidates from becoming obligated to any particular interest and allowing them to raise enough money to compete with a wealthy opponent.[28] Durenberger won the general election by a 53-to-47 percent margin, even though Dayton, according to a Citizens' Research Foundation analysis, gave or lent his campaign more than $6.9 million.

Dayton's heavy spending undoubtedly forced Durenberger to spend more than he would have against almost any other opponent, thus raising the ante for Durenberger and future candidates. Although Dayton lost, his 47 percent of the vote may have resulted from his heavy spending; one might speculate how well another inexperienced 35-year-old without a personal fortune might have done. For a challenger, the incremental value of each additional dollar spent is great, resulting in additional name recognition. Despite defeat, Dayton's increased visibility may serve as a higher plateau from which to launch a future campaign for public office.

New Jersey

In California the two major candidates amassed large sums of other people's money. In Minnesota a wealthy challenger used his own funds, and an incumbent raised a great deal of money from PACs, party, and individuals. In New Jersey's 1982 U.S. Senate election campaign, both candidates were 'wealthy and used a combination of their personal funds and money contributed by individuals and PACs.

The wealthy Republican candidate was Rep. Millicent Fenwick, a popular moderate who was the model for the character Lacey Davenport in the "Doonesbury" comic strip. The wealthy Democratic candidate was Frank Lautenberg, a computer manufacturer with personal assets estimated at $14 million.[29] Lautenberg created his own candidacy by contributing $382,500 to himself in February and March 1982 and lending himself another $1 million between April and June. According to his year-end report to the FEC, Lautenberg lent his campaign $4.4 million, of which about $800,000 was paid back. According to her final FEC report, Fenwick gave her campaign $391,000 and lent it $486,000. As of the January 31, 1983, report, none of the money lent had been repaid to her.

A candidate who partially funds his or her campaign has almost the same advantages as a candidate such as Mark Dayton, who was almost exclusively dependent on his own funds. Lautenberg used his wealth to give himself instant legitimacy as a candidate. As individual and PAC contributions began to flow in, he switched over to lending himself money so that the campaign would not experience spot cash shortages and lose momentum. After he won the Democratic nomination, Lautenberg continued to lend himself money—$2.6 million during the period between July 1 and the general election on November 2. After the election, the campaign committee went to work trying to reimburse the candidate for his loans.

Lautenberg's campaign strategy was to start with positive commercials about himself early in the campaign and to follow up with spot announcements, aired after Labor Day, critical of Fenwick's stands on jobs programs, the nuclear freeze, and other issues in an attempt to erode her favorable image. That Lautenberg was able to do this demonstrates another advantage of wealthy candidates: they can control the timing of their campaigns because they can broadcast their advertising when they want to, not merely when they are able. Lautenberg was able to win an upset victory over Fenwick because he was able to chip away at her image bit by bit, instead of trying to do so in a single media blitz. According to one campaign consultant, the reason negative advertising often does not work is that "people in campaigns try to go for home runs. When you do, you strike out a lot. What you need is three yards and a cloud of dust." [30] To pursue a step-by-step approach, of course, a campaign must be confident it will have the money to fund advertising week after week. In the New Jersey race, such a strategy transformed underdog Lautenberg, who was 20 points behind Fenwick in an early October poll, into a campaign winner.

Independent Expenditures

During the 1981-1982 election cycle, some 70 PACs, 15 other groups, and 7 individuals made nearly $5.7 million worth of independent expenditures for or against congressional candidates, a 143 percent increase over the 1979-1980 total of $2.3 million. Independent expenditures in the later period were more likely to be "negative," that is, to fund messages advocating a candidate's defeat. Such expenditures accounted for 59 percent of the total congressional independent expenditures in 1980 and 78 percent in 1982. As in 1980 the biggest spenders in this category were groups affiliated with the New Right.

Nearly one-fifth of all 1982 independent spending was reported for or against the reelection bid of Sen. Edward M. Kennedy, D-Mass. Kennedy—whose inclusion as a targeted candidate may have been motivated by a desire to increase receipts from conservative contributors—was the focus of $1,078,000 in negative expenditures and $1,350 in positive expenditures. Nevertheless, Kennedy won reelection over Republican Ray Shamie, 61-to-39 percent. Sen. Paul S. Sarbanes, D-Md., also drew the opposition of the New Right; $697,763 was spent independently against him and $30,351 in his favor. Much of the NCPAC spending against Sarbanes came even before Republicans chose a candidate to oppose him. The NCPAC expenditures energized Sarbanes's campaign early, attracting money and volunteers, demonstrating that negative attacks can backfire. Sarbanes won handily, 63-to-37 percent over Republican Lawrence Hogan.

The 1982 elections shattered any illusions that NCPAC—which took credit for defeating four well-known liberal senators in 1980—and other New Right PACs were becoming a dominant factor in the electoral system. In fact, NCPAC turned out to be one of 1982's biggest losers, as 16 of its 17 targeted candidates won reelection. Its only victory, the defeat of Sen. Howard Cannon, D-Nev., probably was due more to his alleged involvement in a well-publicized Teamsters' scandal than to NCPAC's advertising.

State Races

Since the creation of the FEC as a comprehensive repository of federal campaign spending records, political finance literature has been dominated by analysis of and commentary upon presidential and congressional

Table 6-2   Total Cost of Gubernatorial Elections, 1977-1982

Year	Number of Races	Total Campaign Costs, Actual Dollars	Total Campaign Costs, 1967 Dollars	Average Cost Per Election, 1967 Dollars
1977	2	$ 9.1 million	$ 5.0 million	$2.5 million
1978	36	99.7	51.1	1.4
1979	3	32.7	15.0	5.0
1980	13	35.6	14.4	1.1
1981	2	20.0	7.3	3.7
1982	36[1]	192.3	67.7	1.9
	92	$389.2	$160.5	

[1] Data for Illinois, 1982, represents the estimate of expenditures from an Associated Press story published on April 29, 1983, in *The Champaign-Urbana News-Gazette.*
SOURCE: Thad L. Beyle, "The Cost of Becoming Governor," manuscript prepared for publication in *State Government,* Summer 1983.

contests. Because of the relative ease with which federal races can be examined by themselves or in comparison with others, political finance scholars risk overlooking the substantial increases that have occurred in spending for state and local contests in the last several years.

Some of the most dramatic increases have occurred in gubernatorial races. Table 6-2 shows the total cost of gubernatorial elections from 1977 through 1982. In 1982 campaign spending in the 36 gubernatorial races varied significantly, ranging from $23.6 million in New York, where losing candidate Lewis Lehrman spent nearly three times as much as winner Mario Cuomo, to about $250,000 in South Dakota, where Gov. William Janklow handily defeated his Democratic opponent. The average gubernatorial election cost a little more than $5 million, including primaries.[31] Political scientist Thad Beyle cites a number of reasons for increased spending in these races: a decline in the effectiveness of state political party committees, greater use of the mass media, and the increased prestige of state governorships as stepping stones to national office. "Candidates are willing to spend more for the office," writes Beyle, "and they do." [32]

Beyle's observation is illustrated by West Virginia governor Jay Rockefeller who spent $12 million, or about $30 a vote, for reelection in 1980. His broadcasting was so extensive that his campaign advertisements were aired as far away as Washington, D.C., and his computerized direct mail campaign so large that families received eight or ten different letters, each geared to a specific audience.[33]

Higher costs, of course, give advantage to candidates who are personally wealthy or who have access to wealth. "While it is still possible for a middle-class candidate with a good organization and half a million dollars in campaign contributions to win one of the lesser races on the ballot," writes Kaye Northcott, a Texas political activist, "only the wealthy or those bankrolled by the wealthy need apply for the Texas governorship or a berth in the U.S. Senate." [34]

The financing of state races generally is more freewheeling than in federal contests because state campaign finance laws are usually less stringent than their federal counterpart, the FECA. For example, approximately 25 states do not have limits on individual contributions.[35] Although in the last decade nearly every state legislature made substantial changes in its campaign financing or public disclosure laws, as will be described in Chapter 7, gubernatorial campaign costs grew, with a few races marked by particularly heavy expenditures. As with the Senate races mentioned above, these high spending totals were achieved either by wealthy candidates spending their own money, well-connected candidates using other contributors' money, or a combination of the two.

California

The California governor's race paralleled the state's high-spending Senate race, with Democrat Tom Bradley spending $9.48 million and Republican George Deukmejian, the eventual winner, spending $9.06 million, both including primary campaigns. This far surpassed the 1978 combined total of $8.2 million spent by gubernatorial candidates Evelle Younger and Jerry Brown. The heavy spending began in the primaries as the Deukmejian campaign spent $3.6 million to win a narrow upset victory over Lt. Gov. Mike Curb, who spent $4.7 million. Bradley, meanwhile, spent $2.4 million in the Democratic primary, even though he faced insubstantial opposition. A good deal of this money went for television advertising. In California, with its weak parties and diverse regions, broadcast advertising is almost the sole link between statewide candidates and the electorate.

In the general election contest, Deukmejian waged an aggressive advertising campaign that, among other things, sought to link Bradley to Democratic governor Jerry Brown, whose popularity had declined, and himself to President Reagan, who remained popular in his home state. This strategy, along with other campaign efforts, took its toll on Deukmejian's opponent. In October, with Bradley's lead in the polls eroding, his campaign attempted to counter Deukmejian's negative advertising by running commercials hinting that the Republican's campaign smacked of Watergate-type "dirty tricks" tactics. This counterattack, however, was unsuccessful. Deukmejian defeated Bradley by slightly more than 90,000 votes out of nearly 7.9 million cast. A Republican mail drive to encourage absentee voting, while expensive, tipped the balance in favor of Deukmejian although Bradley actually won at the polls on election day.[36] Bradley probably would have been able to salvage victory if the state's Democratic party had been strong enough to mount larger voter registration and get-out-the-vote drives in black and Latino areas. Although black voters cast their ballots overwhelmingly for Bradley, they did not turn out in large numbers. Voting among the state's sizable Latino population was relatively sparse.

Heavy spending also characterized a number of other races in California (Table 6-3). Candidates for statewide and state legislative offices spent $83 million in 1982.[37] Assembly candidates spent $13.9 million in the primaries and $17.4 million during the general election period. In contrast, state Senate candidates, fewer in number than those running for the Assembly, spent $5 million in primary races and $6.9 million in the general election contests. These totals include several high-spending races. The most notable of these involved Democrat Tom Hayden, who spent $2.06 million—much of it contributed by his wife, actress Jane Fonda—in primary and general election contests to win a seat in the 44th Assembly District. He defeated Republican Bill Hawkins, who spent $908,000. Total spending by all candidates for the Assembly seat was $3.3 million. Furthermore, five state Senate races each topped $1 million in spending, driving up the average cost in combined primary and general election spending.

According to the state's Fair Political Practices Commission, the average cost of a legislative seat in California, including primary and general election campaign spending by all candidates, was $429,000 in 1982, up from $210,000 in 1978. The average cost of a California Senate contest was $589,475, and of an Assembly race, $387,839; again, the figures include all primary and general election spending by all candidates for each legislative seat. Incumbents spent more than challengers by an 8-to-1 ratio, up from about 4-to-1 in 1978. Total spending on 1982 state and federal election campaigns in California reached more than $180 million, according to a Citizens' Research Foundation analysis. The spending breakdown is provided in Table 6-3.

Table 6-3 Political Spending on State and Federal Races in California, Primary and General Election, 1981-1982

State Contests	*Expenditures*[1]	
Governor	$25.4	
Lieutenant Governor	4.9	
Superintendent of Public Instruction	3.4	
Attorney General	3.1	
Secretary of State	.81	
Treasurer	.496	
Controller	.955	
Board of Equalization (four seats)	1.4	
Subtotal, Statewide Offices		$ 40,136[2]
State Legislature		
Assembly (80 seats)	$31.3	
Senate (20 of 40 seats up for election)	11.9	
Subtotal, State Legislature		$ 42,825[2]
Ballot Issues		$ 24.3
Federal Contests		
Senate	$21.2[3]	
House of Representatives (45 seats)	21.7[3][4]	
Subtotal, Federal Contests		$ 42.9
Party and Nonparty Administrative and Fund-raising Costs and Individual Out-of-Pocket Expenditures		$ 30.0[5]
Total spending, state and federal		$180,161

[1] Spending in millions of dollars.
[2] Totals and subtotals have been adjusted for transfers among candidates and committees.
[3] Includes coordinated party expenditures.
[4] This figure is an estimate based on a pro-rated share of nationwide House spending.
[5] Estimated as 20 percent of subtotals listed above.
SOURCE: Citizens' Research Foundation compilation based on Federal Election Commission and Fair Political Practices Commission data.

New York

The financing of the gubernatorial race in New York in 1982 was similar to that of the senatorial race in Minnesota discussed above: a wealthy candidate with strong ideological views spent a great deal of his own money to win his party's nomination easily, faced a general election challenger who was financed through traditional sources, and lost in a close race. In New York the wealthy candidate was Lewis Lehrman, major stockholder of a chain of discount drugstores, whose personal fortune has been estimated at about $50 million. Lehrman's views on supply-side economics, balanced budgets, and the gold standard brought him under consideration as a potential secretary of the Treasury in the Reagan administration. To win the state's Republican primary, he spent $5.7 million, $3.7 million of which was lent to the campaign by Lehrman and his twin brother, Gilbert.[38] Lehrman far outspent his nearest Republican rival, Paul Curran, whose expenditures totaled $284,000, and spent three times as much as the best-financed Democratic candidate, New York mayor Edward Koch, who in turn spent twice as much as the Democratic primary winner, Lt. Gov. Mario Cuomo.

In the primary campaign, which began in August 1981, Lehrman spent $3.1 million on advertising, most of it on television. In December 1981 the campaign purchased $50,000 worth of radio and television time, followed by $525,000 in January 1982, and $450,000 in February. In addition, the Lehrman campaign spent nearly $100,000 for polls to determine the effectiveness of his advertising. More than $18,000 was spent for thousands of pairs of red suspenders, which became a trademark of his campaign. According to an inch-thick computer printout the Lehrman campaign submitted to the New York State Board of Elections, primary campaign fund raising collected 24 contributions of $10,000 or more, 74 contributions of $5,000 or more, and 3,525 contributions of less than $100. While there were relatively few contributors, it was remarkable for a candidate as wealthy as Lehrman to attract almost 100 contributions of $5,000 or more, a feat that Nelson Rockefeller rarely accomplished in his campaigns.

During the general election campaign, Lehrman filled the airwaves with so many commercials that the network stations began to limit his advertising, and independent stations carried most of his messages during the final 10 days of the contest. Whereas Mark Dayton's spending became a major issue in the Minnesota senatorial campaign, Lehrman's heavy eleventh-hour spending did not seem to damage his standing with the electorate.

According to Thad Beyle, "Rather than create a voter backlash against so much being spent, the blitz was credited for his late, but unsuccessful surge."[39] After spending about $11 million on his primary and general election campaigns, Lehrman lost to Cuomo, 51-to-48 percent. In both the Dayton and Lehrman campaigns, the heavy spenders lost, but perhaps by not so much as they would have without the enormous sums they were willing to spend.

Texas

Statewide campaigns in Texas always have required large amounts of money to reach the voters. The population of more than 14 million is scattered over a land mass greater than 267,000 square miles. These circumstances have helped shape the two-party system in Texas in which a conservative Democratic party competes with a conservative Republican party. Kaye Northcott, a liberal activist in the Texas Democratic party, has claimed that it would be self-defeating for her party to try to become too liberal because money would flow to the Republicans in such sums that the Democrats soon would become uncompetitive.[40]

According to Northcott, the 1982 Texas gubernatorial primary resembled a high-stakes poker game in which even millionaires found the level of competition too expensive. Oilman Peyton McKnight, who began campaigning for the Democratic nomination in mid-1981, contributed $1.5 million to get his campaign rolling but dropped out in February 1982, nine months before the election, because he was unwilling to spend an additional $1 million to buy the television advertising he thought necessary to win.[41] Buddy Temple, the only son of an east Texas timber baron, also found the race too expensive. After spending $1.3 million, more than 60 percent of it for television advertising, he conceded the runoff election and the nomination to Secretary of State Mark White because he was unwilling to invest an estimated $1.5 million more.[42]

White, a career politician who financed his $1.6 million primary campaign from conventional sources, faced as a general election campaign opponent incumbent governor William Clements, whose fortune from leasing oil well drilling equipment was estimated at $30 million in 1978. Clements spent $7.2 million that year, including $4.5 million of his own money, to be elected the state's first Republican governor in 105 years. Once in office, Clements proved a skilled fund-raiser and was able to reimburse himself all the money he had lent his campaign in 1978. In the 1982 Republican primary, Clements's campaign spent $3 million alone on organizing for the general election contest, for which he said he would spend whatever was necessary to win a second term.[43]

The general election campaign revolved as much around Clements's reputation as an abrasive personality as any substantive issues. Although Clements raised an estimated $12 million for his reelection bid—including more than $3 million at a single fund-raising dinner—challenger White was able to turn the election into a referendum on Clements, and White won 54-to-46 percent.

Ballot Issues

The 1980s have witnessed a boom in the use of the direct initiative, the process by which citizens petition to place measures on the ballot. Initiative sponsors collected more than 16 million signatures to place 52 initiatives—the largest total for any election year since 1932—on the ballot in 1982 in a record 19 states (plus the District of Columbia).[44] Some 41 initiatives appeared on statewide ballots in 1980. Total spending on ballot issues in 1980 was estimated at $40 million.[45] With a greater number of issues and more extensive campaigns in 1982, total spending probably exceeded $50 million.

Although all 50 states allow their electorates to vote on public policy by way of constitutional amendments and bond issues that legislatures place before the electorate, only 23 states allow citizen-initiated access to the ballot. Initiatives are a heritage of the populist reform movement that flourished at the turn of the century. South Dakota enacted the first state initiative provision in 1898; 18 states had the initiative by 1918. Although no states have adopted this procedure since Florida in 1972, legislation that would permit initiatives was introduced in 21 states in 1981 alone. California has become the leader in the use of the initiative; one observer has called its electorate "the largest legislative body in the world."[46]

As the number of initiatives has proliferated, the range of subject matter has broadened. In 1982 initiatives on state ballots ranged from overarching international questions such as the bilateral nuclear weapons freeze to relatively minor issues such as whether Colorado should allow wine to be sold in grocery stores or whether Oregon motorists should be allowed to pump their own gasoline.[47] An initiative on the ballot in Berkeley, California, asked the electorate to outlaw electroshock therapy.[48]

Although some observers see these developments as a healthy indicator of increasing "participatory democracy," others are less encouraged. Sue Thomas, research director of the National Center for Initiative Review, says the initiative represents "single issue politics at its epitome," and questions whether the process takes the pressure off legislatures to address critical issues and places the burden on an electorate that might not be qualified to solve them.[49] Furthermore, public opinion polls indicate that more than half of those interviewed agreed that citizens ought to vote on issues but also thought that issues are often too complicated to be decided by the voter and that interest groups will gain power as a result.[50]

Still other observers are opposed strongly to the increased usage of initiatives, agreeing with political consultant Charles Winner that the initiative process is "being misused and abused as more and more single-purpose and single-interest groups attempt to circumvent the normal process with their quick-fix solutions to complex problems." [51] He warns that if use of the initiative continues to increase, a disjointed stream of computerized plebiscites eventually will replace the deliberative and representative functions of government. He further argues that initiatives "often appeal to the emotions and frustrations of the majority and sometimes to its selfishness," and points to measures such as the initiative passed in California in 1964 that overturned the state's fair housing law. Some observers link that initiative with the environment that provoked the Watts riots in 1965. [52]

Other commentators say that, taken as a whole, the public makes rather intelligent decisions. According to the *Baron Report,* the electorate is "far more discerning and skeptical—and less bigoted—than in many cases, the elites of both 'right' and 'left' assume. Believability and practicality are more important to results than ideology." [53] Moreover, argues Eugene Lee, director of the Institute of Governmental Studies at the University of California, there is nothing to prevent the same information being supplied to the electorate that legislative and administrative decision makers have available. [54] But David Magleby, a professor of political science at Brigham Young University, has argued that the state-published descriptions of ballot measures usually are far too technical to be understood by more than a small percentage of the electorate. He estimates, for example, that California's voter pamphlet requires 18 years of education—the equivalent of a second-year law student—to be understood. [55]

To add to the confusion, groups sometimes take names that deliberately mislead the public. In Washington State a committee that opposed a 1982 initiative to limit interest rates called itself "People for Fair Consumer Credit," even though its supporters were banks and retail chains. [56] In Colorado a group calling itself "Citizens for Common Sense" opposed the sale of wine in grocery stores and argued that this would lead to their selling hard liquor. The group's backers were liquor dealers. [57]

Whatever the degree of dissembling in some ballot measure campaigns, their increasing numbers suggest that certain population groups are highly interested in public policy issues and because legislatures occasionally fail to act on salient issues, the "safety valve" of ballot initiatives exists and is valued by numerous voters.

Some experts believe that the increased use of ballot questions in recent years is due in part to innovations in signature gathering. Petitions usually are circulated by "solicitors," either paid or volunteer, who seek out registered voters at shopping malls, college campuses, sports arenas, and other public places. Although it long has been observed that most people, if asked, will sign a petition without reading it, even monied interests generally have not been willing to hire professional solicitors to obtain a spot on the ballot because of the high costs.[58]

The latest innovation in signature gathering—direct mail—not only generates signatures but also the money to pay for the solicitation. For example, Butcher-Forde Consulting collected 820,000 signatures and a spot on the California ballot in 1980 for Howard Jarvis's initiative to reduce the state income tax. The consulting firm sent out six million pieces of mail to registered voters, asking them to circulate the enclosed petitions and contribute to the effort. Along with the signatures, the campaign received approximately 200,000 individual contributions totaling almost $1.9 million—enough to pay for 90 percent of the signature-gathering costs as well as giving the campaign a large and valuable mailing list.[59] Opponents of mass-mail petitioning say that the technique puts the initiative process even more squarely at the disposal of the special interests. Proponents reply that mailing the petitions allows voters the chance to sit down and examine what they are being asked to sign.[60]

In fact, it appears that the initiative process and direct mail solicitation are mutually reinforcing: both seek out large numbers of like-minded people who are issue-oriented rather than party-oriented. The initiative process is well regarded by both the far right and far left as a way to place their issues on the public agenda, if not enact them into law. Furthermore, national news coverage of state and local initiative campaigns, in addition to increasing coordination among the campaigns themselves, has created a "snowball effect." A measure that proves popular in one state catches on elsewhere, or an initiative that succeeds in several places simultaneously is instantly catapulted onto the national consciousness, if not the national agenda.[61] An example of such a campaign is the nuclear freeze movement, discussed below.

Nuclear Freeze Initiatives

In 1982 a loose-knit coalition of peace activists, church groups, and liberals used the initiative process to place a proposed bilateral nuclear weapons freeze on the national agenda by way of a resolution in the U.S. House of Representatives. Voters in nine states, 35 localities, and the District of Columbia cast more than 19.1 million ballots for or against various nuclear freeze measures. Overall, statewide freeze measures won 57.5 percent of the vote, ranging from 73.7 percent in Massachusetts to 40.7 percent in Arizona, the only state where the measure lost. At the local level, the freeze won even more handily, with 67.7 percent approving. The freeze won in 31 of 35 localities and in the District of Columbia. Freeze measures were placed on six state ballots by direct initiative petitions: California, Arizona, Oregon, Michigan, North Dakota, and Montana. State legislatures placed freeze referenda on ballots in New Jersey, Rhode Island, and Wisconsin, which do not have the initiative.[62]

The freeze movement was successful because it was reasonably well funded and attracted many volunteers. Total state-level spending for the various freeze measures reached nearly $4.6 million, as opposed to $343,000 spent by the anti-freeze forces.[63] Moreover, some 17,000 to 20,000 persons organized to support the freeze in 279 congressional districts in 43 states, according to Karin Fierke, codirector of the Nuclear Weapons Freeze Campaign National Clearing House, a central coordinating body set up in St. Louis in January 1982.[64]

Other Measures

A number of other hotly debated—and more lavishly funded—initiatives made their way onto statewide ballots in 1982. In California, where nearly $24.3 million was spent on ballot measures in 1982,[65] nearly $9.9 million was spent supporting or opposing an initiative that would limit handguns, and nearly $6.4 million was spent for and against a measure that would require a deposit on bottles containing beverages. Since the Supreme Court's decision in *First National Bank of Boston v. Bellotti*, there have been no limits upon how much individuals or groups may contribute to ballot issue campaigns.[66] The Court followed this decision with a ruling in *Citizens Against Rent Control v. City of Berkeley* that limits on corporate contributions in ballot issue campaigns are "clearly a restraint on the right of association." [67] A number of groups have used this doctrine to contribute huge sums to campaigns supporting or, more often, opposing various initiatives. Opposition to California's "bottle bill" was spearheaded by large contributions from the Glass Packaging Institute (nearly $1.2 million), the Can Manufacturers' Institute (almost $700,000), and Anheuser-Busch Brewing Company (more than $350,000). Major contributors to California's nuclear freeze campaign were mostly individuals: Wentworth and Jane Smith Brown ($100,000), Alida Dayton ($85,000), and Norman and Frances Lear ($80,000).[68]

Gun Control

Possibly the most emotionally charged campaign in California in 1982 was fought over an initiative that sought to register all handguns and limit the number of such guns allowed in the state. By the November general election, both sides together had spent $9.9 million—the most ever spent in California on a ballot issue and about 40 percent of the total statewide spending on initiatives—in extensive campaigns that relied on direct mail contributions and broadcast advertisements. The opposition, which spent $7.3 million, also undertook an extensive voter registration campaign among gun owners. Supporters of the measure spent $2.6 million. The leading contributors to the opposition campaign were the National Rifle Association's Institute for Legislative Action, $2.4 million; Gun Owners of America (a group formed by California state senator H. L. Richardson), $478,000; Sturm, Ruger and Company, $220,000; California Rifle and Pistol Association, $200,000; and Smith and Wesson, $158,000. The largest progun control contributor was Handgun Control, which raised $300,000 through direct mail appeals.

Advertising on each side sought to identify that side's position with law and order. Proponents said the initiative was "designed to block access to guns by criminals and the mentally deranged." [69] Opponents portrayed the measure as an attempt to disarm law-abiding citizens who wished to protect their families and property. As opposition advertising began to mount, the polls, which had shown the initiative with a substantial lead as late as Labor Day, began to show an erosion of support. In the last two weeks of the campaign, when it became apparent that the gun control measure might lose, contributions poured in to the opposition campaign to pay for a final advertising push. The antigun control forces raised $702,000 during the final two weeks of the campaign; proponents received $298,000.

By election day, the race was not even close, with the initiative losing 37-to-63 percent. In rural counties, tallies as high as 7-to-1 against the measure were not uncommon, with tiny Modoc County voting 92 percent against. In Los Angeles, where heavy opposition advertising focused on gun ownership as a means of crime prevention, the measure was voted down 42-to-58 percent. According to George Young, director of the opposition campaign, tracking polls conducted for the campaign showed that California voters concluded increasingly that the measure would do little to lessen crime and represented a substantial restriction of constitutional rights.

It is clear that as American politics continue to be characterized by increasingly weak parties and strong special interests, the direct initiative will be a powerful tool for real and symbolic change. It also is clear that this tool can be manipulated by both monied interests and grass-roots popular movements. What remains to be seen is the full potential of the connection between computerized direct mail and the initiative process. That link, if successfully accomplished, could increase the power of the New Right and other fringe movements, which have been highly successful in using direct mail for other purposes, and work to the detriment of both major political parties and the ideological center. In fact, a connection already exists between the New Right and the initiative movement. A component part of the New Right expresses a populist philosophy, demonstrated in its newsletter, *Initiative and Referendum Report,* and that philosophy, as noted, gave rise to the initiative movement at the turn of the century. But the initiative movement is only one manifestation of a larger plebiscitory movement in the nation's politics. It also manifests itself in changes in the presidential selection process, leading to greater direct citizen participation and in the rise of political action committees that allow greater direct financial participation by citizens in election campaigns.

Notes

1. The comparison is still a preliminary one.
2. "Rich Democrats," *Baron Report,* August 30, 1982, 1. See also Adam Clymer, 'Light Wallets Weigh Heavily on Democrats," *New York Times,* October 17, 1982.
3. Steven Roberts, "GOP Challengers Get Low Priority," *New York Times,* September 16, 1983.
4. "Big Spenders," *Broadcasting,* March 7, 1983, 84.
5. Steven Roberts, "Parties Already Working for 1982 Election Races," *New York Times,* January 26, 1982.
6. Julia Malone, "Democrats Confident Despite GOP's High-Tech Lead," *Christian Science Monitor,* March 16, 1982.
7. See Tony Quinn, "How Governor Deukmejian Won in the Mailbox, Not the Ballot Box," *California Journal,* April 1983, 148.
8. See "1982 Post Mortem," *National Journal,* April 2, 1983, 712.
9. David Broder, introduction to *Party Coalitions in the 1980s,* ed. Seymour Martin Lipset (San Francisco: Institute for Contemporary Studies, 1981), 10-11.
10. James R. Dickenson, "GOP Planners See Fall Elections as the Little Truck That Could," *Washington Post,* August 14, 1982.
11. See "GOP Fund Goals Set for '82 Races," *New York Times,* October 29, 1981.
12. Gary C. Jacobson and Samuel Kernell, "Strategy and Choice in the 1982 Congressional Elections," *Political Science* 15 (Summer 1982): 419.

13. Dickenson, "GOP Planners See Fall Elections."
14. Ellen Hume, "Dollars Roll in for State's House Races," *Los Angeles Times,* June 4, 1982.
15. See Rob Gurwitt, "Senate Campaign Strategies: The Early Money Approach," *Congressional Quarterly Weekly Report,* August 14, 1982, 1987.
16. Dickenson, "GOP Planners See Fall Elections."
17. See Richard Bergholz, "Brown Challenged on Hosting Talk Shows," *Los Angeles Times,* December 12, 1981.
18. See Jerry Gillam and Bill Boyarsky, "Loophole Conceals Source of Funds for Goldwater," *Los Angeles Times,* May 23, 1982.
19. Ellen Hume, "Wilson Sweeps into Capital, Cleans up at a Fund-Raiser," *Los Angeles Times,* July 2, 1982.
20. Narda Zacchino and Bill Boyarsky, "Big Business Gets Revenge," *Los Angeles Times,* October 29, 1982.
21. Hume, "Wilson Sweeps into Capital."
22. William Endicott and George Skelton, "Reagan Urges Wilson Victory," *Los Angeles Times,* August 24, 1982.
23. William Endicott, "Kissinger Featured at Wilson Dinner: $60,000 Raised," *Los Angeles Times,* October 21, 1982.
24. Zacchino and Boyarsky, "Big Business Gets Revenge." See also Albert R. Hunt, "Republicans Shudder to Think Jerry Brown May Win Senate Race," *Wall Street Journal,* October 14, 1982.
25. William Endicott, "Wilson Appeals for 'Emergency Contributions,'" *Los Angeles Times,* October 8, 1982.
26. Howell Raines, "A Rich Foe and Reagan Vex GOP Incumbent," *New York Times,* October 8, 1982.
27. "Senators: Questions About Campaign Spending," *Time,* September 27, 1982.
28. Testimony by Sen. David Durenberger before the Senate Committee on Rules and Administration, January 26, 1983.
29. Joseph Sullivan, "A Newcomer in Senate Bid," *New York Times,* June 10, 1982.
30. Fred Barnes, "'Negative' Campaigning Pays Off," *The Sun,* (Baltimore), November 28, 1982. For more on the Lautenberg campaign strategy, see Joseph Sullivan, "Lautenberg's Calculated Campaign," *New York Times,* November 7, 1982.
31. Thad L. Beyle, "The Cost of Becoming Governor," prepared for *State Government,* Summer 1983, 9. On the costs of gubernatorial campaigns, see also Herbert E. Alexander, "Financing Gubernatorial Election Campaigns," *State Government,* Summer 1980, 140-143.
32. Ibid., 1.
33. Donald Baker, "West Virginia's Deep Pockets," *Washington Post,* November 29, 1980.
34. Kaye Northcott, "Getting Elected," *Mother Jones,* November 1982, 16.
35. Citizens' Research Foundation compilation.
36. "1982 Post Mortem," *National Journal,* April 2, 1983, 712.
37. A compilation by Common Cause indicates that heavy giving by special

interests has inflated the cost of state campaigns in California. Twenty such groups gave nearly $10.7 million to California campaigns between January 1975 and December 1980. See Walter Zelman, *Twenty Who Gave $10 Million: A Study of Money and Politics in California* (Los Angeles: Common Cause, 1981.)

38. Frank Lynn, "Spending Mark Set by Lehrman in Primary Race, *New York Times,* August 24, 1982.
39. Beyle, "The Cost of Becoming Governor," 6.
40. Northcott, "Getting Elected," 18.
41. Ibid., 19.
42. Ibid.
43. Ibid., 16.
44. David Schmidt, "Taking the Initiative," *Today,* October 29, 1982.
45. The figure for spending on ballot issues in 1980 is derived from Steven D. Lydenberg, *Bankrolling Ballots, Update 1980: The Role of Business in Financing Ballot Issue Campaigns* (New York: Council on Economic Priorities, 1981).
46. Ibid.
47. Bill Curry, "Initiatives—and Concerns About Their Value—Proliferate Nationwide," *Los Angeles Times,* October 28, 1982.
48. Gladwin Hill, "Now, Therapy by Ballot," *New York Times,* October 31, 1982.
49. Curry, "Initiatives."
50. "An Interview with Sue Thomas," *Initiative and Referendum Report,* January 1983, 1.
51. Charles Winner, "The Abuse of the Initiative Process," *Los Angeles Times,* February 2, 1982.
52. Ibid.
53. "Initiatives & Referendums," *Baron Report,* August 30, 1982, 5.
54. Hill, "Now, Therapy by Ballot."
55. Curry, "Initiatives."
56. Ibid.
57. "Initiatives & Referendums."
58. Ed Koupal, founder of the People's Lobby, estimated that 75 percent of the public would sign an initiative petition, if asked, without bothering to read it.
59. "It Cost Jarvis $2.50/Name for Initiative," *Los Angeles Herald-Examiner,* February 2, 1980.
60. "Popularity of Petition Drives is Snowballing," *Today,* October 29, 1982.
61. Ibid.
62. Schmidt, "Taking the Initiative."
63. "More Complete Freeze Spending Figures: $4 ½ Million in Favor," *Initiative and Referendum Report,* May 1983, 9.
64. Rushworth Kidder, "Growing Grass-Roots Effort for Nuclear Arms Freeze," *Christian Science Monitor,* March 4, 1982.
65. "Final, Official Spending Figures Released in California," *Initiative and Referendum Report,* May 1983, 8.

66. *First National Bank of Boston v. Bellotti,* 435 U.S. 765 (1978).
67. *Citizens Against Rent Control v. City of Berkeley,* 102 S. Ct. 434, quoted at 437 (1981).
68. "Final, Official Spending Figures."
69. "Yes on 15," direct mail letter, Handgun Control, Inc.

Regulation of Political Finance: The States' Experience

7

While the new federal laws governing political financing were being conceived and enacted, some noteworthy experimentation in election reform was taking place in many of the states. In the 1970s almost every state changed its election laws in significant ways. Some laws imposed on candidates for state offices restrictions similar to those governing congressional and presidential elections, but others varied decidedly. Many states that had adopted campaign laws had to change them later to conform to the 1976 U.S. Supreme Court ruling in *Buckley v. Valeo*. In general, that ruling left intact the public disclosure, contribution limitation, and public financing provisions of existing federal (and, by implication, state) election laws. The decision, however, prohibited spending limitations unless they were tied to public financing. While the *Buckley* decision imposed certain similarities in federal and state laws, there remains wide diversity and lack of uniformity; no two states are alike in their political cultures or their election laws.

Disclosure

All 50 states have disclosure requirements, and all but a few call for both pre- and postelection reporting of contributions and expenditures (Table 7-1). Disclosure is based on the concept of the public's right to know the sources of financial support candidates receive and the patterns of their expenditures. Requirements vary by state, but the disclosure laws usually stipulate identification of contributors by name, address, occupation, and principal place of business, plus the amount and date of the contribution. The laws usually require a report of total expenditures and itemization of certain of them including the amount, date, and particulars of each payment.

The states differ as to the threshold amount at which reporting requirements take effect. Colorado, for example, requires itemization of contributions amounting to $25 or more. Louisiana has a reporting requirement for contributions of $1,000 or more. The states also vary as to when the reports must be filed. Alabama requires only one postelection report 30 days after the election, which, of course, does not provide the electorate with this information before they vote. California law calls for filing two preelection reports, 40 days and 12 days before the election, and one postelection report 65 days after the election. Alaska requires two preelection reports, one month and one week prior to the election, and two postelection reports, one 10 days after the election and the final report on December 31.

Challenges to disclosure laws have come in a series of suits by the Socialist Workers Party (SWP) supported by the American Civil Liberties Union at the federal level and in several states.[1] Suits were brought in California, New Jersey, Ohio, Texas, and the District of Columbia, among other jurisdictions. Where the lawsuits have been successful, the states have provided exceptions for minor party disclosure insofar as the listing of contributors is concerned. They have based their actions on the Supreme Court's decision in *Buckley v. Valeo,* which stated that case-by-case exemptions for minor parties may be permitted if there is a "reasonable probability that the compelled disclosure of a party's contributors' names will subject them to threats, harassment, or reprisals from either government officials or private parties." [2]

In 1977 a U.S. District Court ordered the Federal Election Commission (FEC) to develop a full factual record within six months and make specific findings of fact concerning the "present nature and extent of harassment suffered" by the SWP as a result of the disclosure provisions of the act.[3] Evidence introduced by the SWP following the court order convinced the FEC that the threat of harassment was sufficient to warrant exemption of the party from certain disclosure requirements, at least through the 1984 elections. In 1979 the court approved a consent decree to that effect agreed to by both the commission and the Socialist Workers Party.

The state of Ohio, however, appealed its case to the U.S. Supreme Court, and late in 1982 the Court found that hostility against the SWP remained intense and was likely to continue. The justices ruled unanimously that the party need not report the names of its contributors to Ohio and voted 6-to-3 to exempt the party from disclosing the names of recipients of campaign expenditures. The ruling allows exemptions from both state and federal campaign disclosure laws and may apply to other minor parties such as the Libertarian Party and the Communist Party, USA.

Contribution Limits

Contribution limits, sanctioned in the *Buckley* decision, vary by state and by level of candidacy. Approximately 25 states place no limits on donations. Eighteen states have relatively simple restrictions; seven states have rather detailed limitations. Contribution limits for gubernatorial elections range downward from unlimited contributions to as low as $800 per individual in New Jersey's publicly funded primary and general election campaigns. Most statewide individual contribution limits range from $1,000 to $3,000 per election or per calendar year. In New York the limit is based on a specified number of cents per registered voter. Cash contributions usually are prohibited or restricted to $100 or less.

Some states limit contributions for each calendar year, others for each election period (primary and general election treated separately), and still others for each two-year period. Some states have enacted a single contribution limit that is applied to campaigns for all state offices, and others have established different limits for campaigns for various state offices as well as for donations to political or party committees. Some states limit only contributions by individuals (Table 7-1), but others also limit contributions by political or party committees, including political action committees.

Four states—Florida, Kansas, North Carolina, and Wyoming—seek to strengthen the political parties by permitting unlimited contributions to and by party committees while restricting contributions by individuals and other political committees. In addition, Maine permits political party committees to distribute slate cards listing three or more candidates and exempts their costs from the contribution limits.

An innovative approach is used in Connecticut, New York, and Minnesota, where stratified contribution ceilings are imposed, depending upon specific races. Some states allow appropriate officials to recommend adjustments in restrictions or charge a dependent minor's contribution against the parent's limit. Still other approaches provide for exemption of volunteer services, property use, and travel expenses of $500 and less. Others permit unlimited individual contributions to political committees, even though the committees may be restricted in the amount they can contribute to a candidate.

Table 7-1 Regulation of Political Finance by the States

State	Election Commission	Disclosure[1]	Individual Contribution Limits	Expenditure Limits[2]	Public Subsidy[3]	Credit	Deduction[6]	Tax Provisions Checkoff
Ala.		✓						
Alaska	✓	✓	✓			✓		
Ariz.	✓	✓					✓	
Ark.	✓	✓	✓				✓	
Calif.	✓	✓			✓		✓	✓[4]
Colo.		✓						
Conn.	✓	✓	✓					
Del.		✓	✓					
Fla.	✓	✓	✓					
Ga.	✓	✓						
Hawaii	✓	✓	✓	✓	✓		✓	✓
Idaho	✓	✓			✓	✓		✓
Ill.	✓	✓						
Ind.	✓	✓						
Iowa	✓	✓			✓		✓	✓
Kan.		✓	✓					
Ky.	✓	✓	✓		✓		✓	✓
La.	✓	✓						
Maine	✓	✓	✓		✓		✓	✓

	Md.	Mass.	Mich.	Minn.	Miss.	Mo.	Mont.	Neb.	Nev.	N.H.	N.J.	N.M.	N.Y.	N.C.	N.D.	Ohio	Okla.	Ore.	Pa.	R.I.	S.C.	S.D.	Tenn.
	✓	✓	✓	✓		✓·			✓°				✓				✓	✓	✓				
	✓		✓	✓			✓						✓				✓						
				✓												✓							
	✓	✓	✓	✓			✓		✓				✓				✓	✓	✓				
	✓		✓	✓					✓				✓										
	✓	✓	✓	✓			✓		✓	✓		✓				✓			✓				
	✓	✓	✓	✓	✓	✓	✓	✓	✓	✓	✓	✓	✓	✓	✓	✓	✓	✓	✓	✓	✓	✓	✓
	✓	✓		✓		✓			✓		✓	✓		✓	✓		✓	✓		✓	✓	✓	✓

167

Table 7-1 Regulation of Political Finance by the States

State							
Texas			✓				
Utah	✓		✓	✓		✓	
Vt.	✓	✓					
Va.	✓	✓		✓			✓
Wash.	✓	✓					
W.Va.	✓	✓					
Wis.	✓	✓		✓		✓	
Wyo.	✓	✓					
D.C.	✓	✓	✓				

[1] Some states, such as Alabama and South Carolina, require postelection disclosure only.

[2] Under the Supreme Court's *Buckley* ruling (1976), expenditure limits are unconstitutional unless tied to acceptance of public funds. Four states, Michigan, Minnesota, New Jersey, and Wisconsin, have expenditure limits that apply to candidates who accept public funds. Maryland suspended its public funding program with expenditure limits until January 1, 1986. Hawaii ties a contributor's income tax deduction to the candidate's acceptance of expenditure limits.

[3] All the states listed have enacted laws providing for public funding of election campaigns, but in 1981 Oregon's experimental law was not renewed; in 1982 Maryland suspended its public funding program until 1986; and Oklahoma's law awaits amendment to make it conform to the state constitution.

[4] Maryland, Massachusetts, Montana, California, and Virginia have surcharge provisions.

[5] New Jersey enacted a state income tax after the subsidy program, which was applicable to the 1977 gubernatorial elections, became law. The new income tax system included a checkoff, but the 1977 funding was appropriated by the legislature.

[6] Some additional states that used to allow indirect tax deductions tied to the federal tax deduction no longer can do so because the tax deduction under federal law was repealed as of January 1, 1979. The federal tax credit for political contributions remains in force, but there is no indirect benefit for a taxpayer paying state income tax based on the federal system.

SOURCES: Based on data as of July 1979, combined from: *Analysis of Federal and State Campaign Finance Law: Summaries and Quick Reference Charts*, prepared for the Federal Election Commission by the American Law Division of the Congressional Research Service, Library of Congress, Washington, D.C. (December 1977); *The Book of the States, 1976-1977*, XXI (Lexington, Ky.: The Council of State Governments, 1976), 223-226; Karen Fling, ed. "A Summary of Campaign Practices Laws of the 50 States," *Campaign Practices Reports, Report 4* (Washington, D.C.: Plus Publications Inc., October 1978); *Federal-State Election Law Updates: An Analysis of State and Federal Legislation*, prepared for the Federal Election Commission by the American Law Division of the Congressional Research Service, Library of Congress, Washington, D.C. (December 1978).

Restrictions on Business and Labor

Numerous states prohibit direct corporate contributions, but fewer ban direct labor contributions. Twenty-four states restrict contributions by at least some corporations. Some states, for example, restrict campaign contributions by government contractors, but not by other corporations. West Virginia prohibits state contractors from contributing to political candidates, committees, or parties during a contract negotiation period. Oregon bars contributions from most public businesses, such as banks, utilities, and common carriers, as well as companies that can condemn or take land. Others states exclude heavily regulated industries, such as public utilities, banks, and insurance companies, but other corporations may contribute. Seven states—Delaware, Florida, Indiana, Maine, Maryland, Mississippi, and New York—and the District of Columbia permit corporations to contribute but set limits on the amounts they can give.

Although federal law treats corporations and unions alike by prohibiting contributions from either, only 10 states restrict labor union contributions to campaigns. The 10 states are Arizona, Connecticut, New Hampshire, North Carolina, North Dakota, Pennsylvania, South Dakota, Texas, Wisconsin, and Wyoming.[4]

But most states, including those that prohibit direct corporate contributions, now permit corporations and unions to form political action committees that can seek voluntary contributions from employees, stockholders, and members. In recent years business, industry, and trade association PACs have proliferated at the state level as they have at the federal level. Many states limit the amount PACs can donate to candidates, but in 1983 Montana became the first state to place a ceiling on the aggregate amount of money candidates for state legislative office may receive from PACs: $600 from all PACs for House candidates and $1,000 for Senate candidates. This limit is very low, and other states considering such legislation have proposed higher aggregate limits, up to as much as $25,000 from all PACs. The Montana legislation does not apply to gubernatorial candidates. The Montana experience and that of states that may follow suit might provide a means of testing a legislative initiative that has been proposed at the federal level, as noted in Chapter 4, but thus far without enactment.

In the past, corporate and union contributions-in-kind, such as the free provision of office space or furniture or the lending of a car to a candidate, often were not accounted for. Now federal law and most state disclosure provisions consider contributions-in-kind and loans as gifts that must be reported with reasonable estimates of value received, and the value must be within contribution limits where they exist.

In several states, corporations and unions were restricted in their contributions to ballot initiative campaigns, a logical extension of the limits on such contributions to candidates. But in 1978 the U.S. Supreme Court declared unconstitutional a Massachusetts law prohibiting corporations from spending any money to influence the outcomes of ballot issues that did not pertain directly to the corporations' business. This decision in *First National Bank of Boston v. Bellotti* was followed by a U.S. District Court action ruling unconstitutional Florida's state law preventing corporations from spending more than $3,000 on ballot initiatives. In December 1981 the U.S. Supreme Court struck down a Berkeley, California municipal ordinance that limited to $250 the amount an individual or corporation was permitted to contribute to a committee supporting or opposing a ballot measure. One result of these decisions may be greater business involvement in ballot referendum and initiative elections.[5]

Improper Influence

The extent to which campaign contributions are received with expressed or tacit obligations regarding policy, jobs, or contracts cannot be measured, but undoubtedly it is greater at the state and local levels than at the federal level. In many places systematic solicitation of those who benefit from the system occurs.

In Indiana, for example, the Two Percent Club, composed of certain government employees who are assessed 2 percent of their salaries, continues to be a formal basis of financing the party in power.[6] There also have been clear cases of extortion or conspiracy to obtain campaign money in return for favors or preferment. In New Jersey a former Democratic secretary of state was convicted in May 1972 on federal charges of bribery and extortion in seeking $10,000 in political contributions from a company that sought a contract to build a bridge. His successor, a Republican, similarly was indicted and convicted in October of the same year for extorting $10,000 for the state Republican party in return for attempting to fix the awarding of a state highway construction contract. Clearly, corruption crosses party lines.[7]

Another example of the malignant links that can develop between money and politics is the case of former vice president Spiro Agnew. Routine investigations of corruption in Baltimore County, where Agnew had been county executive, led to his grand jury indictment for alleged bribery, extortion, and tax fraud. Witnesses testified that Agnew had pocketed more than $100,000 by using his political office to hand out county and state contracts in exchange for personal payoffs from seven engineering firms and one financial institution. Agnew's resignation from the vice presidency in 1973 was one of the conditions of a plea bargaining agreement, under which he pleaded no contest to a single count of tax evasion.[8]

Criminal Funds

The amount of political money supplied by criminal elements is a subject on which there is little information. Part of the problem is the difficulty in distinguishing campaign gifts from other exchanges of money.

Three decades ago, the Second Interim Report of the Special Senate Committee to Investigate Organized Crime in Interstate Commerce (the so-called Kefauver committee) concluded that one form of "corruption and connivance with organized crime in state and local government" consisted of "contributions to the campaign funds of candidates for political office at various levels by organized criminals. . . ." According to the Kefauver committee, "Not infrequently, contributions are made to both major political parties, gangsters operate on both sides of the street." [9] Little has changed to revise this description.

Unfortunately, the extent of such activity is still unknown. Some scholars have estimated that perhaps 15 percent of the money for state and local campaigns is derived from the underworld.[10] Excluding the federal level where the incidence of such behavior is presumed to be low, this would mean that about $70 million might have come from criminal elements in 1980. If such money is indeed concentrated in nonfederal campaigns, there is special reason to study legislation at the state and local levels designed to regulate such behavior.

Bipartisan Election Commissions

The states vary in their systems of election administration. Thirty states have bipartisan, independent commissions that oversee elections. In most states the governor appoints the commission members. In others, such as Michigan, the secretary of state has administrative enforcement responsibility. In Delaware, Massachusetts, and Montana a single officer is appointed instead of a commission.

The commissions represent an attempt to isolate from political pressures the functions of receiving, auditing, tabulating, publicizing, and preserving the reports of campaign receipts and expenditures. The commissions usually have replaced partisan election officials, such as secretaries of state, who traditionally were repositories of campaign fund reports but whose partisanship as elected or appointed officials did not make them ideal administrators or enforcers of election law. Some commissions have strong powers, including the right to issue subpoenas and to assess penalties, powers that also are available for the administration and enforcement of contribution limits and of public funding in states providing it.

Budget and Legal Problems

Generally, the commissions receive and audit campaign contribution and expenditure reports, compile data, write and implement regulations, and give advisory opinions. They also conduct investigations that include auditing records. Because of the amount of paperwork handled and because of understaffing and underfinancing, most commissions must rely on complaints filed and on investigative newspaper reporting to detect violations. Recently, constraints on most states' budgets have required numerous state agencies, including many election commissions, to cut back their operations. In addition, the commissions have lost their novelty and glamour; after nearly 10 years of existence in some states, they no longer enjoy the level of popular support they once received.

Although independent bipartisan election commissions theoretically are insulated from political pressures, they face many constitutional and enforcement problems. The original method of choosing the Federal Election Commission was challenged successfully in *Buckley v. Valeo* on the ground that congressional appointments violated the constitutional separation of powers. Similarly, an Illinois court ruled that the manner of selection of the bipartisan State Board of Elections contravened the state constitutional prohibition against the legislative appointment of officers of the executive branch.[11] Members of the Illinois board were nominated by the majority and minority leaders of each house of the legislature; each leader nominated two persons, and the governor selected one of the two from each pair. But an Alaska court threw out a suit that contended the Democratic and Republican parties derived unwarranted statutory protection from a law requiring appointment to the state election board from lists submitted by the two parties.[12]

Enforcement

The line between outright bribery and campaign contributions may often be a thin one, but, where there is no accounting whatever of campaign funds or of sources of income, it is easy to rationalize that one was meant to be the other. Statutory disclosure brings at least some discipline to transactions involving money and elected public officials, and, if laws are enforced, even better discipline will result.

Some 30 states require candidates or public officials to disclose their personal finances, but definitions of ethics and conflict of interest are elusive, and laws regulating them can be as difficult to enforce as campaign laws. In some states, such as California, the same commission enforces both areas. Gray areas between compliance and noncompliance sometimes result in antagonisms on the part of state legislators who may work to undercut the administration of such laws. As a result, the responsible offices often exist under severe budget restrictions.

Because the state election commissions have only civil prosecutorial power, they must refer apparent criminal violations to appropriate enforcement officers—normally an attorney general or district attorney, who is a partisan official with discretion to pursue the referrals. Although these officials may be less well equipped than the commissions to deal with election violations because they are usually less well informed on the subject, there is no alternative to referring criminal violations to them.

Early in 1983 a number of campaign financing measures calling for partial public funding of state legislative campaigns and for contribution and expenditure limits were introduced in the California state legislature. Each of the measures would assign enforcement authority to the state attorney general rather than to the state's independent bipartisan election commission, the Fair Political Practices Commission. The proposals in this case indicate that the lawmakers feel more comfortable with election law oversight vested in a partisan officeholder rather than in an independent commission. That such proposals could be offered seriously may be an indication of the declining popularity of election commissions; 10 years ago such proposals would have had almost no chance of success. The erosion of support derives in part from unpopular decisions or enforcement actions such commissions have undertaken.

State Public Funding

Sixteen states provide some type of public financing of state election campaigns (Table 7-2).[13] The states' approaches to collecting and distributing the money vary widely. Funds are collected either by an income tax checkoff or an income tax surcharge procedure. The former permits taxpayers to earmark money, generally a dollar for a single taxpayer or two dollars if a joint return is filed. The money is diverted into a special political fund. If a surcharge is provided, the taxpayers may add a dollar or two to their tax liability; this system uses the tax system as a collection channel for political contributions, usually to a party. With either approach, funds are distributed by the states either to parties or to candidates, or to a combination of both. Taxpayers can designate the party they prefer in most states.

Until 1981, 17 states had forms of public funding, but on January 1 of that year the statutory authority for Oregon's experimental tax checkoff plan expired, and the state legislature chose not to renew it. In 1982 Maryland suspended its income tax surcharge provision and delayed implementation of public funding until January 1, 1986. Oklahoma's Campaign Finance Act, providing for public funding of both candidates and political parties, became effective on January 1, 1980, but has not been operative since its enactment. The state attorney general ruled that some provisions of the act violated the state constitution, and the law awaits amendment by the state legislature. In 1982 California and Virginia undertook surcharge programs, to be noted below.

Tax Checkoff

Of the 19 states that have passed laws that allow taxpayers to make political contributions by using checkoff or surcharge procedures, 13 have used an income tax checkoff provision similar to that of the federal government; 12 are currently using checkoffs. Taxpayer participation in using the income tax checkoff varies by state. Although the checkoff system does not increase tax liability or decrease the amount of the tax refund, participation is relatively low; for election year 1980 (tax year 1979), it ranged from 41 percent in New Jersey to 7.5 percent in North Carolina. The average participation rate is about 20 percent, somewhat below the rate for participation in the federal system.

Tax Surcharge

Six states—Maine, Maryland, Massachusetts, Montana, California, and Virginia—have an income tax surcharge provision. The surcharge in Maine adds to the tax liability a $1 contribution to the party designated; alternatively, $1 of the tax refund may be stipulated for a specific political party.

In Massachusetts, the $1 contribution goes into a general fund for statewide candidates to be distributed on a matching basis. In Maryland, a

Table 7-2   Public Financing of State Elections

Year First Bill on Public Financing Was Passed	States	Years in Which Public Monies Have Been Allocated to Parties/Candidates
1973	Iowa	1974-1982
1973	Maine[1]	1974-1982
1973	Rhode Island	1974-1982
1973	Utah	1975-1982
1974	Maryland[1][2]	——
1974	Minnesota	1976, 1978, 1980-1982
1974	New Jersey	1977, 1981
1975	Idaho	1976-1980
1975	Massachusetts[1]	1978, 1982
1975	Montana[3]	1976-1980
1975	North Carolina	1977-1982
1976	Kentucky	1977-1982
1976	Michigan	1978, 1982
1977	Oregon[4]	1978-1980
1977	Wisconsin	1978, 1980, 1982
1978	Hawaii	1980, 1982
1978	Oklahoma[5]	——
1982	California[1]	——
1982	Virginia[1]	——

[1] States with tax add-ons; all others have tax checkoffs.
[2] In 1982 Maryland suspended its income tax donation provision and delayed implementation of public funding until January 1, 1986.
[3] In 1979 Montana switched from a tax checkoff to a tax add-on system.
[4] Oregon's experimental tax checkoff plan expired on January 1, 1982, and was not renewed by the state legislature.
[5] Oklahoma's Campaign Finance Act became effective on January 1, 1980, but has not been operative since its enactment. The state attorney general ruled that some of its provisions violated the state constitution, and the act awaits amendment by the state legislature.

SOURCE: Ruth S. Jones, "State Public Financing and the State Parties," in *Parties, Interest Groups and Campaign Finance Laws,* ed. Michael Malbin, (Washington, D.C.: American Enterprise Institute, 1976); and Citizens' Research Foundation update.

$2 contribution may be designated for a general campaign fund from which money is distributed to qualified candidates on a matching basis. Montana, in 1979, switched from a checkoff to a surcharge system and other states also are considering changes.

The California income tax add-on procedure is somewhat different from that used in the other four states. Effective January 1, 1983, individual taxpayers have been able to contribute $1, $5, $10, or $25 to the California Election Campaign Fund by adding the amount to their income tax liability and designating the party to receive the donation. Such contributions are not tax deductible, and the individuals using the procedure must lawfully be able to make contributions to qualified political parties in California.

Virginia's tax add-on system also is unique. Only state taxpayers due to receive a refund may participate, by designating $2 of their refunds for use by the state central committee of either the Republican or Democratic parties.

The surcharge participation rate is considerably lower than that of the checkoff system. For the tax year 1979, in Maine, only .5 percent of the taxpayers participated; in Maryland, 2.5 percent; in Massachusetts, 2.8 percent. In Maryland, the payout to candidates had been planned for 1978 but was postponed first until 1982 and then until 1986, because the available funds were inadequate.

Distribution of Funds: To Political Parties

Nine states distribute public funds to political parties.[14] The restrictions on political party use of public funds differ by state. In Idaho, for example, the parties are restricted to using the money for qualified general election expenses, but primary election use is prohibited. In Rhode Island the parties may use the money for administrative costs. In North Carolina the money goes from the parties to specified general election candidates only. In Iowa the money may not be used for primary elections and cannot go to federal candidates if they receive public subsidy. In Utah the money must be proportionally divided among state and county party central committees.

Unlike at the federal level, taxpayers in 10 states may designate the recipient political party. In Minnesota, although taxpayers may check off funds for designated political parties, the parties do not handle the funds. Instead the party-designated money is distributed by the state under a quota system directly to party candidates according to the number of party checkoffs.

In six of the nine states in which parties do handle taxpayer-designated checkoff or add-on funds and in which funds have been distributed, the Democratic party received more funds in 1980 than the Republicans, as shown by the data in Table 7-3. In Rhode Island, the ratio was approximately 3-to-1 in favor of the Democrats; in North Carolina, Kentucky, and Oregon (for 1979), it was almost 2-to-1. Utah, Iowa, and

Table 7-3 Distribution of State Checkoff and Add-on Funds to Political
Parties, 1980[1]

	Taxpayer[2] *Participation Rate*	*Democrats*	*Republicans*	*Other*
Idaho	16.9%	$ 21,103	$ 21,856	$ 2,160[3]
Iowa	16.0	113,930	128,231	——
Kentucky	14.4	143,222	71,225	——
Maine (surcharge)	.5	1,777	1,463	——
Minnesota[4]	18.1	332,394	258,748	13,962[5]
North Carolina	7.5	131,123	65,817	[6]
Oregon (expired)	18.0[7]	152,000	88,000	10,345
Rhode Island	22.0	85,099	30,135	264
Utah	27.5	52,656	98,751	10,133

[1] Beginning in 1983 California and Virginia allowed taxpayers to use an income tax add-on procedure to designate funds for political parties, but data on the initial results of the programs are incomplete. Oklahoma distributes tax checkoff funds to political parties according to a formula established by law. Taxpayers may not designate party recipients.
[2] The states differ in the base used to determine the percentage of taxpayer participation. Iowa, Kentucky, Maine, North Carolina, and Rhode Island figures are based on the total number of individual taxpayers. Idaho, Oregon, and Utah figures are based on the total number of tax returns.
[3] Idaho's general campaign fund, comprised of money not designated by taxpayers for specified parties, received $25,972.
[4] Minnesota allows taxpayers to check off income tax funds for designated political parties but distributes the funds directly to party candidates according to the number of party checkoffs.
[5] In addition, $198,028 was not designated by taxpayers for any specified political party.
[6] In addition, $44,843 was not designated by taxpayers for any specified political party.
[7] Percentage cited for tax year 1978; corresponding distribution amounts estimated for calendar year 1979.

Idaho are the only states in which the Republican party has received more checkoffs than the Democratic party, and in Maine Democrats were favored slightly.

The Democratic edge has caused some observers to express concern about the implications of the system for Republican state parties. They worry that "the strong will get stronger and the weak weaker," leading to one party dominating a state. Yet in Iowa and Idaho the amount checked off for the Republican party suddenly surged ahead of those for the Democratic party in tax year 1979, reversing a trend of the 1970s. In Rhode Island, Minnesota, and Idaho, suits against the checkoffs claimed that the distributions were discriminatory and unconstitutional. In Idaho the suit was dismissed; in Minnesota the court upheld the constitutionality of the checkoff law but required some changes that were made subsequently. In Rhode Island the court determined that the party could not use checkoff funds in favor of an endorsed primary candidate.[15]

In a study of state public campaign financing published in 1980, Ruth S. Jones concluded that, despite some 10 years of experience with the policy, much more systematic analysis and observation will be required in order to understand its consequences.[16] "The relative advantages to majority and minority party organizations and candidates that may follow from different public finance policies," she suggested, "are not immediately apparent." [17] In systems in which funds are collected by party designation and allotted to party organizations, for example, it may appear that the majority party will enjoy an undeniable advantage. But if, as Jones points out, challengers— usually of the minority party—receive more benefit from campaign expenditures than incumbents and if new money is made available through a public financing program to help party organizations revitalize or rebuild themselves, then it appears that any public funding may be more beneficial to the minority party than to the majority party.

In an earlier study, Jones found that in several states where parties used subsidies to hire staff and pay rent "public funds have apparently had a great impact. . . . [S]taff is viewed by most party leaders as the key to expanding the influence and status of the party." [18] She also concluded that those states that distribute public funds to political parties tend to strengthen the party, while those states that disburse public money to candidates tend to weaken the party. Ironically, the states with strong party systems tend to give public funds to candidates, whereas the weak-party states tend to channel public money to the parties.[19]

Distribution of Funds: To Candidates

Seven states—Hawaii, Maryland, Massachusetts, Michigan, New Jersey, Oklahoma, and Wisconsin—distribute money from the public fund directly to candidates. The special case of Minnesota has been described. The states that support candidates with public funds usually do so on a matching incentive basis, and the programs that support candidates with public funds vary, from Hawaii, which provides partial public financing to candidates for a wide variety of state and local offices, to Michigan and New Jersey, which provide public financing for gubernatorial candidates only. The latter two states also provide the most generous level of public funding for election campaigns. In Michigan qualified primary candidates may receive up to $660,000 on a matching basis, and major party general election candidates receive $750,000 in public grants and may raise an additional $250,000 from private sources. Candidates who accept public funds must abide by a $1 million spending limit in both primary and general election campaigns. A complex formula determines the amount of public funds qualified minor party gubernatorial candidates may receive in primary and general election campaigns.

In New Jersey the maximum amount qualified primary candidates may receive in public funds is 20 cents for each voter in the previous presidential election. Based on the number of voters in the 1980 election, the amount was approximately $600,000. The maximum amount a candidate may receive in public funds for the general election is 40 cents per voter, which amounts to about $1.2 million based on the 1980 voter tally. Candidates accepting public funds must abide by expenditure limits that also are based on the number of voters in the previous presidential election. The New Jersey Election Law Enforcement Commission has recommended that the expenditure limits be repealed. The New Jersey experience suggests that spending limits give an advantage to well-known candidates and reduce campaign flexibility, squeezing campaign expenditures for candidates who need to spend more.

Implications of Public Funding

Although public subsidies in campaigns provoke many arguments, scant attention has been paid to the implications that the various state plans have for the political system in general and the two-party system in particular. Questions of fairness, cost, administration, and enforcement need to be asked, assumptions challenged, and an understanding developed of the conditions that ought to be met if subsidies are to be provided. Public financing is not a panacea, and it will bring fundamental changes in the political structure and electoral processes.

Criteria

The main questions raised about public funding are who should receive the subsidy and how and when should it be made. The goal of government subsidization is to help serious candidates. A subsidy system should be flexible enough to permit those in power to be challenged. It should not, however, support candidates who merely are seeking free publicity, and it should not attract so many candidates that the electoral process is degraded. Accordingly, the most difficult policy problems in working out fair subsidies are definitional. How does one define major and minor parties and distinguish between serious and frivolous candidates without doing violence to equality of opportunity or to "equal protection" under the federal or state constitutions? Some parameters must be selected, even if the standards are arbitrary. A certain number of signed petitions or of small contributions, indicating a base of support, can be used to identify a legitimate candidate.

Although it is desirable to increase competition in the electoral arena, there are certain related considerations. One is whether the provisions of government funding can induce two-party competition in predominantly one-party areas by providing funding to minority party candidates. Even with public funding, competition may be extremely hard to stimulate. Another consideration is whether public funding will strengthen the political parties and, if so, whether that is desirable. Still another question is whether government domination of the electoral process will follow government funding.

As the states establish systems of public financing, more people will become concerned about the cost of electing large numbers of officials—a hallmark of this country's political system. In the United States, almost 500,000 public officials are elected over a four-year cycle. Long ballots require candidates to spend money in the mere quest for visibility, and the long ballot and frequent elections combined bring both voter fatigue and low turnout. In New Jersey there are statewide elections at least every six months because the gubernatorial and state legislative campaigns are held in odd-numbered years. New Jersey, however, elects only one statewide public official—the governor—and then lets him appoint the rest. As financial pressures mount, other states may give increasing consideration to reducing the number of elective offices, thus diminishing the amounts of money (whether public or private) needed to sustain the electoral system.

Impact on Parties

When money is given directly to candidates, public funding could accelerate the trend toward candidate independence and further diminish the role of the two major parties. With government funding available and made doubly attractive by limits on private contributions, the candidate's need to rely on party identification is lessened greatly. Supported even partially with government funds, candidates are less beholden to their parties. Although traditionally the parties have not provided much money to candidates, they have eased fund raising by opening access to party workers for volunteer help and to contributors for money. Thus as their obligations to the party are reduced, candidates may become even more independent.

At the least, one can speculate that candidate subsidies will lead to more independence in legislatures and an erosion of party loyalty. A legislator who ignored the demands of the leadership would not be fearful of being frozen out of a reelection bid or denied adequate funds because government would provide at least partial funding. To avoid splintering legislatures and maintain party strength, if policy makers decide that strengthening political parties is desirable, candidate funding—at least in the general election period—could be channeled through the parties.[20]

In a study of the operation and impact of states' experiments with income tax checkoffs to provide political campaign funds, government researcher Jack L. Noragon found some encouraging signs.[21] He noted that the experiments have given a more secure position to the concept that the machinery of government can be used to facilitate the voluntary financial participation of the citizenry in the electoral process. He cited the fact that some states have taken significant steps toward providing near-complete financing of gubernatorial campaigns with a combination of private seed money and public funds. And he observed that

> about a half-dozen states are revitalizing their state and local party apparatuses, which holds out the hope that the election role of political parties may be enhanced, thus balancing the "cult of personality" that has become so apparent in today's election contests.[22]

State Tax Incentives

To the extent that campaigns are financed with public funds, the role of large contributors and special interests is reduced. Where there is less emphasis on private money, there is theoretically less chance for corruption or favoritism. Because it also is desirable to encourage large numbers of people to participate in politics by contributing small sums, the federal government and 17 states provide some form of indirect public support. Of the 41 states that impose an income tax, 14 offer a tax deduction for political donations, usually a deduction from gross income for contributions up to $100. Idaho, Minnesota, Oregon, and the Distirct of Columbia offer tax credits, most of them for one-half the amount of contributions up to a maximum credit of $10. The tax credit provides greater incentive to contribute because it visibly reduces the amount of taxes paid, whereas the deduction simply reduces the amount of income subject to taxation.

Alaska formerly offered an income tax credit, but in 1980 the state legislature repealed the state income tax retroactive to January 1, 1979. The legislature, however, retained a form of tax credit of up to $50 for qualified political donations, offering contributors a cash refund instead of reducing tax liability. As of January 1, 1981, the maximum reimbursable political contribution was raised to $100 for claims representing donations made.

Other forms of direct or indirect government assistance can be suggested. Rather than provide money, governments can supply services that relieve parties and candidates of the need for certain expenditures. Some state governments, for example, provide campaign help through the assumption of greater responsibilities for registration of voters, distribution of voter information pamphlets, and election day activities. Moreover, public funding can help meet the transition costs between election day and inauguration day for the governor-elect.[23]

Among the most important of such services would be government-sponsored universal voter registration. This would reduce the substantial cost to political parties and candidates of performing an essentially public function and would reduce dependence on special interests for their registration activities. Such assistance would, furthermore, be likely to increase voting participation in a nation having complex registration requirements and a highly mobile population.

Testing New Concepts

Some states have been more experimental than the federal government in dealing with public funding, and the results of their pioneering may affect development of federal electoral regulation policy in the future. Until recent years it had been mostly the other way around, with the evolution of federal reforms influencing the adoption of similar changes in the states.

Nine states currently states distribute public funds to political parties and, like the federal government, eight states distribute the money directly to candidates. In the states where taxpayers can specify which party they want to help, the Democrats generally have received more money than the Republicans. But preliminary studies indicate that, Democratic or Republican, the parties are strengthened where public funds are channeled through them—a development that some electoral reformers feel is needed to restore some of the vitality that parties have lost as an intended or unintended result of the vast changes in the American political system.

Notes

1. *Socialist Workers Party v. Jennings,* Civ. No. 74-1328 (D.D.C.).
2. *Buckley v. Valeo,* 424 U.S. at 68.
3. *FEC Record,* March 1977, 6.
4. Wisconsin permits contributions from unions incorporated prior to January 1, 1978.
5. See Karen J. Fling, "The States as Laboratories of Reform," in *Political Finance,* ed. Herbert E. Alexander (Beverly Hills: Sage Publications, 1979). See also the two Supreme Court cases: *First National Bank of Boston v. Bellotti,* 435 U.S. 765 (1978); and *Citizens Against Rent Control v. City of Berkeley,* 454 U.S. 290 (1981).
6. Robert J. McNeill, *Democratic Campaign Financing in Indiana, 1964* (Bloomington, Ind., and Princeton, N.J.: Institute of Public Administration at Indiana University and Citizens' Research Foundation, 1966) 15-19, 35-40.
7. For a discussion of these New Jersey and other state cases, see George Amick, *The American Way of Graft* (Princeton, N.J.: The Center for Analysis of Public Issues, 1976).
8. See *United States v. Spiro T. Agnew,* Crim. A. No. 73-0535, U.S. District Court, District of Maryland, October 10, 1973.
9. *Second Interim Report of the Special Senate Committee to Investigate Organized Crime in Interstate Commerce,* 82d Cong., 1st sess., Report No. 141, 1.
10. According to Alexander Heard, this estimate "embraces funds given in small towns and rural areas by individuals operating on the borders of the law who want a sympathetic sheriff and prosecutor, but who are not linked to crime syndicates. The estimate applies chiefly to persons engaged in illegal gambling and racketeering. It does not extend, for example, to otherwise reputable businessmen who hope for understanding treatment from building inspectors and tax assessors." Alexander Heard, *The Costs of Democracy* (Chapel Hill, N.C.: University of North Carolina Press, 1960) 164, n 73; 154-168; also see Harold Lasswell and Arnold A. Rogow, *Power, Corruption and Rectitude* (Englewood Cliffs, N.J.: Prentice-Hall, 1963) 79-80; and Donald R. Cressey, *Theft of the Nation: The Structure and Operations of Organized Crime in America* (New York: Harper & Row, 1969) 253.
11. *Walker v. State Board of Elections,* Illinois Circuit Court, 7th Judicial Circuit, No. 364-75 (1975).
12. *Abramczyk v. State of Alaska,* Superior Court, 3d Judicial Circuit, No. 72-6426 (1975).
13. For a more detailed analysis of public funding in the states, see Herbert E. Alexander and Jennifer W. Frutig, *Public Financing of State Elections* (Los Angeles: Citizens' Research Foundation, 1982); Ruth S. Jones, "State Public Campaign Finance: Implications for Partisan Politics," *American Journal of Political Science,* 25 (May 1981): 342-361; Jack L. Noragon, "Political Finance and Political Reform: The Experience With State Income Tax Checkoffs," *American Political Science Review,* 75 (September 1981): 667-

687. For case studies and evaluations of two successive experiences with public funding in gubernatorial elections in New Jersey, see *Public Financing in New Jersey: The 1977 General Election for Governor* (Trenton: New Jersey Election Law Enforcement Commission, August 1978) and *New Jersey Public Financing: 1981 Gubernatorial Elections* (Trenton: New Jersey Election Law Enforcement Commission, June 1982).

14. The nine states that distribute funds to political parties are Iowa, Maine, Rhode Island, Utah, Idaho, North Carolina, Kentucky, California, and Virginia. Oregon and Oklahoma were in this group when their programs were enacted.

15. See unpublished paper by James R. Klonoski and Ann Aiken, "The Constitutional Law of Political Parties and the Emergent Dollar Checkoff," University of Oregon School of Law.

16. Jones, "State Public Campaign Finance."

17. Ibid., 361.

18. Ruth S. Jones, "State Public Financing and the State Parties," prepared for the Conference on Parties, Interest Groups and Campaign Finance Laws, September 4-5, 1979, in *Parties, Interest Groups, and Campaign Finance Laws*, ed. Michael J. Malbin (Washington, D.C.: American Enterprise Institute for Public Policy Research, 1979), 296.

19. Jones, "State Public Financing," 303.

20. There is extensive literature on party responsibility. Among the more recent books and articles see *Party Renewal in America: Theory and Practice,* ed. Gerald M. Pomper (New York: Praeger Publishers, 1980); Joel L. Fleishman, *The Future of American Political Parties* (Englewood Cliffs, N.J.: Prentice-Hall, 1982); Austin Ranney, *Curing the Mischief of Faction: Party Reform in America* (Berkeley: University of California Press, 1975); and Herbert E. Alexander, "The Impact of Election Reform Legislation on the Political Party System," (Paper prepared for the annual meeting of the American Political Science Association, San Francisco, California, September 5, 1975. For earlier literature, see Herbert E. Alexander, *Responsibility in Party Finance* (Princeton, N.J.: Citizens' Research Foundation, 1963).

21. Noragon, "Political Finance and Political Reform."

22. Ibid., 686.

23. For a complete discussion of proposals, see Herbert E. Alexander, *Regulation of Political Finance* (Berkeley and Princeton: Institute of Governmental Studies, University of California, and Citizens' Research Foundation, 1966), 16-36.

Past Reform and Future Directions 8

Following the 1982 elections, concern intensified about the high costs of election campaigns at all levels. Richard Schweicker, a former representative and senator from Pennsylvania and former secretary of health and human services in the Reagan administration, summed up the anxieties of many campaign cost critics in a mid-1983 interview. "The cost of campaigning is just out of sight," he said. "It distorts the process." [1] Schweicker, like other critics, decried what he perceived as the increasing dependence of candidates on their own money or on PACs. "More and more when the big campaign bills come in, a Congressman or Senator has to go to one of two sources—either to his own personal wealth or total PAC funding," he maintained. "Neither one, when you're talking big bucks, is really a good answer." [2] Schweicker blamed "single-focus groups," which provide campaign money, for making it more difficult to arrive at legislative consensus. [3]

Reform Proposals

Concern over high campaign costs has been translated into proposals for remedy. Early in 1983, for example, Common Cause attempted to persuade the 98th Congress to pass legislation that would establish a congressional public finance program and reduce the financial role of PACs in election campaigns. [4] Late in 1982 and again in 1983, such legislation was introduced in the House. The so-called Clean Campaign Act of 1983 would limit the aggregate amount candidates could accept from PACs, provide public matching funds for House races, and establish an expenditure limit for candidates accepting the public funds. The legislation also would limit personal and immediate family expenditures.

It may be a measure of the persistence of congressional public funding advocates that they have continued to champion their proposals throughout a period of severe budgetary constraints and unprecedented federal deficits. Although supporting a program that would require expenditure of additional federal funds might appear ill advised in the midst of adverse economic conditions, public funding advocates argue that allowing the current campaign funding system to continue would be even more costly because, they believe, special interests influence members of Congress in very expensive ways. One way is to trigger legislation that provides government subsidies for special interests. Another is to place obstacles in the path of legislation unfavorable to special interests, resulting in revenue loss for the Treasury. In the latter case, for example, financial institutions, particularly banks, defeated a measure that would have required tax withholding of interest payments. "Veto groups"—through direct contributions, campaigns to influence public opinion, and lobbying members of Congress—often are able to stop legislation they oppose.

Public Opinion

Since it was first considered by the Senate in July 1973, the issue of public financing of congressional campaigns has been debated and defeated in Congress three times.[5] Although advocates of congressional public financing have laid claim to considerable popular support for the proposal, the results of public opinion polls on the matter have been mixed at best. For example, in a major national survey in 1977, pollster Louis Harris told respondents that President Carter had proposed that all House and Senate primary and general election campaigns be "publicly financed, as presidential primaries and elections are now financed."[6] When asked their opinions of this proposal, the respondents overwhelmingly supported the idea, with 49 percent in favor and 28 percent opposed. In 1977 and 1979 Gallup polls arrived at similar findings. The Gallup Poll asked, "It has been suggested the government provide a fixed amount of money for the election campaigns of candidates for Congress and that all private contributions from other sources be prohibited. Do you think this is a good idea or a poor idea?"[7] In 1977, 57 percent of the respondents approved of public funding of congressional campaigns and 32 percent disapproved.

The conclusion that popular support existed for public financing of congressional campaigns appeared well substantiated until Harris reworded his survey question in January 1980. This time Harris asked respondents if they would approve of having "all federal elections financed out of public funds contributed by taxpayers." [8] The respondents were overwhelmingly opposed. Only 39 percent supported public funding when the proposal was worded in this manner compared with 58 percent who disapproved. The negative response probably was generated by the phrase "contributed by taxpayers" and by considerations of fiscal restraint. Although public funds for election campaigns have always been paid out of tax dollars, the latter description may have carried a negative connotation that influenced the survey's results.

Just as emotive words may have influenced the 1980 poll results, wording may also have affected the results of the earlier surveys. The 1977 Harris poll told respondents that President Carter had endorsed the plan. Carter's popularity, which was high at the time, may have helped increase the favorable response rate. Similarly, the Gallup polls asked the respondents if they liked a system that prohibits all private contributions. If "private contributions" had a negative connotation, that wording choice may have affected the outcome.

Civic Service Polls. A St. Louis-based survey research group, Civic Service, has been tracking national public opinion since 1977 on assorted political issues, particularly public financing. These surveys, worded differently from the earlier Harris and Gallup polls, produced different results. Civic Service respondents expressed consistent and resounding disapproval toward public financing. A 1978 survey drawn from a nationwide sample found that a majority of those polled agreed that changes were needed in the electoral campaign system, but only 4 percent supported public financing of all federal elections. [9]

The results of the Civic Service polls of February 1980, March 1981, and March 1982 were not much different. [10] The benchmark question in all of the surveys remained constant: "It has been proposed in Congress that the federal government provide public financing for congressional campaigns for the U.S. House of Representatives and Senate. Would you approve or disapprove of the proposal to use public funds, federal money, to pay the costs of congressional campaigns and how strongly do you feel?" The March 1982 poll showed that 4.2 percent of respondents strongly approved, 21.2 percent approved, 36.9 percent disapproved, 28.3 percent strongly disapproved, and 9.4 percent expressed no opinion.

The 1982 findings conform within a small range to the Civic Service surveys conducted in the previous five years. Various degrees of approval for public financing of congressional campaigns were registered by 25.4 percent of the 1982 sample. Disapproval was indicated to some degree by

65.2 percent. Further, in the survey results throughout the period, opposition to public financing of congressional campaigns dominated every subgroup in the sample.

Presidential Campaigns. The 1981 and 1982 Civic Service polls discovered that the disapproval of publicly financed congressional campaigns expressed by most of their respondents also extended to presidential campaign financing. By more than a two-to-one margin respondents disapproved of the existing public funding system for the presidential general election. Upon evaluating alternatives, most respondents favored returning to the system of private contributions. Substantial support was indicated, however, for maintaining the existing campaign contribution ceilings—perhaps because they think too much money is spent on elections.

Judging from the Civic Service survey results, the American public does not appear to be in the mood for any fundamental reforms of congressional campaign finance. There is overwhelming support for the voluntary system of campaign finance in both congressional campaigns and presidential general election campaigns. But the contradictory findings of the Harris and Gallup polls cannot be dismissed outright. Perhaps Americans are disturbed by the idea of using federal money to pay the costs of campaigns, but the Harris and Gallup polls suggest that public attitudes may be altered through the endorsement of an opinon leader or through the manner in which the proposal is made.

Harris Polls. Late in 1982 another poll by the Harris Survey showed results similar to those of 1980: 53 percent of the respondents opposed having all federal elections financed out of federal funds even if expenditure limits were strictly enforced.[11] Harris surveys conducted during the same period found that the majority of respondents considered excessive campaign spending a very serious problem and were suspicious about contributions to political campaigns by organized business and labor groups.[12] They were not bothered by candidates spending large amounts on their own campaigns—perhaps one reason they vote willingly for Rockefellers, Kennedys, and other wealthy candidates. Many respondents criticized political television commercials, and a great majority favored strictly limiting the amount that can be spent on such ads.[13]

The PAC Phenomenon. Recent proposals for election law reform differ from earlier proposals in that they intend to contain campaign costs by combining public funding with lower PAC contribution limits or limits on the total amount candidates might accept from PACs. Some of the problems of unduly restricting PAC growth or limiting their contributions were discussed in Chapter 4. Despite the abundant literature criticizing PACs, following the 1982 elections a revisionist, pro-PAC sentiment began to be expressed in a variety of publications.[14] In general, this literature has sought to clarify the values of diversity and increased participation that PACs have made possible in election campaign finance and to assess the degree of influence PACs have in electoral and legislative politics. According to the Harris Survey, public opinion regarding PACs is mixed. A majority of respondents to a late 1982 survey considered big business and labor union political action committees a bad influence on politics and government but viewed most ideological PACs with favor.[15] William Schneider suggests that people object not to PACs as such but to "self-serving interests." The public seems to include business and labor in that category, he writes, "but not 'causes' such as environmentalism, women's rights and conservatism." [16]

Expenditure Limits

One reason that critics of high campaign costs approve of public funding is that it provides the only constitutionally acceptable way, under the Supreme Court's 1976 *Buckley* ruling, of imposing campaign expenditure limits. But these expenditure limits create problems, and perhaps the major problem is finding a ceiling that is equitable to incumbents and challengers alike. If the ceiling is too high, candidates try to spend up to the limit. If it is too low, the limit tends to hurt challengers, who generally need to spend more money to become well known enough to compete against better known incumbents. In addition, as the 1980 presidential campaign experience demonstrates, expenditure limits tend to trigger independent expenditures and thus to diminish accountability for the uses of campaign money.

The New Jersey Experience. The New Jersey gubernatorial election in 1977, publicly funded for candidates who qualified, illustrates the problem of finding an equitable spending limit. Both major party candidates raised up to the maximum in private contributions (about $500,000 each) and received public funds (a little more than $1 million each) which brought them close to the spending limit ($1,518,576 each). This gave an advantage to the incumbent and eventual winner, Brendan Byrne, who, although burdened with responsibility for an unpopular state income tax, was better known. The limits worked to the disadvantage of his challenger, state senator Ray Bateman. When Bateman wanted to change strategies and revise campaign themes late in the campaign, he was unable to do so and still stay within the limit. The spending limit in this case rigidified the system. In general, spending limits give advantage to candidates who have celebrity status, the backing of superior party organization, or the ability to enlist volunteers.

After the 1977 election, a majority of New Jersey's election commission recommended continued limits on contributions and loans and a cap on the amount of public funds available to the candidates, but with no overall spending limit. This recommendation was passed by the New Jersey legislature, with the surprising support of New Jersey Common Cause, but was vetoed by Governor Byrne. The vetoed bill also would have extended public funding to primary campaigns for governor. The state legislature then passed an amended bill, which included expenditure limits, and Byrne signed it in July 1980.[17] Following the 1981 gubernatorial election, the New Jersey Election Law Enforcement Commission again recommended repealing the expenditure limits.[18]

Floors Without Ceilings. Although the *Buckley* decision ruled out spending limits without public funding, some supporters of public funding would like to try a different approach. They advocate public funding *floors* rather than spending limit *ceilings*. This concept is favored by many of the mature democracies in Western Europe, where government subsidies are given to political parties with no limits on receiving and spending private contributions. The idea is that partial public funding, or a floor, gives candidates at least minimal access to the electorate and provides alternative funds so that candidates can reject private contributions with expressed or tacit obligations attached. At the same time, if this approach were used in the United States, the absence of spending limits would avoid the constitutional issues raised in the *Buckley* case. Some modifications, however, probably would be required to make this system work in the United States, for in other countries subsidies are given not to candidates, but to political parties, based on their parliamentary strength, making for quite different systems.

Public Funding and Political Parties. Some proponents of public financing maintain that the money should be channeled to congressional candidates through the political parties. Among supporters of that proposal are members of the Committee on Party Renewal, a voluntary association of political scientists and practitioners whose goal is to strengthen U.S. political parties. There already has been some experience in funding nonfederal candidates through state or local party committees. That experience was summarized in Chapter 7.

At present, portions of the Federal Election Campaign Act work to separate the candidate from the party. Limits on party activity for and contributions to candidates are imposed concurrently with limits on individual or interest-group activity and contributions. According to proponents of party renewal, the parties should be unrestricted in their ability to help candidates. The greater the dependence of the candidate upon the party, they maintain, the greater the leverage the party has in the potential to withhold funds, the greater the chance to achieve some policy coherence and discipline among candidates on the ticket, the greater the potential to mobilize party majorities for policy votes in Congress, and the more national unity and cooperation there will be on issues. This, they point out, holds true both for the majority party and the minority party. Strengthening the parties could lead to more sharply defined policy and issue differences between them, which some consider desirable in a two-party system.[19]

Political scientist Gary Jacobson, however, cautions that as long as congressional incumbents can rely on sources of campaign support other than their national party committees, party renewal advocates should be careful not to overestimate the unity parties might be able to achieve.[20] That, he maintains, is the hard lesson labor supporters of congressional Democrats have learned. "When many Democrats elected in the early 1970s with heavy labor backing decided, with an eye to district voters, not to support legislation dear to labor," he writes, "they could do so in full knowledge that business and trade PACs could more than make up for the loss if labor money were withdrawn."[21] In fact, despite the generous assistance Republican national committees offered their candidates in 1980 and 1982, thus far there have been no visible efforts by the party to allocate funds to candidates in a disciplinary fashion, nor have any serious efforts been made by the party to gain influence over the selection of party whips in Congress.

Supporters of public funding through the parties contend that it would serve three desirable ends: 1) Public funding would give candidates an alternative funding source, enabling them to refuse special-interest or PAC gifts at their discretion. 2) Presuming the parties would be allowed to retain a percentage of the public funds to finance their federal election activities, such as voter registration and voter turnout, the new funding would enable them to strengthen both themselves and their relationships with their candidates. 3) Stronger political parties would have incentive to reform themselves, to be more issue oriented than job oriented, and to root out the corruption that has developed from time to time in the past.

The legacy of past abuses is opposition to strengthening the parties.

Early in the twentieth century parties were or were thought to be corrupt; they often were described as closed clubs dominated by a leader or a small clique, who designated party hacks as candidates for public office. According to some observers, state and local parties often continue to be bastions of the corrupt, holding governments in thrall to the politics of patronage and graft. For them, the proposed solution to provide public funding through the parties is unacceptable. Chapter 7 outlined the ways in which at least some states have channeled public funding through the parties.

1984 and Beyond

Despite the concern about high campaign costs demonstrated in current campaign finance reform proposals, there are several indications that the costs of running for public office, particularly for the presidency, will remain high. Ironically, some of the circumstances that may contribute to continued high costs are the result of efforts to increase grass-roots participation in the presidential selection process.

Hunt Commission

Following a mandate of the Democratic party's 1980 convention, DNC chairman Charles Manatt appointed a commission to examine the presidential selection process. The Commission on Presidential Nominations, chaired by Gov. James B. Hunt of North Carolina, conducted hearings throughout the nation and early in 1982 submitted its recommendations to the DNC. One suggestion accepted by the national committee was that the campaign calendar be shortened by requiring that all primaries and caucuses, except Iowa's and New Hampshire's, take place during a 13-week period between the second Tuesday in March and the second Tuesday in June. Under the new plan the Democratic Iowa caucuses were scheduled to start no earlier than 15 days before the beginning of the period, and the New Hampshire primary to be held no earlier than 7 days before.

In fact shortening the primary season put even greater emphasis on raising money early. In 1980 George Bush was able to capitalize on his surprise win in Iowa by using the five-week period before the New Hampshire primary to build up his campaign treasury. Under the Hunt Commission schedule, candidates had to be funded for both Iowa and New Hampshire in advance of the Iowa caucuses because the New Hampshire primary was only one week later. And if candidates did well in either of those contests, they might not have enough time to raise the money to see them through the next deluge of primaries and caucuses. The concentrated primary period would seem to give an immense advantage to candidates with ample funds to carry them through the early part of the primary season when the nominee might well be chosen.

Several suggestions were made to assist the lesser-known candidates, who generally have greater difficulty raising campaign funds. One remedy would be to double the amount of the individual contribution matchable by public funds from the current $250 to $500. Another suggestion was to offer qualified candidates a 2-for-1 match—two public dollars for every dollar raised privately—up to $250 from each individual contributor. Whatever method may be preferred, unless greater amounts of public funds are made available early in the primary season, the advantages enjoyed by front-runners will be augmented, and other candidates will have less opportunity to prove their popularity in later primaries. They simply will not have the money to survive the rapid succession of early contests.

Early Starts

On February 2, 1983, Sen. Alan Cranston of California formally announced his candidacy for the 1984 Democratic presidential nomination. By announcing so far in advance, Cranston continued a trend started by George McGovern in 1971, repeated by several Democratic candidates, including Jimmy Carter on December 12, 1974, and repeated once again by Republican candidates in 1978 and 1979. Three other Democratic candidates followed Cranston in announcing during February, and by April 21 the ranks of Democratic presidential contenders had reached six. In addition to Cranston, they included former vice president Walter Mondale, former Florida governor Reubin Askew, Sen. Gary Hart of Colorado, Sen. Ernest Hollings of South Carolina, and Sen. John Glenn of Ohio. These decisions to begin the formal, public side of the presidential campaigns many months before the party's nominating convention assured that costs of seeking the nomination would be correspondingly high.

Mondale followed the example of 1976 Republican candidates Reagan, Bush, Connally, and Dole and managed a head start of sorts over his Democratic rivals by establishing a political action committee that served as a shadow presidential committee for him during 1981 and 1982. As noted in Chapter 5, the money spent by Mondale's PAC, called the Committee for the Future of America, did not count against his overall or state expenditure limits once he announced his candidacy in February 1983. During the 1981-1982 election cycle, the PAC reported raising almost $2.2 million and spending a like amount.

Sen. Edward M. Kennedy established a similar PAC following the 1980 election when he was still thought to be a strong potential contender for the 1984 Democratic nomination. But following a successful Senate reelection campaign in 1982, Kennedy withdrew as a presidential candidate. His Fund for a Democratic Majority raised $2.3 million during the 1981-1982 election cycle and spent $2.2 million.

Straw Polls

In 1979 Republican and Democratic candidates and potential candidates for the presidency expended considerable energy and money trying to influence the outcome of straw polls conducted in a number of states late in the year. The polls were intended by state party officials to attract media attention and to energize rank-and-file party members. Candidates felt obliged to participate in them to persuade the media and the public that they commanded enough support to be considered serious candidates.

In 1983 the pattern was repeated, with the significant difference that straw polls were conducted even earlier in the preelection year, requiring greater expenditures of time and funds earlier than ever. By mid-1983 the Democrats already had conducted four such polls—at state party conventions in California, Massachusetts, and Wisconsin, and at a Young Democrats meeting in Alabama. Political scientist Thomas E. Mann suggests that the decision of the Hunt Commission to shorten the primary season may be responsible in part for increased emphasis on straw polls. As noted, that decision encouraged candidates to raise money and build organizations in 1983. "It heightened the tension of 1983 activities," said Mann, "because the candidates felt they had less time [in 1984] to do the things that needed to get done." [22]

The current system of presidential campaign funding takes account of increasing campaign costs in that the expenditure limits for publicly funded candidates are adjusted for inflation. For example, presidential prenomination candidates could spend up to $10.9 million each in 1976 and up to $14.7 million each in 1980—in both cases not counting the fund-raising overage of 20 percent or compliance costs. In 1984 the amount will reach about $19.6 million. But the contribution limits, which went into effect in 1975, have remained the same: $1,000 for individuals and $5,000 for PACs. In mid-1983 a $1,000 contribution, measured in 1975 dollars, was worth only about $530. Consequently, although candidates are allowed to spend higher amounts, the unchanging contribution limits make it increasingly difficult for them to meet rising costs.

Table 8-1   Federal Income Tax Checkoff

Tax Year	Approximate Percentages of Taxpayers Using Checkoff[1]	Approximate Amount[2]
1972[3]	7.0	$ 12,900,000
1973	13.6	17,300,000
1974	24.2	31,900,000
1975	25.8	33,700,000
Total available for 1976 presidential election (approx.)		95,900,000
Total payout to candidates and conventions		70,800,000
Total remaining after 1976 election		$ 25,100,000
1976	27.5	36,600,000
1977	28.6	39,200,000
1978	25.4	35,900,000
1979	27.4	38,800,000
Total available for 1980 presidential election (approx.)		$175,600,000
Total payout to candidates and conventions		100,600,000
Total remaining after 1980 election		$ 75,000,000
1980	28.7	41,000,000
Balance		$116,000,000

[1] Percentage figures are compiled by the IRS on the basis of fiscal years. Therefore they are not directly comparable to the tax-year dollar figures.

[2] Subject to minor discrepancies due to the unresolved status of some repayments and miscellaneous disbursements, as well as to rounding.

[3] In its first year, the tax checkoff form was separate from the 1040 form and was not readily available. In 1974 the tax checkoff form was included on the front page of the 1040 form. It also allowed taxpayers who had not checked off for 1972 to do so retroactively, for a total of $12.9 million.

SOURCE: Testimony of Thomas E. Harris before the Committee on Rules and Administration, U.S. Senate, *Federal Election Reform Proposals of 1977,*

Income Tax Checkoff

The success of public financing in the 1976 and 1980 presidential campaigns depended on taxpayers' willingness to earmark a small portion of their federal tax liabilities—$1 for individuals and $2 for married couples filing jointly—for the Presidential Election Campaign Fund. The tax checkoffs provided sufficient funds to cover the more than $100 million certified to 1980 presidential prenomination and general election candidates and to the major parties for their national nominating conventions. By the end of 1981, taxpayers had shown enough support for the tax checkoff to ensure adequate funds, including increases caused by a rise in the cost of living, for the 1984 payouts to eligible candidates and parties.

The extent of support for the program is indicated by the data in Table 8-1, which show both the approximate percentages of taxpayers using the checkoff and the amount checked off for each year since the program began in 1972. The number of persons using the checkoff rose significantly when, starting in 1974, the checkoff option was shown on the front page of the 1040 form.

About $176 million was available for the 1980 payout of $100 million. Including a carry-over of more than $75 million following the 1980 payout, the presidential campaign fund may be expected to have more than $200 million on hand to finance the 1984 presidential elections.

The Financial Future

A systemic condition exists in election campaign financing, but particularly in the financing of congressional campaigns. Candidates want to win. Campaign costs are high. There are only a limited number of local people who can or will give. So candidates start early to gear up their fund raising, based on where they think the money is.

When candidates are unable to finance a campaign adequately from constituents within a state or district, they seek funds from political action committees, political parties, lobbyists, out-of-staters, or, if possible, they spend their own funds. Another layer of sources is added when presidential candidates or party leaders, through their personal PACs, contribute to favored party candidates.

If the reasons for high campaign costs are clear, so are their consequences. The higher the costs, the more need for a candidate to raise money. The greater the concern about where the money comes from, the more concern there is about the public policy interests of groups that have the money or are willing to give it.

Campaign spending, however, should be considered the tuition the American people must spend for their education on the issues. Admittedly, many campaigns are not edifying, but, through all the political verbiage, issues are brought forward, and the nation determines its agenda. The people elected to office then determine public policies that affect all of us— an educational, if not always pleasing, process.

In every society in which free elections are held, someone has to incur expenses and someone has to pay the bills. But of our immense resources,

Americans are willing to spend only sparingly for politics. The personal contributions by candidates to their own campaigns, the debts they are willing to assume, the continual efforts to raise money, are ample testimony to the need for the allocation of more of our resources to politics.

Private Financing

Even with public financing in force for presidential elections and under consideration for congressional elections, a dependence on some forms of private financing is certain to continue. Improved solicitation and collection systems are essential if tax or matching incentives are to work effectively. The political party, of course, is one possible "collection agency." The party can go beyond merely funding party committees to financing its candidates' campaigns as well.

Other important collection systems include associational networks existing in membership groups. Labor unions, corporations, dairy cooperatives, trade associations, and professional groups can solicit for political funds effectively because of two characteristics: 1) they are made up of large groups of like-minded persons, and 2) they have ready-made channels for communicating with their members. Whether at meetings, through their people in the field, or even by mail, such groups possess internal and therefore inexpensive means of raising money to be used for political purposes.

Collection systems with bipartisan potential exist at places of employment. With safeguards (perhaps through the use of a neutral trusteeship program), even government employees could be asked on a nonpartisan basis to contribute. While such sources of funds may be controversial, their potential is immense if properly tapped.

Political scientist Carleton Sterling has criticized the political reformer for seeking ". . . a direct dialogue between candidates and voters both free of outside influences." [23] Politics devoid of the influence of interest groups is not realistic. Politics probably cannot be sterilized and purified to the degree that would satisfy the most zealous reformers. Politics is about people and groups of people, their ideas, interests, and aspirations. Because people seek political involvement partly through groups, a politics in which groups are shut out or seriously impaired is difficult to envision.

Government subsidies represent one alternative source of funds. But given the struggle to provide public funding at just the presidential level, private solicitation for campaigns at lower levels will be necessary in the indefinite future.

Participation as a Goal

If voting is the most important individual act in politics, then financial participation may be the second most important. Those who would replace private financing with total government funding might succeed unwittingly in changing fundamental balances in the political system. Critics who minimize individual efforts ignore history: a system of free elections cannot survive without voluntarism. In whatever form or quantity elections draw upon government assistance, freely contributed money and services still will be needed.

Success in attracting individuals to charitable giving has not been a matter of accident or a spontaneous result of general good will toward organizations with good causes. Rather, it reflects a serious effort to educate the public in its responsibilities and to organize collection systems. Political responsibilities must be similarly learned.

The value of contributing small sums for political activity is neither taught in schools nor widely understood as an act of good citizenship, although voting is both honored and respected, at least in principle. The challenge is to associate contributing with voting as an act of good citizenship, to upgrade and dignify political giving, and to gain for the popular financing of politics the public approval accorded voting.

The major changes in our political finance laws in the 1970s have not always resulted in systematic or consistent reform. One reason for this uneven progress is that various aspects of the problem have been dealt with separately and at different times by the major actors in government— Congress, the president, the Federal Election Commission, and the Supreme Court.

What the 1971 Federal Election Campaign Act, the 1974 Amendments, and many state laws have lacked has been a philosophy about regulation that is both constitutional and pragmatically designed to keep the election process open and flexible rather than rigid, exclusionary, and fragmented. It is not yet clear whether the 1976 and 1979 Amendments or the revision of state laws following *Buckley v. Valeo* will lead to the openness and flexibility a democratic and pluralistic society require.

Notes

1. Robert D. Hershey, Jr., "A Political Insider's New Views From the Outside," *New York Times,* June 21, 1983.

2. Ibid.
3. Recent literature criticizing high campaign costs abounds: see, for example, Elizabeth Drew, *Politics and Money: The New Road To Corruption* (New York: Macmillan, 1983); Mark Green, "Political PAC-Man," *New Republic*, December 13, 1982, 18-25; "Running With the PACs," *Time*, October 25, 1982, 20-26.
4. Don Irwin, "Common Cause Attacks Election Funding," *Los Angeles Times*, February 2, 1983.
5. For information about congressional efforts from 1973 through 1979 to enact legislation to provide public funding for congressional campaigns, see Herbert E. Alexander, *Financing the 1976 Election* (Washington, D.C.: CQ Press, 1979), 654-660, and Alexander, *Financing the 1980 Election* (Lexington, Mass.: D. C. Heath, 1983), 18-26.
6. Louis Harris, *The Harris Survey* (New York: The Tribune Company Syndicate, May 1977), 4.
7. George H. Gallup, *The Gallup Poll: Public Opinion 1972-1977* (Wilmington, Del.: Scholarly Resources, 1978), 2:1060-1061; and *The Gallup Poll: Public Opinion 1979* (Wilmington, Del.: Scholarly Resources, 1980), 103-104.
8. Louis Harris, "Limit on Political Action Committee Campaign Contributions Favored," *ABC News-Harris Survey* (New York: Chicago Tribune-N.Y. News Syndicate, April 3, 1980), 2.
9. See Roy Pfautch, "Campaign Finance: The Signals from the Polls," *Public Opinion*, August-September 1980, 52.
10. The following is a condensation of the February 1980, March 1981, and March 1982 reports by Civic Service, Inc., "Attitudes Toward Campaign Financing," (St. Louis, Mo.: Civic Service).
11. "Public Financing of Federal Elections Opposed by Most Americans," *The Harris Survey*, January 10, 1983, 1.
12. "Americans Call Heavy Spending a Serious Problem," *The Harris Survey*, January 3, 1983, 1.
13. "Public Fed Up With Political TV Ads," *The Harris Survey*, January 6, 1983, 1.
14. See, for example, Herbert E. Alexander, *The Case for PACs* (Washington, D.C.: Public Affairs Council, 1983); Andrew Mollison, "What's Right With PACs," *New Leader*, March 7, 1983, 3-4; Michael Malbin, "The Problems of PAC-Journalism," *Public Opinion*, December-January 1983, 15-16+; Simon Lazarus, "PAC Power? They Keep Losing," *Washington Post*, April 3, 1983.
15. "Americans Call Heavy Spending a Serious Problem," 1.
16. William Schneider, "Campaign Financing: Curb Special-Interest Giving But Don't Go Public," *National Journal*, February 26, 1983.
17. Herbert E. Alexander, "Financing Gubernatorial Election Campaigns," *State Government*, Summer 1980, 140-143.
18. New Jersey Election Law Enforcement Commission, "Public Financing Conclusions and Recommendations: New Jersey's 1981 Gubernatorial Elections," Trenton, N.J., June 10, 1982.
19. Other proposals to strengthen the parties have been made by the Campaign

Study Group of Harvard University's Institute of Politics. They include creating an additional tax credit for contributions to political parties and easing reporting requirements for state and local party committees that contribute to federal candidates. See *Campaign Practices Reports,* July 10 1979, 9.

20. Gary C. Jacobson, *The Politics of Congressional Elections* (Boston: Little, Brown & Co., 1983), 194.
21. Ibid.
22. Quoted in Robert Shogan, "Straw Polls Stir Enthusiasm But Generate Fear," *Los Angeles Times,* June 20, 1983.
23. Carleton W. Sterling, "Control of Campaign Spending: The Reformer's Paradox," *American Bar Association Journal* 59 (October 1973): 1153.

Appendix

Federal Election Campaign Act of 1971*

The Federal Election Campaign Act of 1971 (FECA) was the first comprehensive revision of federal campaign legislation since the Corrupt Practices Act of 1925. The act established detailed spending limits and disclosure procedures. P.L. 92-225 contained the following major provisions:

General

- Repealed the Federal Corrupt Practices Act of 1925.
- Defined "election" to mean any general, special, primary, or runoff election, nominating convention or caucus, delegate-selection primary, presidential preference primary, or constitutional convention.
- Broadened the definitions of "contribution" and "expenditure" as they pertain to political campaigns, but exempted a loan of money by a national or state bank made in accordance with applicable banking laws.
- Prohibited promises of employment or other political rewards or benefits by any candidate in exchange for political support, and prohibited contracts between candidates and any federal department or agency.
- Provided that the terms "contribution" and "expenditure" did not include communications, nonpartisan registration, and get-out-the-vote campaigns by a corporation aimed at its stockholders or by a labor organization aimed at its members.
- Provided that the terms "contribution" and "expenditure" did not include the establishment, administration, and solicitation of voluntary contributions to a separate segregated fund to be utilized for political purposes by a corporation or labor organization.

Contribution Limits

- Placed a ceiling on contributions by any candidate or his immediate family to his own campaign of $50,000 for president or vice president, $35,000 for senator, and $25,000 for representative.

Spending Limits

● Limited the total amount that could be spent by federal candidates for advertising time in communications media to 10 cents per eligible voter or $50,000, whichever was greater. The limitation would apply to all candidates for president and vice president, senator, and representative, and would be determined annually for the geographical area of each election by the Bureau of the Census.

● Included in the term "communications media" radio and television broadcasting stations, newspapers, magazines, billboards, and automatic telephone equipment. Of the total spending limit, up to 60 percent could be used for broadcast advertising time.

● Specified that candidates for presidential nomination, during the period prior to the nominating convention, could spend no more in primary or nonprimary states than the amount allowed under the 10-cent-per-voter communications spending limitation.

● Provided that broadcast and nonbroadcast spending limitations be increased in proportion to annual increases in the Consumer Price Index over the base year 1970.

Disclosure and Enforcement

● Required all political committees that anticipated receipts in excess of $1,000 during the calendar year to file a statement of organization with the appropriate federal supervisory officer, and to include such information as the names of all principal officers, the scope of the committee, the names of all candidates the committee supported, and other information as required by law.

● Stipulated that the appropriate federal supervisory officer to oversee election campaign practices, reporting, and disclosure was the Clerk of the House for House candidates, the Secretary of the Senate for Senate candidates, and the Comptroller General for presidential candidates.

● Required each political committee to report any individual expenditure of more than $100 and any expenditures of more than $100 in the aggregate during the calendar year.

● Required disclosure of all contributions to any committee or candidate in excess of $100, including a detailed report with the name and address of the contributor and the date the contribution was made.

● Required the supervisory officers to prepare an annual report for each committee registered with the commission and make such reports available for sale to the public.

● Required candidates and committees to file reports of contributions and expenditures on the 10th day of March, June, and September every year, on the 15th and 5th days preceding the date on which an election was held, and on the 31st day of January. Any contribution of $5,000 or more was to be reported within 48 hours after its receipt.

● Required reporting of the names, addresses, and occupations of any lender and endorser of any loan in excess of $100 as well as the date and amount of such loans.

● Required any person who made any contribution in excess of $100, other than through a political committee or candidate, to report such contribution to the commission.

● Prohibited any contribution to a candidate or committee by one person in the name of another person.

● Authorized the office of the Comptroller General to serve as a national clearinghouse for information on the administration of election practices.

● Required that copies of reports filed by a candidate with the appropriate supervisory officer also be filed with the secretary of state for the state in which the election was held.

Miscellaneous

● Prohibited radio and television stations from charging political candidates more than the lowest unit cost for the same advertising time available to commercial advertisers. Lowest unit rate charges would apply only during the 45 days preceding a primary election and the 60 days preceding a general election.

● Required nonbroadcast media to charge candidates no more than the comparable amounts charged to commercial advertisers for the same class and amount of advertising space. The requirement would apply only during the 45 days preceding the date of a primary election and 60 days before the date of a general election.

● Provided that amounts spent by an agent of a candidate on behalf of his candidacy would be charged against the overall expenditure allocation. Fees paid to the agent for services performed also would be charged against the overall limitation.

● Stipulated that no broadcast station could make any charge for political advertising time on a station unless written consent to contract for such time had been given by the candidate, and unless the candidate certified that such charge would not exceed his spending limit.

Revenue Act of 1971*

The Revenue Act of 1971, through tax incentives and a tax checkoff plan, provided the basis for public funding of presidential election campaigns. P.L. 92-178 contained the following major provisions:

Tax Incentives and Checkoff

● Allowed a tax credit of $12.50 ($25 for a married couple) or a deduction against income of $50 ($100 for a married couple) for political contributions to candidates for local, state or federal office. [NOTE: The Revenue Act of 1978, P.L. 96-600, raised the tax credit to $50 on a single tax return, $100 on a joint return. As in the 1971 Act, the credit equaled 50 percent of the contribution, up to those limits. The 1978 law eliminated the tax deduction for political contributions while increasing the tax credit.]

• Allowed taxpayers to contribute to a general fund for all eligible presidential and vice presidential candidates by authorizing $1 of their annual income tax payment to be placed in such a fund.

Presidential Election Campaign Fund

• Authorized to be distributed to the candidates of each major party (one which obtained 25 percent of votes cast in the previous presidential election) an amount equal to 15 cents multiplied by the number of U.S. residents age 18 or over.

• Established a formula for allocating public campaign funds to candidates of minor parties whose candidates received 5 percent or more but less than 25 percent of the previous presidential election vote.

• Authorized payments after the election to reimburse the campaign expenses of a new party whose candidate received enough votes to be eligible or to a minor party whose candidate increased its vote to the qualifying level.

• Prohibited major party candidates who chose public financing of their campaign from accepting private campaign contributions unless their share of funds contributed through the income tax checkoff procedure fell short of the amounts to which they were entitled.

• Prohibited a major party candidate who chose public financing and all campaign committees authorized by the candidate from spending more than the amount to which the candidate was entitled under the contributions formula.

• Provided that if the amounts in the fund were insufficient to make the payments to which each party was entitled, payments would be allocated according to the ratio of contributions in their accounts. No party would receive from the general fund more than the smallest amount needed by a major party to reach the maximum amount of contributions to which it was entitled.

• Provided that surpluses remaining in the fund after a campaign be returned to the Treasury after all parties had been paid the amounts to which they were entitled.

Enforcement

• Provided penalties of $5,000 or one year in prison, or both, for candidates or campaign committees that spent more on a campaign than the amounts they received from the campaign fund or who accepted private contributions when sufficient public funds were available.

• Provided penalties of $10,000 or five years in prison, or both, for candidates or campaign committees who used public campaign funds for unauthorized expenses, gave or accepted kickbacks or illegal payments involving public campaign funds, or who knowingly furnished false information to the comptroller general.

Federal Election Campaign Act Amendments of 1974*

The 1974 Amendments set new contribution and spending limits, made provision for government funding of presidential prenomination campaigns and national nominating conventions, and created the bipartisan Federal Election Commission to administer election laws. P.L. 93-443 contained the following major provisions:

Federal Election Commission

● Created a six-member, full-time bipartisan Federal Election Commission to be responsible for administering election laws and the public financing program.

● Provided that the president, Speaker of the House and president pro tem of the Senate would appoint to the commission two members, each of different parties, all subject to confirmation by Congress. Commission members could not be officials or employees of any branch of government.

● Made the Secretary of the Senate and Clerk of the House ex officio, nonvoting members of the FEC; provided that their offices would serve as custodian of reports for House and Senate candidates.

● Provided that commissioners would serve six-year, staggered terms and established a rotating one-year chairmanship.

Contribution Limits

● $1,000 per individual for each primary, runoff, or general election, and an aggregate contribution of $25,000 to all federal candidates annually.

● $5,000 per organization, political committee, and national and state party organization for each election, but no aggregate limit on the amount organizations could contribute in a campaign nor on the amount organizations could contribute to party organizations supporting federal candidates.

● $50,000 for president or vice president, $35,000 for Senate, and $25,000 for House races for candidates and their families to their own campaign.

● $1,000 for independent expenditures on behalf of a candidate.

● Barred cash contributions of over $100 and foreign contributions.

Spending Limits

● Presidential primaries—$10 million total per candidate for all primaries. In a state presidential primary, limited a candidate to spending no more than twice what a Senate candidate in that state would be allowed to spend.

● Presidential general election—$20 million per candidate.

● Presidential nominating conventions—$2 million each major political party, lesser amounts for minor parties.

● Senate primaries—$100,000 or eight cents per eligible voter, whichever was greater.

● Senate general elections—$150,000 or 12 cents per eligible voter, whichever was greater.

● House primaries—$70,000.

● House general elections—$70,000.

● National party spending—$10,000 per candidate in House general elections;

$20,000 or two cents per eligible voter, whichever was greater, for each candidate in Senate general elections; and two cents per voter (approximately $2.9 million) in presidential general elections. The expenditure would be above the candidate's individual spending limit.

● Applied Senate spending limits to House candidates who represented a whole state.

● Repealed the media spending limitations in the Federal Election Campaign Act of 1971 (P.L. 92-225).

● Exempted expenditures of up to $500 for food and beverages, invitations, unreimbursed travel expenses by volunteers, and spending on "slate cards" and sample ballots.

● Exempted fund-raising costs of up to 20 percent of the candidate spending limit. Thus the spending limit for House candidates would be effectively raised from $70,000 to $84,000 and for candidates in presidential primaries from $10 million to $12 million.

● Provided that spending limits be increased in proportion to annual increases in the Consumer Price Index.

Public Financing

● Presidential general elections—voluntary public financing. Major party candidates automatically would qualify for full funding before the campaign. Minor party and independent candidates would be eligible to receive a proportion of full funding based on past or current votes received. If a candidate opted for full public funding, no private contributions would be permitted.

● Presidential nominating conventions—optional public funding. Major parties automatically would qualify. Minor parties would be eligible for lesser amounts based on their proportion of votes received in a past election.

● Presidential primaries—matching public funds of up to $5 million per candidate after meeting fund-raising requirement of $100,000 raised in amounts of at least $5,000 in each of 20 states or more. Only the first $250 of individual private contributions would be matched. The matching funds were to be divided among the candidates as quickly as possible. In allocating the money, the order in which the candidates qualified would be taken into account. Only private gifts, raised after January 1, 1975, would qualify for matching for the 1976 election. No federal payments would be made before January 1976.

● Provided that all federal money for public funding of campaigns would come from the Presidential Election Campaign Fund. Money received from the federal income tax dollar checkoff automatically would be appropriated to the fund.

Disclosure and Enforcement

● Required each candidate to establish one central campaign committee through which all contributions and expenditures on behalf of a candidate must be reported. Required designation of specific bank depositories of campaign funds.

● Required full reports of contributions and expenditures to be filed with the

Federal Election Commission 10 days before and 30 days after every election, and within 10 days of the close of each quarter unless the committee received or expended less than $1,000 in that quarter. A year-end report was due in nonelection years.

- Required that contributions of $1,000 or more received within the last 15 days before election be reported to the commission within 48 hours.
- Prohibited contributions in the name of another.
- Treated loans as contributions. Required a cosigner or guarantor for each $1,000 of outstanding obligation.
- Required any organization that spent any money or committed any act for the purpose of influencing any election (such as the publication of voting records) to file reports as a political committee.
- Required every person who spent or contributed more than $100, other than to or through a candidate or political committee, to report.
- Permitted government contractors, unions, and corporations to maintain separate, segregated political funds.
- Provided that the commission would receive campaign reports, make rules and regulations (subject to review by Congress within 30 days), maintain a cumulative index of reports filed and not filed, make special and regular reports to Congress and the president, and serve as an election information clearinghouse.
- Gave the commission power to render advisory opinions, conduct audits and investigations, subpoena witnesses and information, and go to court to seek civil injunctions.
- Provided that criminal cases would be referred by the commission to the Justice Department for prosecution.
- Increased existing fines to a maximum of $50,000.
- Provided that a candidate for federal office who failed to file reports could be prohibited from running again for the term of that office plus one year.

Miscellaneous

- Set January 1, 1975, as the effective date of the act (except for immediate pre-emption of state laws).
- Removed Hatch Act restrictions on voluntary activities by state and local employees in federal campaigns, if not otherwise prohibited by state law.
- Prohibited solicitation of funds by franked mail.
- Preempted state election laws for federal candidates.
- Permitted use of excess campaign funds to defray expenses of holding federal office or for other lawful purposes.

Federal Election Campaign Act
Amendments of 1976*

The 1976 Amendments revised election laws following the Supreme Court decision in *Buckley v. Valeo*. The Amendments reopened the door to large contributions through "independent expenditures" and through corporate and union political action committees. P.L. 94-283 contained the following major provisions:

Federal Election Commission

● Reconstituted the Federal Election Commission as a six-member panel appointed by the president and confirmed by the Senate.
● Prohibited commission members from engaging in outside business activities; gave commissioners one year after joining the body to terminate outside business interests.
● Gave Congress the power to disapprove individual sections of any regulation proposed by the commission.

Contribution Limits

● Limited an individual to giving no more than $5,000 a year to a political action committee and $20,000 to the national committee of a political party (the 1974 law set a $1,000-per-election limit on individual contributions to a candidate and an aggregate contribution limit for individuals of $25,000 a year, both provisions remaining in effect).
● Limited a multicandidate committee to giving no more than $15,000 a year to the national committee of a political party (the 1974 law set only a limit of $5,000 per election per candidate, a provision remaining in effect).
● Limited the Democratic and Republican senatorial campaign committees to giving no more than $17,500 a year to a candidate (the 1974 law set a $5,000-per-election limit, a provision remaining in effect).
● Allowed campaign committees organized to back a single candidate to provide "occasional, isolated, and incidental support" to another candidate. (The 1974 law had limited such a committee to spending money only on behalf of the single candidate for whom it was formed.)
● Restricted the proliferation of membership organization, corporate, and union political action committees. All political action committees established by a company or an international union would be treated as a single committee for contribution purposes. The contributions of political action committees of a company or union would be limited to no more than $5,000 overall to the same candidate in any election.

Spending Limits

● Limited spending by presidential and vice presidential candidates to no more than $50,000 of their own or their families' money on their campaigns, if they accepted public financing.
● Exempted from the law's spending limits payments by candidates or the national committees of political parties for legal and accounting services required to comply with the campaign law, but required that such payments be reported.

Public Financing

● Required presidential candidates who received federal matching subsidies and who withdrew from the prenomination election campaign to give back leftover federal matching funds.

● Cut off federal campaign subsidies to a presidential candidate who won less than 10 percent of the vote in two consecutive presidential primaries in which he ran.

● Established a procedure under which an individual who became ineligible for matching payments could have eligibility restored by a finding of the commission.

Disclosure and Enforcement

● Gave the commission exclusive authority to prosecute civil violations of the campaign finance law and shifted to the commission jurisdiction over violations formerly covered only in the criminal code, thus strengthening its power to enforce the law.

● Required an affirmative vote of four members for the commission to issue regulations and advisory opinions and initiate civil actions and investigations.

● Required labor unions, corporations, and membership organizations to report expenditures of over $2,000 per election for communications to their stockholders or members advocating the election or defeat of a clearly identified candidate. The costs of communications to members or stockholders on issues would not have to be reported.

● Required that candidates and political committees keep records of contributions of $50 or more. (The 1974 law had required records of contributions of $10 or more.)

● Permitted candidates and political committees to waive the requirement for filing quarterly campaign finance reports in a nonelection year if less than a total of $5,000 was raised or spent in that quarter. Annual reports would still have to be filed. (The exemption limit was $1,000 under the 1974 law.)

● Required political committees and individuals making an independent political expenditure of more than $100 that advocated the defeat or election of a candidate to file a report with the election commission. Required the committee and individual to state, under penalty of perjury, that the expenditure was not made in collusion with a candidate.

● Required that independent expenditures of $1,000 or more made within 15 days of an election be reported within 24 hours.

● Limited the commission to issuing advisory opinions only for specific fact situations. Advisory opinions could not be used to spell out commission policy. Advisory opinions were not to be considered as precedents unless an activity was "indistinguishable in all its material aspects" from an activity already covered by an advisory opinion.

● Permitted the commission to initiate investigations only after it received a properly verified complaint or had reason to believe, based on information it obtained in the normal course of its duties, that a violation had occurred or was about to occur. The commission was barred from relying on anonymous complaints to institute investigations.

● Required the commission to rely initially on conciliation to deal with alleged campaign law violations before going to court. The commission was allowed to refer alleged criminal violations to the Department of Justice for action. The attorney general was required to report back to the commission within 60 days an action taken on the apparent violation and subsequently every 30 days until the matter was disposed of.

● Provided for a one-year jail sentence and a fine of up to $25,000 or three times the amount of the contribution or expenditure involved in the violation, whichever was greater, if an individual was convicted of knowingly committing a campaign law violation that involved more than $1,000.

● Provided for civil penalties of fines of $5,000 or an amount equal to the contribution or expenditure involved in the violation, whichever was greater. For violations knowingly committed, the fine would be $10,000 or an amount equal to twice the amount involved in the violation, whichever was greater. The fines could be imposed by the courts or by the commission in conciliation agreements. (The 1974 law included penalties for civil violations of a $1,000 fine and/or a one-year prison sentence.)

Political Action Committees

● Restricted the fund-raising ability of corporate political action committees. Company committees could seek contributions only from stockholders and executive and administrative personnel and their families. Restricted union political action committees to soliciting contributions only from union members and their families. However, twice a year the law permitted union and corporate political action committees to seek campaign contributions only by mail from all employees not initially included in the restriction. Contributions would have to remain anonymous and would be received by an independent third party that would keep records but pass the money to the committees.

● Permitted trade association political action committees to solicit contributions from member companies' stockholders, executive and administrative personnel, and their families.

● Permitted union political action committees to use the same method to solicit campaign contributions that the political action committee of the company uses. The union committee would have to reimburse the company at cost for the expenses the company incurred for the political fund raising. (Other provisions of the 1976 Amendments apply to PACs. See Contribution Limits and Disclosure and Enforcement provisions.)

*Some provisions have been declared unconstitutional and some have been superseded by later amendments or repealed.

Federal Election Campaign Act
Amendments of 1979*

The 1979 Amendments were enacted to lighten the burden the law imposed on candidates and political committees by reducing paperwork, among other changes. P.L. 96-187 contained the following major provisions:

Disclosure

● Required a federal candidate to file campaign finance reports if he or she received or expended more than $5,000. Previously any candidate, regardless of the amount raised or spent, had to file.

● Allowed local political party organizations to avoid filing reports with the FEC if expenditures for certain voluntary activities (voter registration and voter turnout drives for presidential tickets and purchase of buttons, bumper stickers, and other materials) were less than $5,000 a year. If other types of expenditures were more than $1,000 a year, then such a group would be required to file. Previously local political party organizations were required to file when any class of expenditure exceeded $1,000 a year.

● Permitted an individual to spend up to $1,000 on behalf of a candidate or $2,000 on behalf of a political party in voluntary expenses for providing his home, food, or personal travel without it being counted as a reportable contribution.

● Eliminated the requirement that a political committee have a chairman, but continued the requirement that each have a treasurer.

● Allowed ten days, instead of the previous five, for a person who received a contribution of more than $50 on behalf of a candidate's campaign committee to forward it to the committee's treasurer.

● Required a committee's treasurer to preserve records for three years. Previously, the FEC established the period of time that committee treasurers were required to keep records.

● Required a candidate's campaign committee to have the candidate's name in the title of the committee. Also, the title of a political action committee was required to include the name of the organization with which it was affiliated.

● Reduced to six from eleven the categories of information required on registration statements of political committees. One of the categories eliminated had required political action committees to name the candidates supported. That requirement meant that PACs were forced frequently to file lists of candidates to whom they contributed when that information already was given in their contribution reports.

● Reduced to nine from twenty-four the maximum number of reports that a candidate would be required to file during a two-year election cycle. Those nine reports would be a preprimary, a pregeneral, a postgeneral, four quarterly reports during an election year, and two semiannual reports during the nonelection year. The preelection reports would be due 12 days before the election; the postgeneral report would be due 30 days after the election; the quarterly reports would be due 15 days after the end of each quarter, and the semiannual reports would be due July 31 and January 31.

● Required presidential campaign committees to file monthly reports, as well as pre- and postgeneral reports, during an election year if they had contributions or expenditures in excess of $100,000. All other presidential campaign committees would be required to file quarterly reports, as well as pre- and postgeneral reports, during an election year. During a nonelection year presidential campaign committees could choose whether to file monthly or quarterly reports.

● Required political committees other than those affiliated with a candidate to file either monthly reports in all years or nine reports during a two-year election cycle.

● Provided that the FEC be notified within 48 hours of contributions of $1,000 or more that were made between 20 days and 48 hours before an election. Previously the period had been between 15 days and 48 hours before an election.

● Required the names of contributors to be reported if they gave $200 or more instead of $100 or more.

● Required expenses to be itemized if they were $200 or more instead of $100 or more.

● Increased the threshold for reporting independent expenditures to $250 from $100.

Federal Election Commission

● Established a "best effort" standard for the FEC to determine compliance by candidates' committees with the law. This was intended to ease the burden on committees, particularly in the area of meeting the requirement of filing the occupations of contributors.

● Allowed any person who had an inquiry about a specific campaign transaction—not just federal officeholders, candidates, political committees, and the national party committees—to request advisory opinions from the FEC.

● Required the FEC to respond to advisory opinion requests within 60 days instead of within a "reasonable time." If such a request were made within the 60-day period before an election, the FEC would be required to issue an opinion within 20 days.

● Provided that within five days of receiving a complaint that the election campaign law had been violated the FEC must notify any person alleged to have committed a violation. The accused has fifteen days in which to respond to the complaint.

● Required a vote of four of the six members of the FEC to make the determination it had "reason to believe" a violation of the law had occurred. An investigation then would be required, and the accused had to be notified.

● Provided that four votes of the FEC were necessary to determine "probable cause" that a violation had occurred. The commission then would be required to attempt to correct the violation by informal methods and to enter into a conciliation agreement within 90 days. Commission action required the vote of four FEC members.

● Narrowed the scope of the FEC's national clearinghouse function from all elections to federal elections.

● Eliminated random audits of committees by the FEC and required a vote of four FEC members to conduct an audit after it had determined that a committee had not substantially complied with the election campaign law.

● Required secretaries of state in each state to keep copies of FEC reports on file for only two years compared with the previous requirement that all House candidate reports be retained for five years and all other reports for ten years.

● Provided an expedited procedure for the Senate, as well as for the House, to disapprove a regulation proposed by the FEC.

Enforcement

● Retained the substance of the existing law providing for civil and criminal relief of election campaign law violations.

● Continued the prohibition on the use of the contents of reports filed with the FEC for the purpose of soliciting contributions or for commercial purposes, but added the exception that the names of PACs registered with the FEC may be used for solicitation of contributions.

● Permitted political committees to include 10 pseudonyms on each report to protect against illegal use of the names of contributors. A list of those names would be provided to the FEC and would not be made public.

Political Parties

● Allowed state and local party groups to buy, without limit, buttons, bumper stickers, handbills, brochures, posters, and yard signs for voluntary activities.

● Authorized state and local party groups to conduct voter registration and get-out-the-vote drives on behalf of presidential tickets without financial limit.

Public Financing

● Increased the allotment of federal funds for the Democrats and Republicans to finance their nominating conventions to $3 million from $2 million.

Miscellaneous

● Permitted buttons and similar materials, but not commercial advertisements, that promoted one candidate to make a passing reference to another federal candidate without its being treated as a contribution to the second candidate.

● Permitted leftover campaign funds to be given to other political committees, as well as charities.

● Prohibited anyone, with the exception of members of Congress at the time of P.L. 96-187's enactment, to convert leftover campaign funds to personal use.

● Continued the ban on solicitation by candidates for Congress or members of Congress and by federal employees of other federal workers for campaign contributions, but dropped the prohibition on the receipt of such contributions by federal employees. An inadvertent solicitation of a federal employee would not be a violation.

● Permitted congressional employees to make voluntary contributions to members of Congress other than their immediate employers.

● Continued the ban on solicitation and receipt of contributions in a federal building. But it would not be a violation if contributions received at a federal building were forwarded within seven days to the appropriate political committee and if the contribution had not been directed initially to the federal building.

*Some provisions have been declared unconstitutional.

Bibliography

Books

Adamany, David. *Campaign Finance in America*. North Scituate, Mass.: Duxbury Press, 1972.

——. *Financing Politics: Recent Wisconsin Elections*. Madison, Wis.: University of Wisconsin Press, 1969.

Adamany, David, and Agree, George E. *Political Money: A Strategy for Campaign Financing in America*. Baltimore: The Johns Hopkins University Press, 1975.

Agranoff, Robert. *The Management of Election Campaigns*. Boston: Holbrook Press, 1976.

——. *The New Style in Election Campaigns*. Boston: Holbrook Press, 1976.

Alexander, Herbert E. *Financing the 1960 Election*. Princeton, N.J.: Citizens' Research Foundation, 1962.

——. *Financing the 1964 Election*. Princeton, N.J.: Citizens' Research Foundation, 1966.

——. *Financing the 1968 Election*. Lexington, Mass.: Lexington Books, 1971.

——. *Financing the 1972 Election*. Lexington, Mass.: Lexington Books, 1976.

——. *Financing the 1976 Election*. Washington, D.C.: CQ Press, 1979.

——, with the assistance of Brian A. Haggerty. *Financing the 1980 Election*. Lexington, Mass.: Lexington Books, 1983.

——. *Money in Politics*. Washington, D.C.: Public Affairs Press, 1972.

——, ed. *Campaign Money: Reform and Reality in the States*. New York: The Free Press, 1976.

——, ed. *Political Finance*. Beverly Hills: Sage Publications, 1979.

Alexander, Herbert E., and Frutig, Jennifer W. *Public Financing of State Elections: A Data Book and Election Guide to Public Funding of Political Parties and Candidates in Seventeen States*. Los Angeles: Citizens' Research Foundation, 1982.

Alexander, Herbert E., and Haggerty, Brian A. *Political Reform in California: How Has It Worked?* Los Angeles: Citizens' Research Foundation, 1980.

——. *The Federal Election Campaign Act: After a Decade of Reform*. Los Angeles: Citizens' Research Foundation, 1981.

Alexander, Herbert E., and Molloy, J. Paul. *Model State Statute: Politics, Elections and Public Office*. Princeton, N.J.: Citizens' Research Foundation, 1974.

215

Barber, James David, ed. *Choosing the President.* Englewood Cliffs, N.J.: Prentice-Hall, 1974.

Berg, Larry L.; Hahn, Harlan; and Schmidhauser, John R. *Corruption in the American Political System.* Morristown, N.J.: General Learning Press, 1976.

Bernstein, Carl, and Woodward, Bob. *All the President's Men.* New York: Simon & Schuster, 1974.

Bickel, Alexander M. *Reform and Continuity: The Electoral College, the Convention, and the Party System.* New York: Harper & Row, Publishers, 1971.

Bishop, George F.; Meadow, Robert G.; Jackson-Beeck, Marilyn, eds. *The Presidential Debates: Media, Electoral, and Policy Perspectives.* New York: Praeger Publishers, 1979.

Bradshaw, Thornton, and Vogel, David, eds. *Corporations and Their Critics.* New York: McGraw-Hill, 1981.

Bretton, Henry. *The Power of Money.* Albany, N.Y.: State University of New York Press, 1980.

Broder, David S. *The Party's Over: The Failure of Politics in America.* New York: Harper & Row, Publishers, 1972.

Caddy, Douglas. *The Hundred Million Dollar Payoff.* New Rochelle, N.Y.: Arlington House, Publishers, 1974.

Chester, Edward W. *Radio, Television and American Politics.* New York: Sheed & Ward, 1969.

Claude, Richard O. *The Supreme Court and the Electoral Process.* Baltimore: The Johns Hopkins Press, 1970.

Common Cause. *A Common Cause Guide to Money, Power & Politics in the 97th Congress.* Washington, D.C.: Common Cause, 1981.

Congressional Quarterly. *Dollar Politics.* 3d ed. Washington, D.C.: Congressional Quarterly, 1982.

Crotty, William J. *Decision for the Democrats: Reforming Party Structure.* Baltimore: The Johns Hopkins University Press, 1978.

——. *Political Reform and the American Experiment.* New York: Thomas Y. Crowell Co., 1977.

——, ed. *Paths to Political Reform.* Lexington, Mass.: D. C. Heath & Co., 1980.

Davis, James W. *Presidential Primaries: Road to the White House.* Westport, Conn.: Greenwood Press, 1980.

Demaris, Ovid. *Dirty Business: The Corporate-Political Money-Power Game.* New York: Harper's Magazine Press, 1974.

DeVries, Walter, and Tarrance, Lance, Jr. *The Ticket-Splitter: A New Force in American Politics.* Grand Rapids, Mich.: William B. Eardmans Publishing Co., 1972.

Domhoff, G. William. *Fat Cats and Democrats: The Role of the Big Rich in the Party of the Common Man.* Englewood Cliffs, N.J.: Prentice-Hall, 1972.

Drew, Elizabeth. *Politics and Money: The New Road to Corruption.* New York: Macmillan, 1983.

Dunn, Delmer. *Financing Presidential Campaigns.* Washington, D.C.: The Brookings Institution, 1972.

Epstein, Edwin M. *The Corporation in American Politics.* Englewood Cliffs, N.J.:

Prentice-Hall Inc., 1969.

Fleishman, Joel, ed. *The Future of American Political Parties.* Englewood Cliffs, N.J.: Prentice-Hall, 1982.

Frazer/Associates. *The PAC Handbook.* Washington, D.C.: Frazer/Associates, 1981.

Gilson, Lawrence. *Money and Secrecy: A Citizen's Guide to Reforming State and Federal Practices.* New York: Praeger Publishers, 1972.

Graber, Doris A. *Mass Media and American Politics.* Washington, D.C.: CQ Press, 1980.

Greenfield, Jeff. *The Real Campaign.* New York: Summit Books, 1982.

Greenwald, Carol. *Group Power: Lobbying and Public Policy.* New York: Praeger Publishers, 1977.

Grief, Edward A. *Fighting to Win: Business Political Power.* New York: Harcourt Brace Jovanovich, 1981.

Heard, Alexander. *The Costs of Democracy.* Chapel Hill, N.C.: University of North Carolina Press, 1960.

Heidenheimer, Arnold J., ed. *Comparative Political Finance: The Financing of Party Organizations and Election Campaigns.* Lexington, Mass.: Lexington Books, 1970.

Hess, Stephen. *The Presidential Campaign: The Leadership Selection Process After Watergate.* Washington, D.C.: The Brookings Institution, 1974.

Hiebert, Ray; Jones, Robert; Lotito, Ernest; and Lorenz, John, eds. *The Political Image Merchants: Strategies in the New Politics.* Washington, D.C.: Acropolis Books Ltd., 1971.

Jacobson, Gary C. *Money in Congressional Elections.* New Haven, Conn.: Yale University Press, 1980.

___. *The Politics of Congressional Elections.* Boston: Little, Brown & Co., 1983.

Jacobson, Gary C., and Kernell, Samuel. *Strategy and Choice in Congressional Elections.* New Haven, Conn.: Yale University Press, 1981.

Kelley, Stanley, Jr. *Political Campaigning: Problems in Creating an Informed Electorate.* Washington, D.C.: The Brookings Institution, 1960.

___. *Professional Public Relations and Political Power.* Baltimore: The Johns Hopkins Press, 1956.

King, Anthony, ed. *The New American Political System.* Washington, D.C.: American Enterprise Institute for Public Policy Research, 1978.

Kraus, Sidney. *The Great Debates: Background—Perspective—Effects.* Bloomington, Ind.: Indiana University Press, 1962.

Ladd, Everett Carll, Jr. *Where Have All the Voters Gone? The Fracturing of America's Political Parties.* New York: W. W. Norton & Co., 1978.

Leonard, Dick. *Paying for Party Politics: The Case For Public Subsidies.* London: PEP, 1975.

Leuthold, David A. *Electioneering in a Democracy: Campaigns for Congress.* New York: John Wiley & Sons, 1968.

Lipset, Seymour Martin, ed. *Emerging Coalitions in American Politics.* San Francisco: Institute for Contemporary Studies, 1978.

McCarthy, Max. *Elections for Sale.* Boston: Houghton-Mifflin Co., 1972.

McGinniss, Joe. *The Selling of the President, 1968.* New York: Trident Press, 1969.

MacNeil, Robert. *The People Machine: The Influence of Television on American Politics.* New York: Harper & Row, Publishers, 1968.

Maisel, Louis, ed. *Changing Campaign Techniques: Elections and Values in Contemporary Democracies.* Beverly Hills: Sage Publications, 1976.

Malbin, Michael J., ed. *Parties, Interest Groups, and Campaign Finance Laws.* Washington, D.C.: American Enterprise Institute for Public Policy Research, 1980.

May, Ernest R., and Fraser, Janet, eds. *Campaign '72: The Managers Speak.* Cambridge: Harvard University Press, 1973.

Mazmanian, Daniel A. *Third Parties in Presidential Elections: Studies in Presidential Selection.* Washington, D.C.: The Brookings Institution, 1974.

Mickelson, Sig. *The Electric Mirror: Politics in an Age of Television.* New York: Dodd, Mead & Co., 1972.

Minow, Newton N.; Martin, John Bartlow; and Mitchell, Lee M. *Presidential Television.* New York: Basic Books, 1973.

Napolitan, Joseph. *The Election Game and How to Win It.* Garden City, New York: Doubleday & Co., 1972.

Nichols, David. *Financing Elections: The Politics of an American Ruling Class.* New York: New Viewpoints, 1974.

Nie, Norman H.; Verba, Sidney; and Petrocik, John R. *The Changing American Voter.* Cambridge: Harvard University Press, 1976.

Nimmo, Dan. *The Political Persuaders.* Englewood Cliffs, N.J.: Prentice-Hall, 1970.

Ornstein, Norman J., and Elder, Shirley. *Interest Groups, Lobbying, and Policymaking.* Washington, D.C.: CQ Press, 1978.

Overacker, Louise. *Money in Elections.* New York: Macmillan, 1932.

Patterson, Thomas E. *The Mass Media Election.* New York: Praeger Publishers, 1980.

Patterson, Thomas E., and McClure, Robert D. *The Unseeing Eye: The Myth of Television Power in National Politics.* New York: G. P. Putnam's Sons, 1976.

Peabody, Robert L.; Berry, Jeffrey M.; Frasure, William G.; and Goldman, Jerry. *To Enact A Law: Congress and Campaign Financing.* New York: Praeger Publishers, 1972.

Pinto-Duschinsky, Michael. *British Political Finance, 1830-1980.* Washington, D.C.: American Enterprise Institute for Public Policy Research, 1981.

Pollock, James K., Jr. *Party Campaign Funds.* New York: Alfred A. Knopf, 1926.
——. *Money and Politics Abroad.* New York: Alfred A. Knopf, 1932.

Polsby, Nelson W. *The Consequences of Party Reform.* Oxford, U.K.: Oxford University Press, 1983.

Pomper, Gerald; Baker, Ross K.; Jacob, Charles E.; McWilliams, Wilson Carey; Plotkin, Henry A.; Pomper, Marlene M., eds. *The Election of 1976: Reports and Interpretations.* New York: David McKay Co., 1977.

Pomper, Gerald M., ed. *The Election of 1980: Reports and Interpretations.* Chatham, N.J.: Chatham House Publishers, 1981.

Rae, Douglas W. *The Political Consequences of Electoral Laws.* New Haven: Yale University Press, 1967.

Ranney, Austin. *Curing the Mischiefs of Faction: Party Reform in America.* Berkeley: University of California Press, 1975.

___, ed. *The Past and Future of Presidential Debates.* Washington, D.C.: American Enterprise Institute for Public Policy Research, 1979.

Rosenbloom, David Lee. *The Election Men: Professional Campaign Managers and American Democracy.* New York: Quadrangle Books, 1973.

Sabato, Larry J. *The Rise of Political Consultants: New Ways of Winning Elections.* New York: Basic Books, 1981.

___. *Goodbye to Good-Time Charlie: The American Governorship Transformed.* 2d ed. Washington, D.C.: CQ Press, 1983.

Schwarz, Thomas J. *Public Financing of Elections: A Constitutional Division of the Wealth.* Chicago: The American Bar Association, Special Committee on Election Reform, 1975.

Shannon, Jasper B. *Money and Politics.* New York: Random House, 1959.

Steckmest, Francis W. *Corporate Performance: The Key to Public Trust.* New York: McGraw-Hill, 1981.

Steinberg, Arnold. *Political Campaign Management: A Systems Approach.* Lexington, Mass.: Lexington Books, 1976.

___. *The Political Campaign Handbook: Media, Scheduling, and Advance.* Lexington, Mass.: Lexington Books, 1976.

Stewart, John G. *One Last Chance: The Democratic Party, 1974-76.* New York: Praeger Publishers, 1974.

Sundquist, James L. *Dynamics of the Party System: Alignment and Realignment of Political Parties in the United States.* Washington, D.C.: The Brookings Institution, 1973.

Thayer, George. *Who Shakes the Money Tree? American Campaign Financing Practices from 1789 to the Present.* New York: Simon and Schuster, 1973.

Van Doren, John. *Big Money in Little Sums.* Chapel Hill: Institute for Research in Social Science, University of North Carolina, 1956.

Viguerie, Richard A. *The New Right: We're Ready to Lead.* Falls Church, Va.: The Viguerie Co., 1981.

White, George H. *A Study of Access to Television for Political Candidates.* Cambridge: John F. Kennedy Institute of Politics, May 1978.

White, Theodore H. *The Making of the President, 1960.* New York: Atheneum Publishers, 1961.

___. *The Making of the President, 1964.* New York: Atheneum Publishers, 1965.

___. *The Making of the President, 1968.* New York: Atheneum Publishers, 1969.

___. *The Making of the President, 1972.* New York: Atheneum Publishers, 1973.

___. *America in Search of Itself.* New York: Harper & Row, 1982.

Woodward, Bob, and Bernstein, Carl. *The Final Days.* New York: Simon & Schuster, 1976.

Reports and Articles

Accountants for the Public Interest. *Study of the Federal Election Commission's*

Audit Process. Report by Accountants for the Public Interest to the Federal Election Commission. New York, September 10, 1979.

Adamany, David. "Money, Politics and Democracy: A Review Essay." *The American Political Science Review* 71, no.1 (March 1977).

——. "Political Finance in Transition." *Polity* 14 (Winter 1981).

Agree, George E. "Public Financing After the Supreme Court Decision," *The Annals* (The American Academy of Political and Social Science) 425 (May 1976.)

Alexander, Herbert E. "Communications and Politics: The Media and the Message." *Law and Contemporary Problems*, pt. 1 (Spring 1969).

——. "Financing Presidential Campaigns." In *History of American Presidential Elections 1789-1968*, edited by Arthur M. Schlesinger and Fred L. Israel, 3869-3897. New York: Chelsea House Publishers, 1971.

——. "The High Cost of TV Campaigns." *Television Quarterly* 5, no. 1 (Winter 1966).

——. "The Impact of the Federal Election Campaign Act on the 1976 Presidential Campaign: The Complexities of Compliance." *Emory Law Journal* 22, no. 2 (Spring 1980).

——. "The Obey-Railsback Bill—Its Genesis and Early History." *Arizona Law Review* 22, no. 2 (1980).

——, ed. Political Finance: Reform and Reality." *The Annals* (The American Academy of Political and Social Science) 425 (May 1976).

Alexander, Herbert E., and Molloy, J. Paul. *Model State Statute: Politics, Elections and Public Office.* Princeton, N.J.: Citizens' Research Foundation, August 1974.

American Bar Association, Special Committee on Election Reform. *Symposium on Campaign Financing Regulation* (Tiburon, Calif.: April 25-27, 1975).

Anonymous. "Developments in the Law—Elections." *Harvard Law Review* 88, no. 6 (April 1975).

Cantor, Joseph E. *Political Action Committees: Their Evolution and Growth and Their Implications for the Political System.* Congressional Research Service, The Library of Congress. Washington, D.C.: Government Printing Office, May 7, 1982.

Cohen, Richard E. "Public Financing for House Races—Will It Make a Difference?" *National Journal*, May 12, 1979.

Committee for Economic Development. *Financing a Better Election System: A Statement on National Policy by the Research and Policy Committee of the Committee for Economic Development.* New York: December 1968.

Common Cause. *How Money Talks in Congress: A Common Cause Study of the Impact of Money on Congressional Decision-Making.* Washington, D.C.: Common Cause, 1979.

——. *1972 Congressional Campaign Finances.* 3 vols. Prepared by the Campaign Finance Monitoring Project. Washington, D.C.: Common Cause, 1974.

——. *1972 Federal Campaign Finances: Interest Groups and Political Parties.* 10 vols. Prepared by the Campaign Finance Monitoring Project. Washington, D.C.: Common Cause, 1974.

____. *1974 Congressional Campaign Finances.* 5 vols. Prepared by the Campaign Finance Monitoring Project. Washington, D.C.: Common Cause, 1976.

____. *1976 Federal Campaign Finances.* 3 vols. Prepared by the Campaign Finance Monitoring Project. Washington, D.C.: Common Cause, 1977.

____. *Twenty Who Gave $10 Million: A Study of Money and Politics in California.* Los Angeles: Common Cause, 1981.

Congressional Research Service. *Nomination and Election of the President and Vice President of the United States.* Compiled by Thomas M. Durbin, Rita Ann Reimer, and Thomas B. Riby. Congressional Research Service, Library of Congress for the U.S. Senate Library, under the direction of Francis R. Valeo, Secretary of the Senate. Washington, D.C.: Government Printing Office, 1976.

Epstein, Edwin M. "An Irony of Electoral Reform." *Regulation* (May/June 1979).

Federal Election Commission. *Federal Election Commission, Review of the Political Campaign Auditing Process.* Report by Arthur Andersen & Co. to the Federal Election Commission, Washington, D.C.: September 1979.

Fling, Karen, ed. "A Summary of Campaign Practices Laws of the 50 States." *Campaign Practices Reports* Report 4 (October 1978).

The Hansard Society for Parliamentary Government. *Paying for Politics: The Report of the Commission Upon the Financing of Political Parties.* The Hansard Society for Parliamentary Government, July 1981.

Harvard University. *An Analysis of the Impact of the Federal Election Campaign Act, 1972-1978.* Report by the Campaign Finance Study Group to the Committee on House Administration of the U.S. House of Representatives, Institute of Politics, John Fitzgerald Kennedy School of Government, Harvard University. May 1979.

Hogan, Bill; Kiesel, Diane; and Green, Alan, "The New Slush Fund Scandal." *New Republic,* August 30, 1982, 21-25.

____. "The Senate's Secret Slush Funds." *New Republic,* June 20, 1983, 13-20.

Jacobson, Gary C. "The Effects of Campaign Spending in Congressional Elections," *American Political Science Review* 72, no. 2 (June 1978).

Jones, Ruth S. "State Public Financing and the State Parties." In *Parties, Interest Groups, and Campaign Finance Laws,* edited by Michael J. Malbin. Washington, D.C.: American Enterprise Institute for Public Policy Research, 1980.

Kirby, James C., Jr. *Congress and the Public Trust.* The Association of the Bar of the City of New York Special Committee on Congressional Ethics, 1970.

Lyndenberg, Steven D. *Bankrolling Ballots, Update 1980: The Role of Business in Financing State Ballot Question Campaigns.* Council on Economic Priorities, 1981.

Malbin, Michael J. "Campaign Financing and the Special Interests." *Public Interest* 56 (Summer 1979).

____. "Labor, Business, and Money—A Post-Election Analysis." *National Journal,* March 19, 1977.

____. "Neither a Mountain nor a Molehill." *Regulation* (May/June 1979.)

Moore, Jonathan, and Albert C. Pierce, eds. *Voters, Primaries and Parties.* Selections from a Conference on American Politics. Institute of Politics, John Fitzgerald Kennedy School of Government, Harvard University, 1976.

Patterson, Thomas E. "It's Not the Commercials, It's the Money." Report of the 1982 Aspen Institute Communications Policy Workshop, November 7-9, 1982.

President's Commission on Campaign Costs. *Financing Presidential Campaigns,* Washington, D.C.: Government Printing Office, April 1962.

Rosenbloom, David Lee. *Electing Congress: The Financial Dilemma.* Report of the Twentieth Century Fund Task Force on Financing Congressional Campaigns, 1970.

Rosenthal, Albert J. *Federal Regulation of Campaign Finance: Some Constitutional Questions,* edited by Milton Katz. Princeton, N.J.: Citizens' Research Foundation, 1972.

Schwarz, Thomas J. *Public Financing of Elections: A Constitutional Division of the Wealth.* Chicago: American Bar Association, Special Committee on Election Reform, 1975.

Twentieth Century Fund. *Voters' Time.* Report of the Twentieth Century Fund Commission on Campaign Costs in the Electronic Era. New York, 1969.

U.S. Congress. House. Committee on House Administration. *Public Financing of Congressional Elections.* Hearings on a Bill to Amend the Federal Election Campaign Act of 1971 to Provide for the Public Financing of General Election Campaigns for the House of Representatives and for Other Purposes. 95th Cong., 1st sess. Washington, D.C.: Government Printing Office, 1977.

U.S. Congress. Senate. Select Committee on Presidential Campaign Activities. *Final Report.* Pursuant to S. Res. 60, February 7, 1973. Senate Report No. 93-981. 93d Cong., 2d sess. Washington, D.C.: Government Printing Office, 1974.

——. Select Committee on Presidential Campaign Activities. *Election Reform: Basic References.* Pursuant to S. Res. 60. Committee Print. 93d Cong., 1st sess. Washington, D.C.: Government Printing Office, 1973.

——. *Senate Campaign Information: A Compilation of Federal Laws and Regulations Governing United States Senate Elections in 1978.* Compiled by the Senate Library under the direction of J. S. Kimmitt, Secretary of Senate; Roger K. Haley, Librarian. Washington, D.C.: Government Printing Office, 1978.

Winter, Ralph K., Jr. *Watergate and the Law: Political Campaigns and Presidential Power.* Domestic Affairs Study No. 22. Washington, D.C.: American Enterprise Institute for Public Policy Research, 1974.

——, in association with John R. Bolton. *Campaign Financing and Political Freedom.* Domestic Affairs Study No. 19. Washington, D.C.: American Enterprise Institute for Public Policy Research, 1973.

Index

Adams, John Quincy - 5
Advertising. *See also* Mass media.
  Election, 1982 - 127, 139, 152
  FECA provisions - 213
  Institutional - 80
  Political, in the past - 5-6
  Proliferation of consulting firms - 17
  Related costs of TV and radio - 10-14, 115
Afghanistan - 122
Agnew, Spiro T. - 170-171
Aikens, Joan - 48
Alabama - 164
Alaska - 164
Ambassadorships - 65-66
Amendments, Constitutional. *See* Constitution.
American Civil Liberties Union - 164
American Conservative Union - 108
American Medical Political Action Committee (AMPAC) - 101
Anderson, John B.
  Compliance costs - 130
  Direct mail - 130
  Fund raising - 131
  Matching funds - 118, 130
Appendix - 201-214
Arizona - 169
Ashmore-Goodell Bill - 34
Askew, Reubin - 193

Baker, Howard H., Jr., R-Tenn. - 119
Ballot initiatives - 154-159
Baron Report - 155
Bentsen, Lloyd, D-Texas - 142
Beyle, Thad - 148, 152
Bibliography - 215-222
Bipartisan Election Commissions
  Budgets - 172
  Enforcement - 172-173
Book of the Democratic Convention of 1936 - 81
Bradley, Tom - 149-150
Brandeis, Louis D. - 19
Broadcast industry. *See* Radio; Television.
Brown, Edmund G. "Jerry," Jr. - 122, 141-142, 149
Bryan, William Jennings - 6, 32, 56
Buchanan, James - 6
Buckley v. Valeo
  Campaign disclosure - 163-164
  Contribution limits - 165
  Events leading to - 38
  Free speech rights - 141
  Highlights - 40-42
  Independent expenditures - 126
  Self-contributions - 26, 138, 141
  Separation of powers - 172
Bush, George
  Campaign spending - 21, 114
  Fund raising - 192
  Political action committee - 117
Business and Labor. *See also* Political action committees (PACs).
  Ban on corporate giving - 32, 33
  Convention financing - 81-83
  Corporate giving - 79-83
  Financing history - 56-57
  Fund-raising practices - 79-82
  Illegal gifts - 86-88
  Labor union contributions - 33, 83-85
  State ballot issues, participation - 170
  State limits - 169-170
Byrne, Brendan - 189-190

California
  Ballot issues - 154
  Campaign disclosure, state - 164
  Candidate spending limits - 115
  Congressional election, 1982 - 141-144
  State elections, 1982 - 149-150, 151 (chart)
California Rifle and Pistol Association - 158
Campaign Finance Study Group - 46
Campaign reform. *See* Federal Election Campaign Act.
Campaigns, Congressional. *See also* Election, 1972; Election, 1974; Election, 1976; Election, 1978; Election, 1980; Election, 1982.
  Checkoff funds - 173-174
  Disclosure requirements - 33
  Election, 1980 - 132-134

Election, 1982 - 137-147
Expenditures, 1972-1982 (chart) - 138
Financial future - 196-198
Ideological committees - 108-110
Increasing costs of - 9-10
Incumbency advantages - 102-104, 139-140
Individual contributors - 98
Interest group giving - 10
Political action committee contributions - 96,
98-99, 137-147
Private financing - 197
Public funding - 185-189
Campaigns, General. *See also* Minor parties;
Prenomination campaigns; Primaries.
Corporate and labor contributions - 83-85,
169-179
Election, 1980 - 124-134
Financial future - 196-198
Get-out-the-vote drives - 125-126
Gubernatorial - 8
History - 5-6, 7 (chart)
Ideological committees - 108-110
Independent spending - 129-130
National party funds - 126-128
Organization - 21
Political action committees - 71-72
Public funding - 64, 126-128, 185-198
Rising costs - 8-17, 134
State and local - 8, 147-154, 163-182
State ballot issues - 154-159, 170
Campaigns, Presidential, Vice Presidential
Campaign calendar - 192
Direct mail appeals - 67-70
Escalation of costs - 8-17
History - 5-6, 7 (chart)
Impact of TV and radio - 10-15
Increase in primaries - 17
Independent expenditures - 116
Prenomination - 24-25, 96, 113-124
Public funding - 15, 62-63, 96, 118, 188
Spending, 1860-1976 (chart) - 7
Spending, 1980 (charts) - 121, 123
Candidates
Conservative - 108-109
Distribution of funds - 178-179
Financial inequalities of - 3
Fringe - 67, 122
Ideological. *See* Issue-oriented politics.
Incumbent - 102-104, 138-139
Minor party. *See* Minor parties.
Nonpublic funded - 141
Wealthy - 2-3, 25-30, 141, 144, 146
Cannon, Howard, D-Nev. - 147
Carter, Jimmy
Advertising - 127
Ambassadorships - 66

Campaign strategy - 122-124
Communications costs - 13
Compliance costs - 15-16, 127
Direct mail - 69
FEC appointments - 47-48
Fund-raising costs - 16, 21
Incumbency advantage - 122
Independent expenditures (charts) - 123, 125
Matching funds - 118
Media spending - 12, 13-14
Party funding - 127
Personal wealth - 26
Prenomination spending - 25, 122
Primaries - 69
Public funding - 20, 62-63, 126, 186-187
Casey, William - 120
Caucuses - 192
Center for Public Financing of Elections - 41
Charleston Gazette - 6
Checkoff. *See* Taxes, tax law.
*Citizens Against Rent Control v. City of
Berkeley* - 157
Citizens for the Republic
Circumventing finance limits - 118
Direct mail appeals - 70
Fund raising - 119-120
Citizens' Research Foundation
California campaign spending, 1982 - 150
Financial disclosure - 61
Personal contributions - 145
Presidential campaign costs - 8
Civic Service - 92-93, 187
Civil Service Reform Act (1883) - 31, 57
Clean Air Act - 102
Clean Campaign Act of 1983 - 185
Clearinghouse on Election Administration -
52
Clements, William - 153
Collins, Thomas - 68
Colorado - 164
Commission on Campaign Costs (Kennedy) -
31, 33-34
Commission on Presidential Nominations -
192
Committee for the Future of America - 193
**Committee for the Reelection of the Presi-
dent (CRP)** - 69, 87
Committee on Party Renewal - 190
Committee on Political Education (COPE) -
92
**Committee to Investigate Organized Crime
in Interstate Commerce** - 171
Committees, Candidate
Direct mail appeals - 70
Political action - 117-118
Committees, National party
Annual budgets - 2

Convention financing - 82-83
Democratic
  Congressional candidate support - 137-138
  Election, 1980 - 119-121
  Fund raising - 56, 119-121
  Media outlays - 127
Direct mail appeals - 71-72
History - 5
Republican
  Congressional candidate support - 133, 137-138
  Fund raising - 119-121
  State candidate support - 176-178
Common Cause
  Buckley v. Valeo - 41
  Disclosure suit against Nixon - 61
  Election commission study - 46
  Electoral reform proposals - 185
  PACs - 106, 185
Computer technology
  Ballot initiatives - 158-159
  Campaign costs - 139
  Data banks - 140
  Election, 1982 - 139-140
Congress. *See also* Campaigns, Congressional.
  Campaign advertising - 23
  Clerk of the House - 36, 39
  Election regulation - 32
  Legislative veto - 40
  Secretary of the Senate - 36
Congress: The Heartbeat of Government - 81
Congressional Research Service - 52
Connally, John B. - 14, 116, 117, 119
Connecticut - 165, 169
Constitution
  First Amendment - 14
  Nineteenth Amendment - 4
  Twenty-sixth Amendment - 4
Contributions, Campaign
  Checkoff funds. *See* Taxes, tax law.
  Congressional elections - 27
  Corporate. *See* Business and labor.
  Criminal funds - 171
  Direct mail. *See* Direct mail.
  FECA limits on - 15, 201, 205, 208
  Foreign - 88
  Illegal - 85-88
  In-kind - 169
  Laundered money - 86-88
  Limits by states - 163-182
  Reporting of. *See* Federal Election Campaign Act.
  Restrictions - 15, 19, 169-170
  'Seed money' - 68
  Straight party - 71-72
  Supreme Court ruling - 26, 40-42

Voluntary disclosure - 60-61
Contributors. *See also* Political action committees (PACs).
  Ambassadorships - 65-66
  Ballot initiatives - 157
  Direct mail - 67-72, 116
  Entertainers - 116
  Foreign nationals - 88
  Government employees - 31, 56-57
  Groups - 79-110
  History - 55-59
  Individuals - 33, 41-42, 55-75, 79, 98
    Largest in 1968 - 59
    Largest in 1972 - 59-62
    Largest in 1976 - 64
  Patterns in donating - 72-73
  Self-contributors - 26-28, 141, 185
  Wealthy families - 25-28
Convention books - 81
Conventions, Nominating
  Corporate and labor contributions - 84
  Disclosure regulations - 205
  Fund raising, program books - 81-82
  History - 81
  Host-city bids - 82
  Public funding - 82-83
Corrupt Practices Act. *See* Federal Corrupt Practices Act (1925).
Crane, Philip M., R-Ill. - 119
Cranston, Alan, D-Calif. - 193
Cuomo, Mario - 148
Curb, Mike - 149
Curran, Paul - 152

Dayton, Mark - 27, 144-146
Dees, Morris - 68, 69
Democratic Congressional Campaign Committee - 137
Democratic National Committee
  Budgets - 2
  Campaign spending, 1980 - 126-128, 133
  Campaign spending, 1982 - 137
  Convention financing - 83
  Direct mail appeals - 72
Democratic Senatorial Campaign Committee - 137, 143
Deukmejian, George - 140, 149-150
Direct mail
  Ballot initiatives - 158-159
  Broad-based solicitation - 60, 140
  Computer technology - 23, 148
  Costs - 13, 16
  Fund raising - 67-72, 140
  Issue-oriented - 156
  McGovern campaign - 67-68
  Nixon campaign - 68-69

Political party committees - 71-72
Primaries - 69-70
Disclosure, Campaign finance
Buckley v. Valeo - 38, 40-42
By states - 163-165
Challenges to disclosure laws - 164
Compliance costs - 8
Effect of laws - 19
Exemption from - 164
FECA requirements - 202-203, 206-210
History - 31-35, 60-61
Need for - 18-19
Dodd, Thomas, D-Conn. - 34
Dole, Robert, R-Kan. - 117, 119
Dornan, Robert, R-Calif. - 142
Douglas, Stephen A. - 6
Draft Ford Committee - 119
Durenberger, David, R-Minn - 27, 144-145

Eisenhower, Dwight D.
Congressional party majorities - 22
Finance reform - 33
Personal wealth - 25
Election, 1952 - 25
Election, 1960 - 24
Election, 1964
Prenomination spending - 25
Radio costs - 12
Election, 1968
Large contributors - 59
Spending
Prenomination - 25
Radio costs- 12
Television costs - 12-13
Election, 1972
Corporate role - 87
Direct mail appeals - 67-69
Illegal funding - 85-88
Large contributors - 59-62
Spending - 8
Prenomination - 25
Radio costs - 12
Television costs - 12-13
Voluntary disclosure - 60
Election, 1974 - 25
Election, 1976
Direct mail appeals - 69
Independent expenditures - 63-64
Public funding - 43, 62-63
Spending - 8
Prenomination - 25, 121
Radio costs - 12
Election, 1978 - 27
Election, 1980
Broadcasting regulation - 14-15
Direct mail appeals - 70

FECA effects
Contribution limits - 116-118
Spending limits - 114-115
State limits - 115-116
Fund raising - 118-124, 128-129
Ideological committees - 109
Independent spending - 129-131
Labor contributions - 85
Spending
Compliance costs - 15-16, 127-128
Congressional - 132-134
Fund raising costs - 16
Prenomination - 25, 113-124
Radio costs - 12
Election, 1982
Incumbents - 139-140
Political action committee support - 137-139
Spending
Advertising - 139-140
Congressional spending - 138-147
State races - 147-153
Electorate
Growth - 2, 4
Individuals contributing - 55-75
Eliot, Charles William - 32
Elliott, Lee Ann - 48
Expenditures, Campaign. *See also* Federal
Election Campaign Act.
Buckley v. Valeo - 190
Communications expenditures. *See* Mass media.
Compliance-related - 15-16
Democratic spending, 1980 (chart) - 123
Election, 1980 - 118-124
Escalating costs - 8-18
Independent - 129-130
Limits - 15, 19, 189-192
Media outlays. *See* Mass media.
Republican spending, 1980 (chart) - 121

Fairness doctrine - 14-15
FCC. *See* Federal Communications Commission
(FCC).
FEC. *See* Federal Election Commission (FEC).
FECA. *See* Federal Election Campaign Act
(FECA).
Federal Communications Commission (FCC)
Campaign broadcasting - 14-15
Fairness doctrine - 14-15
Television campaign costs - 12
Federal Corrupt Practices Act of 1925 - 31,
32-33, 60, 61
**Federal Election Campaign Act of 1971
(FECA)**
Amendments, 1974
Background - 37-38

Congressional opposition - 38
Contribution limits - 205
Convention financing - 82
Court action. *See Buckley v. Valeo.*
Disclosure and enforcement - 206-207
Election commission - 38, 205
Individual contributions - 63, 79
Matching funds qualifications - 113
Political action committees - 90-91
Provisions - 23, 204-207
Public funding - 38, 62, 206
Reporting requirements - 113
Self-contributions - 26
Spending limits - 38, 205
State limits - 113
Amendments, 1976
Contribution limits - 208
Disclosure and enforcement - 209-210
Election commission - 208
Individual contribution limit - 26, 91
Matching funds qualifications - 114
Political action committees - 91-92, 210
Provisions - 42-43, 206-210
Public funding - 42, 209
Reporting requirements - 15, 91
Spending limits - 208-209
Wealthy candidates - 26-27
Amendments, 1979
Convention financing - 83
Disclosure and enforcement - 211-212, 213
Election commission - 212-213
Excess campaign contributions - 45
Exempt candidates - 44
FEC requirements - 44
Fund raising - 126
Political parties - 213
Provisions - 43-45, 210-214
Public funding - 213
Reporting requirement changes - 15, 44
Volunteer activities - 80-81, 126
Background, early reforms - 19
Compliance costs - 15-16, 127
Constitutional challenge. *See Buckley v. Valeo.*
Contribution limits - 201
Disclosure - 164
Fund raising limits - 113
Impact - 114-118
Media expenditures - 35
Political action committees - 89-90
Provisions - 201-203
Public funding - 190-191
Reporting requirements - 36, 99
Results - 131-132
Self and family contributions - 35-36
Spending limits - 202

State limits - 115-116
Federal Election Commission (FEC)
Advisory opinions (AO) - 48-49
Appointments - 47-48
Audit policy revisions - 51
Audits - 50-51
Clearinghouse on Election Administration - 52
Compliance action - 49-50
Congressional opposition - 39
Draft committees - 117
Establishment - 38-39
Evolution - 45-52
FECA provisions - 205, 208, 212-213
Independence - 38-39
Matching funds requirement - 15
Membership - 38
Open meetings - 51-52
Publications - 52
Reconstitution - 42-43, 208
Structure - 46-47
Fenwick, Millicent
Election, 1982 - 146
Personal wealth - 27
Finance Committee for the Reelection of the President - 87
Finance reports. *See* Disclosure, campaign finance.
Financing, Political. *See also* Contributions, campaign; Expenditures, campaign; Taxes, tax law.
History - 55-59
Private. *See* Contributors.
Public. *See* Public Funding.
Regulation
Reform 18-19, 31-52
States - 163-182
Tax incentives to contributors. *See* Taxes, tax law.
Finch, Cliff - 122
First Amendment - 40-41, 141
First National Bank of Boston v. Bellotti - 157, 170
Florida - 154, 165, 169
Ford, Gerald R.
Direct mail - 69
FEC nominations - 47
Incumbency advantage - 122
Media spending - 12
Personal wealth - 26
Prenomination spending - 25
Primaries - 69
Public funding - 38, 43, 62
Ford, Henry - 32
Franked mail - 207
Free speech - 40-41, 141

Freneau, Philip - 5
Friedersdorf, Max - 47
Fund for a Conservative Union - 108
Fund Raising. *See also* Contributions, Campaign; Direct mail.
  Ambassadorships - 65-66
  Costs - 16-17
  Dinners - 58
  Direct mail. *See* Direct mail.
  Election, 1982 - 140, 143
  Expenses - 16-17
  History - 56-58
  Party conventions - 81-82
  Proliferation of consulting firms - 17
  Solicitations, broad-based - 60
  Spending limits - 113
  Technological advances - 139

Gallup Polls - 73, 186,
Gaylord, Joe - 140
Gazette of the United States. - 5
General Accounting Office - 60
Glenn, John, D-Ohio - 193
Goldwater, Barry Jr. - 142
Gompers, Samuel - 32
Gore, Albert - 35
Grant, Ulysses S. - 56
Grants. *See* Public funding.
Gubernatorial campaigns
  Election, 1980 - 10
  Election, 1982 - 147-153
  Public funding - 189-190
Gun Owners of America - 158

Hamilton, Alexander - 5
Handgun Control, Inc. - 158
Handgun control initiatives - 157-158
Hanna, Mark - 57
Harriman, E. H. - 58
Harris, Louis - 186
Harris Survey - 188
Harris, Thomas - 48
Harrison, William Henry - 6
Hart, Gary, D-Colo. - 193
Hatch Act (1940) - 33, 207
Hayakawa, S. I. - 141-142, 144
Hayes, Rutherford B. - 56
Heinz, John, R-Pa. - 27
Helms, Jesse, R-N.C. - 70
Hollings, Ernest, D-S.C. - 193
House campaigns - 9-10, 133-134
Hughes, Charles Evans - 32
Humphrey, Hubert H.
  Disclosure - 60
  Labor support - 85
  Personal wealth - 26

Television campaigning - 12
Hunt Commission - 192-193
Hunt, James B. - 192

Ickes, Harold L. - 57
Immigration and Naturalization Service - 40
Incumbents
  Election, 1976 support - 121
  Election, 1980 support - 122
  Election, 1982 support - 138-140
Independent Action - 71
Independent expenditures
  Congressional campaign, 1982 - 147
  Growth - 63-64
  Presidential campaign, 1980 - 129-130
Indiana - 169, 170
Initiative and Referendum Report - 159
Interest groups. *See also* Political action committees; Presidential political action committees.
  New Right - 109-110, 147
  Power of - 8-10, 147
  Single-issue groups - 154-158
Internal Revenue Service - 81
Iowa - 115, 120, 192
Issue-oriented politics
  Gun control - 157-158
  Ideological groups - 155
  Impact of new technology - 159
  Nuclear freeze - 156-157
  State ballot issues - 154-159
  Taxes - 156

Jackson, Andrew - 6, 55
Jacobson, Gary - 140, 191
Janklow, William - 148
Jefferson, Thomas - 5, 55
Johnson, Lyndon B.
  Finance reform proposals - 34
  Personal wealth - 25
  Prenomination spending - 25
Jones, Ruth S. - 178
Justice Department - 50

Kansas - 165
Kefauver Committee - 171
Kennedy, Edward M., D-Mass.
  Campaign spending - 21, 147
  Draft committees - 117
  Political action committee - 118, 194
Kennedy, John F.
  Campaign spending - 20
  Personal wealth - 25
  Prenomination spending - 24
  Reform proposals - 33

Kennedy, Robert -
  Finance reform proposals - 35
  Prenomination spending - 25
  Wealthy donors - 59
Kernell, Samuel - 140
King, Rufus - 5
Kissinger, Henry - 143
Koch, Edward - 152

Labor Unions. *See* also Political action committees (PACs).
  Campaign contributions - 33
  Political support - 83-85
  Smith-Connally Act - 83
Landon, Alfred - 22
LaRouche, Lyndon - 122
'Laundered money'. *See* Money.
Lautenberg, Frank, D-N.J. - 27, 146-147
Law Enforcement Assistance Administration
  - 83
League of Women Voters - 41
Legislation, Reform
  Early reform efforts - 31-35
  Federal Election Campaign Act (FECA) of
  1971 - 35-36, 88-90, 201-203
    Amendments, 1974 - 37-38, 90-91, 204-
    207
    Amendments, 1976 - 42-43, 91, 207-210
    Amendments, 1979 - 43-45, 210-214
    Constitutionality, 40-42
  History - 31-35, 57
  Impact of - 131-132
  Political action committees - 106-108, 185
  Proposals - 106-108
  Public financing, congressional - 185
  Veto power, congressional - 39-40, 208, 213
Legislative veto - 40
Lehrman, Lewis - 27, 148, 151-152
Lewis, John L. - 83
Liberty League - 22
Library of Congress
  Congressional Research Service - 52
Lincoln, Abraham -
  Campaign spending - 12, 20
  Newspaper support - 6
Lindsay, John - 60
Lobbying. *See* Legislation, Reform.
Long Act (1966) - 34-35
Long, Russell, D-La. - 34
Louisiana - 164

McCarthy, Eugene J.
  Prenomination spending - 25
  Wealthy donors - 59
McCloskey, Matthew - 58
McCloskey, Paul N., R-Calif. - 60

McCloskey, Pete - 142
McCormick, Cyrus H. - 56
McDonald, Danny - 48
McGarry, John W. - 47
McGovern, George
  Candidacy, 1984 - 193
  Direct mail - 67-68
  Fund raising - 61
  Labor support - 85
  Large contributions - 61
  Media spending - 13
  Prenomination spending - 25
  Voluntary disclosure - 60
  Wealth - 26
McKinley, William - 6, 57
McKnight, Peyton - 153
Maine - 169
Manatt, Charles - 192
Maryland - 169
Mass Media. *See* also Advertising.
  Direct mailing. *See* Fund raising
  Election, 1968 - 12, 13
  Election, 1972 - 12, 13
  Election, 1976 - 12
  Election, 1980 - 12, 14-15, 127
  Equal air time - 14-15
  Media spending limits - 35
  News coverage - 22
  Newspapers, pamphlets and books - 5-6
  New technology impact - 23
  Professionalizing politics - 17-18
  TV and radio spending - 10-15
Massachusetts - 171
Matching funds. *See* Public funding.
Michigan - 171
Minnesota - 165, 176
Minor Parties
  Disclosure - 164
  Public funding - 130
  Socialist Workers Party - 164
Mississippi - 169
Mondale, Walter F.
  Political action committee - 118
Money. *See* also Contributors.
  Close elections and - 20-21, 25-28
  Foreign - 88
  'Laundered' - 86-88
  Media competition and - 10-15
  Power and - 3
  Seed - 68
Montana - 169, 171, 175
Mott, Stewart R. - 59, 61
Muskie, Edmund S. - 60

Nast, Thomas - 56
National Committee for an Effective

Congress - 71, 108
National Congressional Club - 71, 108
National Conservative Political Action Committee (NCPAC)
  Congressional compaign, 1982 - 147
  Direct mail activities - 71
  Growth - 108, 110
National Gazette - 5
National Publicity Law Association (NPLA) - 32
National Republican Congressional Committee
  Congressional spending - 133
  Direct mail activities - 71
National Republican Senatorial Committee
  Direct mail appeals - 71
  Election, 1982 support - 137, 143
National Rifle Association - 158
National Sustaining Fund - 69
New Hampshire - 115, 120, 169, 192
New Jersey - 145-147, 170, 189-190
New Right - 109, 147, 159
New York - 115, 151-152, 165, 169
Newberry, Truman - 32
Newberry v. United States - 32
Newspapers - 5-6
Newton, Wayne - 143
Nixon, Richard
  Ambassadorships - 65-66
  Broadcast spending - 12-13
  Campaign spending - 20
  Common Cause suit - 61
  Contributions - 61-62
  Direct mail - 68-69
  Disclosure - 61
  Finance reform proposals - 37
  Fund raising - 58
  Illegal gifts - 85-88
  Labor support - 83
  Prenomination spending - 25
  Resignation - 122
  Wealth - 26
Noragon, Jack L. - 181
North Carolina - 165, 169
North Dakota - 169
Northcott, Kaye - 149, 153
Nuclear freeze initiatives - 156-157

PACs. *See* Political action committees (PACs).
Pennsylvania - 169
Political action committees (PACs). *See also*
Business and labor.
  Antiproliferation provisions - 91
  Contribution limits - 52, 79, 88-92, 169
  Contributions (chart) - 103
  Corporate - 88-94

Direct-mail use - 70
Disbursements, receipts - 92, 95 (chart), 96 (chart)
Establishment - 90-91
FECA provisions - 210
Ideological committees - 108-110, 117
Incumbency support - 102-104, 138-139
Labor - 88-94, 169
Legislative influence - 100-102
Legislative proposals - 106-108, 185
Nationalization - 97-99
New Right - 109, 137, 147, 159
Partisanship - 104-106
Presidential PACs - 116-118
Proliferation - 18, 94-97
Public opinion - 188-189
Registered (chart) - 94
Reporting requirements - 91
Restrictions by states - 169
Role of - 18
Solicitation guidelines - 92-94
Spending, 1978 - 105
Spending, 1980 - 10, 105
Spending, 1982 - 105, 137-139, 142-143
Political Parties
  Convention financing - 83
  Declining influence - 99
  Direct mail appeals - 71-73
  Distribution of checkoff funds - 176-178, 177 (chart)
  Election funding, 1980 - 126-127
  European - 4
  FECA provisions - 213
  Funding limits - 100
  History - 4
  National Committees. *See* Committees, National party.
  Newspaper printing - 5-6
  Political action committee financing - 104-106, 105 (chart)
  Public funding - 62-65, 176-178, 180-181, 190-192
  Renewal of - 100
  Reporting requirements - 44
Prenomination campaigns
  Contribution limits - 116-118
  Election, 1980 - 113-124
  Financing - 96
  Importance - 24-25
  Independent expenditures - 116-118
  Matching funds - 62, 113, 118, 193
  Reform proposals - 192-194
  Straw polls - 194
Presidential Election Campaign Fund
  Election, 1976 - 8
  Revenue Act provisions - 37, 204

Success - 195-196
Presidential nominations - 192
Presidential political action committees
  Campaign limits - 116-118
  Early starts - 193-194
President's Club - 34
Pressler, Larry, R-S.D. - 119
Primaries
  Campaign calendar - 192
  Corporate and labor contributions - 84
  Cost of - 17-18
  Direct-mail strategy - 67-70
  Increase in - 17
  Public funding - 63
Printing - 5-6
ProPAC - 71
Public Funding
  Background - 62-63
  Checkoffs - 36-37, 174, 195-196, 195 (chart)
  Compliance requirements - 15-16, 127
  Congressional campaigns - 141
  Conventions - 82-83
  Credits - 36-37, 100
  Criteria - 179-180
  Disbursements - 62-63, 176-179
  FECA impact - 114-118
  FECA provisions - 206, 209, 213
  Fund raising limits - 113
  Implications - 179-181
  Kennedy commission proposals - 33
  Opposition to - 33-34
  Political parties and - 176-178, 190-192
  Prenomination spending - 96, 113-124
  Presidential elections - 64-65, 118-124
  Reform proposals - 190-192
  Regulations - 55
  Spending limits - 41, 190
  State public funding - 173-181, 175 (chart)
  Tax surcharge - 174-176
Public Opinion Surveys - 186-189

Radio. *See also* Mass media.
  Election, 1980 - 127
  FECA provisions - 203
  History - 10-12
  Recent rise in use - 15
Rae, Douglas - 19
Reagan, Ronald
  Appointees - 66-67
  Campaign costs - 20-21, 121 (chart)
  Campaign strategy - 21, 119-121
  Compliance costs - 16, 127
  Direct mail - 70
  FEC nominations - 48
  Fund raising - 16, 143
  Media spending - 12, 127

Party funds - 126-127
Prenomination spending - 16, 25, 114, 117-120
Presidential PAC - 118
Primaries - 120
Public funding - 114, 120, 126-127
Reform. *See* Legislation, Reform.
Reiche, Frank P. - 48
Republican National Committee
  Budgets - 2
  Campaign spending, 1980 - 121 (chart), 126-128
  Campaign spending, 1982 - 137, 143
  Convention financing - 83
  Direct mail appeals - 69, 71-72
  Tax incentives and checkoff - 203-203
Revenue Act of 1971
  Background - 19
  Enforcement - 204
  Presidential Election Campaign Fund - 204
  Provisions - 36-37, 99, 203-204
  Tax incentives and checkoff - 203-204
Revenue Act of 1978 - 37
Rockefeller, Nelson A. - 59, 152
Rockefeller, John D. "Jay" - 27, 148
  Prenomination spending - 25
Roosevelt, Franklin D.
  Fund raising - 58
  Personal wealth - 25
Roosevelt, Theodore - 58

Sarbanes, Paul S., D-Md. - 147
Sears, John - 120
Schneider, William - 189
Schweicker, Richard - 185
Seith, Alex - 27
Senate campaigns
  Financing - 1
  Spending, 1980 - 9-10, 133
  Spending, 1982 - 138
Separation of Powers. *See Buckley v. Valeo.*
Shamie, Ray - 147
Smith-Connally Act (1943) - 33, 83
South Dakota - 154, 169
Specter, Arlen, R-Pa. - 27
Staebler, Neil - 47
State elections
  Finance regulation
    Bipartisan election commissions - 171-173
    Chart - 166-168
    Contribution limits - 165, 169-171
    Disclosure - 163-165
    Public funding - 173-179
    Restrictions - 115
    Spending, 1980 - 10
    Spending, 1982 - 147- 153

Tax incentives - 181-182
Stevenson, Adlai
  Media costs - 12
  Personal wealth - 25
Stewart, Potter - 41
Stone, W. Clement - 59, 61
Straw polls - 119, 194
Sun Oil Company - 90
SunPAC - 90-91
Supreme Court
  Ballot issue campaigns - 157
  Campaign broadcasting regulation - 14-15
  Campaign expenditure limits - 40-42
  Disclosure exemption - 164
  Federal Election Commission appointments - 38
  Independent expenditures - 126
  Legislative veto - 40
  Personal funding restrictions - 141
  Separation of powers - 172
Supreme Court cases
  Buckley v. Valeo - 38, 40-42, 126, 138, 141, 163, 164, 172
  Citizens Against Rent Control v. City of Berkeley - 157
  First National Bank of Boston et al. v. Bellotti - 157, 170
  Newberry v. United States - 32
Survey Research Center - 73-74

Taft-Hartley Act (1947) - 33
Taxes, tax law
  Ballot issues - 156
  Checkoffs - 8, 36-37, 174, 195-196, 195 (chart), 203
  Corporate advertising deductions - 81
  Credits - 36-37, 100
  Deductions - 36-37
  Incentives - 181-182, 203-204
  Long Act - 34-35, 37
  State incentives - 181-182
  State laws - 174
  Surcharge - 174-176

Television. *See also* Mass media.
  Broadcasting costs increase - 10-15
  Broadcasting regulation - 14, 203
  Campaign strategies - 13
  Election, 1980 - 115, 127
  Election, 1982 - 152-153
  History - 12-14
Temple, Buddy - 153
Texas - 153, 169
Third parties. *See* Minor parties.
Thomson, Vernon - 48
Tilden, Samuel J. - 56
Tillman Act (1907) - 32
Truman, Harry S - 33
Twenty-sixth Amendment - 4

U.S. Chamber of Commerce - 34
Udall, Morris K., D-Ariz. - 69
Unions. *See Business and labor.*
United Mine Workers - 83

Vanderbilt, Cornelius - 56
Virginia - 176
Voter registration. *See also* Electorate.
  Civil rights movement - 4
  Information pamphlets, books - 85
  Registration drives - 71, 85, 125
  Turnout - 85, 142
  Twenty-sixth Amendment - 4
  Universal voter registration - 182

Wallace, George C. - 60, 67, 69
Watergate - 35, 85-87
Wealthy families. *See* Contributors.
Weicker, Lowell P., Jr., R-Conn. - 119
White, Mark - 153
Williams, John - 35
Wilson, Pete - 141-145
Wisconsin - 169
Women - 4
Wyoming - 169

Zagoria, Samuel - 47